CHRIST CONSCIOUS LEADERSHIP

CHRIST CONSCIOUS LEADERSHIP

Barbara Benjamin

Introduction by
The Reverend Troy P. DeCohen

Nepperhan Press
Yonkers, NY

2012
Nepperhan Press, LLC
Yonkers, NY 10702

First Edition

© 2012 by Barbara Benjamin

All rights reserved. No part of this book may be reproduced, stored in a retrieval system, or transmitted, in any form or by any means, electronic, mechanical, photocopying, recording, or otherwise, without the written permission of Nepperhan Press, LLC.

Printed in the United States of America

Library of Congress Control Number: 2012945365

ISBN: 978-0-9839412-6-2

Cover photograph by Barbara Benjamin

Dedicated to the Christ in each of us

ACKNOWLEDGMENTS

During the past twenty years, as a consultant, educator and executive mentor, I have been privileged to work with many extraordinary leaders from a variety of professional disciplines. It is with a deep sense of gratitude that I acknowledge the contribution that each of them has made to my conviction that outstanding leadership arises from the Christ consciousness of each leader.

I am especially grateful to Fr. Joseph F. Girzone for his enduring friendship and guidance, to Dr. Orest Bedrij who generously shared both his extensive knowledge of physics and his unreserved enthusiasm for this project, and to Fr. Philippe Charles whose consistent and profound responses to the work in progress inspired, informed, and enhanced my efforts. I am also grateful to many others who have encouraged and supported this work with their insight and feedback: Tanya Bickley, Dr. Hollace Bristol, Fr. James Francis Healy, Sr. Claude Marie Jablonski, Gaitre Lorick, Dr. Clancy McKenzie, and Fr. Joe LaMar.

I also extend my heartfelt thanks to Marie Milton whose production editing experience and expertise made a vital contribution to the clarity of the final draft, and to Karen Weinstein whose artistic vision and talent is reflected in the book's form and design.

Above all, I thank a loving God for the opportunity to use whatever gifts I may have for advancing Christ conscious leadership in the world.

CONTENTS

INTRODUCTION
The Reverend Troy P. DeCohen … xi

PREFACE … xvii

SECTION ONE
THE GOOD NEWS – EVOLVING AND SURVIVING … 1
  1 Christ: The Eternal Absolute … 3
  2 Consciousness and the Soul … 56
  3 Leadership at a Crossroad … 100

SECTION TWO
THE WAY TO CHRIST CONSCIOUS LEADERSHIP … 143
  4 Unity – *The First Step* … 145
  5 Love – *The Second Step* … 170
  6 Detachment – *The Third Step* … 197
  7 Commitment – *The Fourth Step* … 226
  8 Action – *The Fifth Step* … 253

SECTION THREE
YOUR CHRIST CONSCIOUS LEADERSHIP PROFILE … 281
  9 Introspection and Creative Action Plans … 283

NOTES … 323
INDEX … 365
ABOUT THE AUTHOR … 379

INTRODUCTION

Since the start of the twenty-first century, leadership has been questioned and challenged throughout the world. We have witnessed the struggles of leaders to make clear, concise, and beneficial decisions for the people they serve. They appear to have stumbled along the way, whereas their past decision-making abilities, guidance, and influences have availed them little. The old paradigms do not work, and the matrix that once brought prosperity and power lacks strength and affluence. In the Middle East, long-lasting regimes and leaderships have crumbled under the weight of people's need to be free. These systems of governments have failed because the leadership could not interpret the writings on the wall and, therefore, they continued in a direction that tore at the fabric of their societies. This was seen as well with American and European banking institutions which have crumbled because of the lack of insight and intuitiveness of their leaders. Once these were prestigious models of systems and financial structures that created wealth, stability, and commerce throughout the world, structures which governments and industries depended upon to maintain monetary support and the flow of currency. However, as a result of their inability to see the changing landscape, they have become the borrowers and have amassed great debt for societies to climb out from.

Needless to say, religious institutions have not been immune from the failures of church leadership.

Western Christian movements have been under attack by the rise of immoral behaviors, unpleasant rhetoric, and the exploitation of prosperity ministries. These instances have caused many believers to discontinue their relationships with the church and their denominational affiliations. In addition, with the rise of extremist and radical fundamentalists who have used the sovereignty of God as a guise to commit heinous acts of terror against God's creation, many have questioned religion and its leaders as to the purpose of practicing a faith that promotes violence. Humankind is one, and there is no distinction in that which God has created. We cannot say, "I hate my brother," and say, at the same time, "I love God." Regardless of theology, faith formation, or religious practices, we are all created by the One.

In the first century c.e., Apostle Paul had been confronted by the same complexities of faith formations, societies, and failed leadership throughout his missionary journeys. He had witnessed the failures of government and society and the failures of religions as he sought to evangelize the message of Christ. And as he considered these things, he wrote to the Church of Rome and said: "Be not conformed to this world but be transformed by the renewing of your mind" (Romans 12:2). Paul recognized there were issues and problems that existed within society that had caused a collapse in the moral, ethical, and cultural development of the people and would, thus, create obstacles for the prospective and believing body to fully embrace and receive Christ. Furthermore, he realized these areas of concerns had crept into the church and had caused great harm with the conversion of the Gentiles. Leadership had eroded, and the behaviors in the church were no different from those in the world. So Paul understood that transformation was needed to break the bonds of societal conformity. He realized that people were following customs and traditions without questioning purpose or having conscious thought of what the outcome would be, and because their thoughts had become diluted, disengaged, and desirous to please only self, they could no longer distinguish godly practice from worldly customs. They relinquished themselves to following societal norms without critical thought. Conventionality only was the practice. The masses did as the leadership dictated, and the people became polluted by the influences around them. So Paul stated to them that a transformation was needed to break the chains of this bondage and the mental imprisonment that isolated them. However, as Paul thought about the mind and how it should transform and what it should transform into, he needed a model of perfection, a model of leadership that was conscious of the people it served. So he considered Jesus as the model, and he expressed this in his epistle to the Philippians where he said: "Let this mind be in you which was also in Christ Jesus" (Philippians 2:5).

Christ consciousness was the needed element to turn the poison of conformity into a personal process of transformation. Jesus epitomized transformational leadership, causing those who followed him to acquire new insights into life and to critically consider thoughts and ideas outside of the practicing cultural norms. He changed humanity by affecting the lives of those around him through sayings, expressions, ideas, and practical and supernatural occurrences. He used basic elements to convey his message, as when he said "Greater love has no one than this, that one lay down his life for his friends" (John 15:13).

Love was and is at the center of Jesus' leadership. Love and concern shaped him into a servant leader where the needs of others took precedence and the cause of liberation took priority in order to transform the world. He was vocal to government, he criticized religious sects, he stood up against injustices, he sought the welfare of others, and he was beaten, ridiculed, and killed because he stood for something that was incomprehensible for the world to fathom. Nonetheless, he rose to lead a people into the realm of brotherhood and into a world of citizenry that declare we are all God's children. Paul knew Christ consciousness was the answer to creating leaders and believers who would promote a concept and a movement that would change the lives of others and change the world. He encouraged it and proclaimed it at every corner and in every synagogue, arena, and amphitheater that he traveled to in the first century C.E. He knew intuitively and by faith that Jesus' model of leadership was the method to use to affect and change the direction that society was heading toward. The world needs leaders who are transformational, transparent, inspirational, and humble, who have the abilities to comprehend instinctively, deliberately, and intuitively, and who understand the world's changing landscapes of politics, economics, beliefs, ideologies, and natural resources. For without such leaders, there will be no help to relieve the stressors and struggles that lie ahead. "He said follow me" (Matthew 4:19).

As it was during the time of Jesus, so it is today. For every citizen in every culture in the world, developing the consciousness of the anointed one, the Eternal Absolute, is the only answer for the transformation of individuals and nations, for understanding our unity in God, and for building global peace.

The Reverend Troy P. DeCohen, Pastor
Mount Vernon Heights Congregational Church

PREFACE

Today, wherever we turn, we are being bombarded with doomsday predictions of Armageddon, with warnings that we are soon to run out of the vital resources needed to sustain a rapidly escalating world population, and with warnings that our current oppositional behavior in relating to one another is bringing us to the precipice of mutual annihilation. And across the board, all these predictions and warnings are fueled by solid and alarming facts. We know that water resources continue to diminish rapidly, with four thousand children dying every day because of diseases caused by dirty water or poor sanitation. We know that an estimated one billion people are underfed and undernourished, while an equal number of people suffer from obesity. We also know that since the end of World War II, the proliferation of civil and international conflicts and nuclear weapons continues to pose a threat to global security.

In response to these realities, there is a widespread call for change. We are being told that we have to change the way we protect and allocate our dwindling resources, the way we address international conflict, and the way we think about ourselves in relation to others and to our environment. Governments, torn between immediate political and economic pressures and long-range solutions, try valiantly, though ineffectively, to address this call for change. Well-intentioned individuals, torn between habitual patterns of thought and behavior, find themselves overwhelmed by the erosion of all that is familiar in their environment. And those in traditional leadership positions in our families, schools, churches, financial and corporate organizations, and local and national governments attempt to adopt new strategies as fast as they can find them, but to no avail.

Certainly humanity has faced many challenges in the past and adapted to those challenges in order to survive, but those adaptations have been physical and social adaptations, and many have taken hundreds of thousands of years to occur. We don't seem to have the option this time of waiting that long. This time it seems that our adaptation has to be faster than the depletion of our resources, faster than the explosion of our population, and faster than the eruption of global conflicts and the production of annihilating weapons. We seem, in fact, to be in a race against time for our very survival, and the odds of our winning this race seem slim.

But how real is this perception?

In light of everything our wisdom literature teaches us, from the Upanishads to the Koran, there is no race, and we are not facing a doomsday scenario that threatens our survival. We are, rather, coming quite naturally upon a new dimension in the evolution of our conscious awareness of our souls, an evolution that is our established and promised destiny. This new dimension invites us to discover our indwelling unity with God, the

"Christ in you" (Colossians 1:27) that the apostle Paul speaks of, and to manifest that unity through actions that fulfill God's plan to establish his kingdom on earth.

To move forward into this new dimension in our spiritual evolution, we need perspective, guidance, and introspection. We need to gain a sense of where we have been, where we are, and where we are headed, physically, socially, and spiritually, and we need to become aware of the innate tools we have for consciously engaging in our continuing evolution. We also need to understand how the scientific and technological innovations that are shaping the world we live in can facilitate our spiritual progress. Above all, we need perspective, guidance, and introspection to help us relinquish our habitual patterns of thought and behavior, to turn the kaleidoscope of our consciousness so that we can begin to perceive new patterns of thought and behavior that reflect our unity with each other and with Christ, the Eternal Absolute.

Structured to provide that perspective and guidance, as well as to provide an opportunity for personal introspection, *Christ Conscious Leadership* is divided into three sections. Section One, "The Good News: Evolving and Surviving," offers a comprehensive reflection of historic and current forces that have brought us to this point in our evolution and prepared us for the next step in our spiritual development. Chapter 1, "Christ: The Eternal Absolute," reveals the timeless, universal human longing for unity with the Christ and explores the revelation of the Christ in religious history and in our daily lives. Chapter 2, "Consciousness and the Soul," examines past and current theories on the evolution of human consciousness and the nature of the soul. This chapter highlights the interaction of human ingenuity with our intellectual, emotional, and intuitive perceptions and the impact of ingenuity on the development of technology, the generation of change, and our emerging consciousness. Chapter 3, "Leadership at a Crossroad," redefines the nature and the role of the leader in a digital, networked world, where central and hierarchical authority is rapidly being replaced by anonymous individuals who are empowered by a level playing field of information to connect with anyone, anywhere and make a lasting difference in any sphere of influence. Such unknown and unnamed individuals are already demonstrating their power to challenge and overthrow governments, to influence thought across the globe, and to create new forms of communication. In such a digitally interconnected world, now only fifteen years old, where every individual's thoughts, words, and actions are having a potentially significant impact on the course of human events, the imperative for every individual to develop a Christ conscious state of mind is clear. We are now all empowered to make a difference, and our state of mind will determine our destiny.

In Section Two, "The Way to Christ Conscious Leadership," five steps are presented for achieving and manifesting Christ consciousness in our interactions with each other and with our environment: Unity, Love Detachment, Commitment, and Action. Chapter 4, "Unity," provides reflections and examples for developing an awareness of the oneness of all existence and for applying that awareness in our perception of ourselves and our interactions with others. Drawing on the lessons in the Gospels and other wisdom literature and referring to the latest understanding of universal law provided by the quantum physicists, this chapter focuses on the first, most critical step in becoming a Christ conscious leader. Chapter 5, "Love," explores Jesus' new commandment: "A new commandment I give to you, that you love one another; even as I have loved you, that you also love one another" (John 13:34), and offers steps for becoming receptive to Divine Love and for becoming a vehicle of Divine Love for others. Chapter 6, "Detachment," reveals a pivotal step on the way to becoming a Christ conscious leader, highlighting the need to separate from our familiar and ingrained habits and thoughts that keep us tied to old perceptions of reality. Once detached from those influences that impede transformation and growth, we are now prepared to make commitments and take actions that will contribute to building God's kingdom on earth. Chapter 7, "Commitment," explores how we can make a commitment to God's purpose, to our life's work, and to our continual transformation. In Chapter 8, "Action," we begin to see how our emerging Christ consciousness can now be applied to discerning and answering God's call to action and to generating an enduring peace for all mankind.

Opportunities for introspection, self-assessment, and action planning are presented in Section Three, "Your Christ Conscious Leadership Profile." Focusing on each of the five steps in Section Two, Chapter 9, "Introspection and Creative Action Plans," provides exercises to gain insight into our personal challenges and strengths in our process of becoming Christ conscious leaders. This chapter also provides a template for applying our ingenuity and our intellectual, emotional, and intuitive tools of perception to creating Action Plans for our continual transformation and growth.

The Indo-European root word for *leadership* is *kla*, meaning *load*. As this root word took on new connotations, it came to mean *carry your load*. In the emerging reality of leadership as the expression of the state of mind of each individual on the globe, carrying our load becomes an immeasurable personal responsibility, a responsibility that we cannot possibly fulfill without developing a new consciousness, Christ consciousness. It is to this end, to helping us each carry our load, that the pages of *Christ Conscious Leadership* are dedicated.

SECTION ONE

THE GOOD NEWS

–

EVOLVING AND SURVIVING

> The darkness drops again; but now I know
> That twenty centuries of stony sleep
> Were vexed to nightmare by a rocking cradle,
> And what rough beast, its hour come round at last,
> Slouches towards Bethlehem to be born?
>
> The Second Coming
-William Butler Yeats

1

CHRIST
THE ETERNAL ABSOLUTE

The story of humanity is an adventure filled with passionate, faith-filled testimonies to the Eternal Absolute, a primal source that defines our ideals and values, our yearning for unity and perfection, and our inherent sense of our indwelling divinity. In Hinduism, one of the oldest recorded religions, the Brahman, the Ultimate Reality represented in many gods and goddesses, is the Eternal Absolute. In Taoism, it is the Tao of Heaven, the source of all creation; and in Judaism, it is Yahweh, the creator of heaven and earth. For Christians, Jesus Christ reveals the relationship of the Father, the Son, and the Holy Spirit as the Eternal Absolute; and for Muslims, it is Allah, the Light of the heavens and the earth.

Whether a culture views the Eternal Absolute as pantheistic or monotheistic, as a powerful, personified natural force, or as a supreme being, the Christ always represents the most revered ideals of that culture: irrefutable Truth, unconditional Love, supreme Wisdom, infinite Freedom, eternal Life, and inherent, divine Unity, life without duality, the Alpha and the Omega of all existence. We find these ideals in the prayers and sacred books of all major religions. In the Upanishads, the Hindus describe the Brahman as "the Whole....speech...mind...and breath,"[1] the source of all unity, the source of all that exists and part of all that exists. The Brahman is an infinite, indestructible, universal Soul, the Absolute Principle in a continually changing world. In the Tao Te Ching, the Tao, "the world's mother,"[2] is described as divine, the Eternal, unceasing, peaceful, and profound. In Judaism, Yahweh represents the unity of all existence and instructs Moses: "I am who I am...Say this to the people of Israel, 'I am has sent me to you'....This is my name for ever" (Exodus 3:14-15).[3] Christian ideals are embodied in the words and actions of Jesus and in his commandments: "You shall love the Lord your God with all your heart, and with all your soul, and with all your mind....You shall love your neighbor as yourself" (Matthew 22:37-40); and "love one another as I have loved you" (John 15:12). And throughout the Koran, Allah is described as "the Compassionate, the Merciful,"[4] the Lord of the Worlds, the Everlasting, the All-Forgiving Creator, All-Hearing, All-Knowing.

In some cultures, these revered ideals are achieved by loving, following, and worshiping God, and by receiving God's grace; in others, by becoming self-less, distancing oneself from any personal ego identity, and regaining original unity with God. For the major world cultures, these ideals describe a state of being which all individuals have the potential to achieve, either in a single lifetime or in many reincarnations. And in almost every culture, there is an acknowledgment that most of humanity falls short of achieving this state of being.

The explanations of why we fall short of these revered ideals differ in context and symbolism from culture to culture, but in every culture, one perception emerges: the way we choose to exercise our free will determines our destiny.

Hindus believe that the Brahman, the universal Soul, endowed all creation with free will. When this free will is misused, one experiences separation from Brahman, duality, and suffering. One's iniquities, often in a previous life cycle, are the cause for all of life's hardships and pain, and one will carry the consequences of one's actions in continuous lifetimes, until one becomes Brahman again: "An ocean, a seer alone without duality, becomes he whose world is Brahman....This is man's highest path. This is his highest achievement. This is his highest world. This is his highest bliss."[5]

Seeing parallels in the perceptions of both Taoism and Christianity, Hieromonk Damascene, an Eastern Orthodox priest, in his book, *Christ the Eternal Tao*,

The Lord saw that the wickedness of man was great in the earth and that every imagination of the thoughts of his heart was only evil continually. And the Lord was sorry that he had made man on the earth, and it grieved his heart.

Genesis 6:5-6

> *What one does in life determines who he is. Those who practice evil become evil. Those who perform acts that are pure, themselves become pure. We are what we do in life. It is our will that determines our fate.*
>
> Brihadaranyaka Upanishad[7]

explores free will as it is understood in both religions: "When man, in wrongly using his free will, first departed from the Way (Tao), he corrupted his primal simplicity and became fragmented."[6]

Damascene elaborates:

> Before his primordial departure from the Way, man had experienced only that which was natural to him. Now...he also experienced what was unnatural to him. Thus he self-willfully usurped the "knowledge of good and evil," destroying the primal simplicity and bringing duality into the world.
>
> Before, man had been spontaneous....At every step, he freely chose...to act according to nature, according to the Way. Now, however, at every step he had to stop and think, to calculate: "Should I follow the Way or not?" Thus he became a complex being, inwardly divided, and always vacillating.[8]

To live according to the Tao requires living in the natural order of things, in "the perpetual round of beginning and return" to man's original state of perfection. No amount of civilization or cultural development can ever replace this Way.[9]

Jews, Christians, and Muslims share a similar understanding of how man became separated from God and from his original state of perfection. In Genesis, we read of how Adam and Eve were tempted to "be like God, knowing good and evil" (Genesis 3:5). In the Judaic and Christian traditions, Adam and Eve are punished for yielding to this temptation, and through their actions, all mankind suffers.

The Catechism of the Catholic Church explains: "The first man was not only created good, but was also established in friendship with his Creator and in harmony with himself and with the creation around him....in an original state of holiness and justice...to share in... divine life."[10]

The Catechism continues:

> Man, tempted by the devil, let his trust in his Creator die in his heart and, abusing his freedom, disobeyed God's command.... In that sin man preferred himself to God and by the very act scorned him. He chose himself over and against God....Created in a state of holiness, man was destined to be fully "divinized" by God in glory. Seduced by the devil, he wanted to "be like God," but "without God, before God, and not in accordance with God...." The harmony in which they had found themselves, thanks to original justice, is now destroyed....Harmony with creation is broken: visible creation has become alien and hostile to man.[11]

A similar story is told in the Koran, but Allah, the All-Forgiving God, does not punish all mankind for the choices made by Adam and Eve. Both Adam and Eve, exercising their free will, made an "error in judgment" which does not condemn the rest of mankind. Every human being, after Adam and Eve, remains free to choose to serve God or to serve his own desires.[12] Every person, therefore, has ultimate responsibility for his own decisions, his own actions, and his own consequences.

Whatever the details of the story of humanity's fall from unity with God may be from one culture to another, in each story, the misuse of our free will to gratify our personal egos, to live without God, and to reinforce an illusion of control leads to duality and suffering. And whatever the details of the story may be from one culture to another, humanity yearns to regain its lost paradise.

These yearnings radiate in the fervent words of the Chandogya Upanishad:

> ...this Soul of mine with the heart is greater than the earth, greater than the atmosphere, greater than the sky, greater than these worlds.
>
> Containing all works, containing all desires, containing all orders, containing all tastes, encompassing this whole world, the unspeaking, the unconcerned – this is the Soul of mine with the heart, this is Brahman. Into him I shall enter on departing hence.[13]

For the Hindu seeker, his awareness of his Brahman Soul prevails over all other human experiences and all existence, and he is consumed with the joy of anticipating the impending unity with the Ultimate Reality.

The same yearnings are found in the Tao TeChing. Here, the man who seeks the path of return to the Tao recognizes his limitations, while those who do not seek this path appear more competent:

> I have the mind of an idiot
> So chaotic and dull!
> Ordinary men are bright and intelligent.
> I alone am chaotically dull!
> Ordinary men are farsighted.
> I alone am blindly chaotic.
>
> Most men follow the groove,
> I alone am stubborn and boorish!
> I alone differ from other men,
> Because I value feeding from the Mother.[14]

How complacent and self-satisfied we can become when we content ourselves with the status quo and "follow the groove," concerned only with our pursuit of feeling good from moment to moment. We do, then, appear "bright and intelligent" and "farsighted." Not so for those who yearn to return to paradise, those who "value feeding from the Mother." In comparison to the perfection of the Eternal Absolute, such seekers do perceive themselves as "chaotic and dull" and "stubborn and boorish." It is this genuine humility that prepares them to be *disciples*, taken literally from the Indo-European root of the word, *dek*, those who can *accept...take in...learn.*[15]

Humanity's profound yearning to return to the original state of unity with God also resonates throughout the Psalms in the Old Testament. We hear that yearning in Psalm 42(1-2): "As a hart longs for flowing streams,

> *Enter by the narrow gate; for the gate is wide and the way is easy, that leads to destruction, and those who enter by it are many. For the gate is narrow and the way is hard, that leads to life, and those who find it are few.*
>
> Matthew 7:13-14

so longs my soul for thee, O God. My soul thirsts for God, for the living God. When shall I come and behold the face of God"; and, again, in Psalm 84(1-2): "How lovely is thy dwelling place, O Lord of hosts! My soul longs, yea, faints for the courts of the Lord; my heart and flesh sing for joy to the living God."

But longing, alone, would not bring a man back to unity with God. Repeatedly, the psalmist reaches out to God for help in purifying himself: "Search me, O God, and know my heart! Try me and know my thoughts! And see if there be any wicked way in me, and lead me in the way everlasting" (Psalm 139:23-24). As in the traditions of Taoism, such longing must also be accompanied by humility: "The sacrifice acceptable to God is a broken spirit; a broken and contrite heart, O God, thou wilt not despise" (Psalm 51:17). Such atonement and humility could lead to salvation as one leaves behind the temptations of personal ego and moves toward unity in God's love.

Beyond one's personal desire to "dwell in the house of the Lord for ever" (Psalm 23:6), the Israelites yearned for the coming of a Messiah, an anointed one, who would bring the kingdom of heaven to earth, overcoming all evil and oppression suffered by the nation of Israel and restoring the harmony mankind enjoyed in the Garden of Eden. Found throughout the Old Testament, messianic prophesies culminate in the words of Isaiah: "Behold, a young woman shall conceive and bear a son, and shall call his name Immanuel" (Isaiah

7:14). "And the government will be upon his shoulder, and his name will be called Wonderful, Counselor, Mighty God, Everlasting Father, Prince of Peace. Of the increase of his government and of peace there will be no end" (Isaiah 9:6-7).

Judaic-Christians find the fulfillment of their yearning for a Messiah and for regaining paradise in the birth, life, Crucifixion, and Resurrection of Jesus: "In the beginning was the Word, and the Word was with God, and the Word was God....And the Word became flesh and dwelt among us, full of grace and truth; we have beheld his glory, glory as of the only Son from the Father" (John 1:1-14). Dwelling among them, Jesus teaches his followers to pray for the kingdom of God on earth and to follow his commandments, and he fulfills their longing for salvation through his sacrifice on the Cross.

In *Paradise Regained*, the English poet John Milton writes ecstatically of humanity's return to paradise through the redemption of Jesus Christ:

> True Image of the Father, whether throned
> In the bosom of bliss, and light of light
> Conceiving, or, remote from Heaven,
>   enshrined
> In fleshly tabernacle and human form,
> Wandering the wilderness – whatever place,
> Habit, or state, or motion, still expressing
> The Son of God, with Godlike force endued
> Against the attempter of thy Father's throne
> And thief of Paradise! Him long of old
> Thou didst rebel, and down from Heaven cast
> With all his army; now thou hast avenged

At that time, the broken will be made perfect; the bent will be straightened; the empty will be filled; the worn out will be renewed; those having little will obtain much; and those having much will be overcome.

Tao Te Ching 22

> Supplanted Adam, and, by vanquishing
> Temptation, hast regained lost Paradise,
> And frustrated the conquest fraudulent.
> He never more henceforth will dare set foot
> In paradise to tempt; his snares are broke.
> For, though that seat of earthly bliss be failed,
> A fairer Paradise is founded now
> For Adam and his chosen sons, whom thou,
> A Saviour, art come down to reinstall;
> Where they shall dwell secure, when time shall be,
> Of tempter and temptation without fear....
> Hail, Son of the Most High, heir of both Worlds,
> Queller of Satan! On thy glorious work
> Now enter, and begin to save Mankind.[16]

Jesus, in conquering the "thief of Paradise," does not simply give mankind hope of returning to Paradise but goes beyond that timeless yearning to establish "a fairer Paradise," more secure than the original Garden of Eden. Beyond anything mankind has ever experienced or imagined, this new Eden is free of Satan's temptations and "without fear."

The expressions of yearning to regain paradise are no less fervent in Islam, one of the three major Abrahamic religions. The Koran (9:72) reveals the joys of this paradise:

> God has promised the men and women who believe in Him gardens watered by running streams, in which they shall abide for ever: goodly mansions in the gardens of Eden: and, what is more, they shall have grace in God's sight. That is the supreme triumph.

There they shall hear no idle talk, but only the voice of peace.

The Koran 19:62

And, like Moses, the believer prays: "Lord, reveal Yourself to me, that I may look upon You" (The Koran 7:143).

Transcending diverse generations and shifting national boundaries, this yearning to reestablish unity with God remains a vital force in the human heart.

Stirring the Soul

Simply surviving is a daily concern for everyone. This reality has shaped human existence from the beginning of time. We must find ways to feed, clothe, and shelter ourselves and our families, whether we are hunting and gathering like the indigenous peoples of Sri Lanka and Australia, farming like the rice growers in Indonesia, catching the morning express into the financial canyons of Wall Street like the brokers of global capital, or telecommunicating like the programmers of cyberspace. Even as the definition of survival changes with the continuous introduction of modern technologies, the challenges of survival remain an all-consuming concern, and the more closely we become connected to each other, the more we persist in viewing our survival as a competitive activity, a battle to control what is perceived as limited resources. As a consequence, we continue to develop more and more sophisticated technologies for competing with and defeating each other, so that now we are fully equipped to annihilate each other.

There is no sin greater than desire.
There is no misfortune greater than discontent.
There is no calamity greater than greed.
Tao Te Ching 46

As in all of human history, we continue to use our social and religious differences as a barely veiled justification for violent oppositional behavior. However, today that violent behavior threatens to destroy not only our alleged competitors but also the very environment in which we all live.

Rene Girard, historian and honorary chair of the Colloquium on Violence and Religion, suggests that, since the beginning of human history, our violent behavior results from a "rivalry that exists at the very heart of human relations. This rivalry, if not thwarted, would permanently endanger the harmony and even the survival of the human community."[17] Whether, as Girard contends, this rivalry is basic in human nature, a "mimetic desire"[18] to have what others have, or whether it is, as many psychologists suggest, an Oedipal phenomenon, or simply a sibling battle waged over securing what is perceived as limited parental love, our history provides overwhelming evidence that we are oppositional, and often violent, in our behavior toward each other.

To allay the tension of this ongoing violent battle with each other, we find many ways to gratify ourselves, to escape from the harsh realities we have created, and to temporarily numb our consciousness. From i-pods to the Mall of America, with its more than five hundred stores, fifty restaurants, seven nightclubs, and fourteen movie theaters, we can distract ourselves and "plug in" to another world indefinitely. And when media and malls fail to provide a satisfying escape, we can

> *...even the most intimate relationships have become part of competition and rivalry.*
>
> *Reaching Out*
> Henri J. M. Nouwen[19]

turn to an unlimited supply of chemical and behavioral alternatives. On June 20, 2010, in an article in "The Money Times," Neka Sehgal reported: "CDC statistics reveal misuse of prescription pain drugs up 111% in 4 years." The report further stated that "ED (Emergency Department) visits involving misuse of anti-anxiety drugs such as Valium, Klonopin, Ativan and Xanax, increased 89 percent from 2004 to 2008."[20] Similar data is found in a 2010 report from the Substance Abuse and Mental Health Services Administration: "In 2009, nearly one quarter (23.7 percent) of persons aged 12 or older participated in binge drinking. This translates to about 59.6 million people."[21] The report defines binge drinking as "...having five or more drinks on the same occasion on at least 1 day in the 30 days prior to the survey."[22]

The statistics for illicit drug use in the United States are equally significant: "In 2009, an estimated 21.8 million Americans aged 12 or older were current (past month) illicit drug users….This estimate represents 8.7 percent of the population aged 12 or older."[24] Illicit drugs are defined as "marijuana/hashish, cocaine (including crack), heroin, hallucinogens, inhalants, or prescription-type psychotherapeutics used nonmedically."[25] The report points out that "among those aged 50 to 59, the rate of past month illicit drug use increased from 2.7 percent in 2002 to 6.2 percent in 2009," a statistic that reflects the aging of the baby boomers who have a higher rate of lifetime illicit drug use than previous generations.[26]

> *We live in a society whose whole policy is...to create as many new desires and synthetic passions as possible, in order to cater to them with the products of our factories and printing presses and movie studios and all the rest.*
>
> *The Seven Storey Mountain*
> Thomas Merton[23]

Burdened with an overriding concern to win our survival battles and absorbed by the many distractions we enjoy in our environment, we often find little time to be introspective, to contemplate our relationships with each other and with God, our purpose in life, and, indeed, the very meaning of life itself. It is as if we go from birth to grave competing against others for our survival and then finding ways to escape from the stress of this battle.

Yet, no matter how desperate our struggle to survive and no matter how enticing our distractions, in all times and in all cultures, our yearning to reunite with the Eternal Absolute remains constant in our consciousness. Whether in the person of a holy man or woman, or in the sacred writings and rituals of our culture, or in acts of compassion and unconditional love that we may witness, the presence of the Christ always stirs our souls, invoking us to move past our familiar state of mind and toward the ecstasy of growth and change.

St. Teresa of Avila, in *Interior Castle*, suggests that God is present in our daily lives and stirs our souls in the most ordinary ways: "His appeals come through the conversations of good people, or from sermons, or through the reading of good books."[27] St. Teresa goes on to suggest that "there are many other ways…in which God calls us. Or they come through sickness and trials, or by means of truths which God teaches us at times when we are engaged in prayer."[28]

Most stirrings of the soul that we experience are, unfortunately, short lived. We will go to church and come out with a glow of brotherly love and peace that will fade as soon as we get behind the wheel of our car and start charging through the busy parking lot on the way to our next destination. We may read an inspirational book, like Walsch's *Conversations with God,* and be moved to tears. Then, in a few hours, we are seduced by life's distractions and forget both the words we read and their effect on us. After a crisis like 9/11, we may come together as one nation united with God in compassion and caring for each other, but in the ensuing months and years, we simply forget and return to our self-absorbed lives. Worse, we lose all sense of God and community and continue to engage in habitual, narcissistic, greedy behaviours that fuel economic instability across the globe.

There are other times when our souls experience such a deep stirring that it has a permanent effect on our awareness of our union with God and this, in turn, changes both our perceptions and our actions. We become less self-absorbed and begin to understand our interdependence and interconnection with God, with all of humanity, and with all that exists in the universe. Among us, there are so many anonymous people whose ordinary, daily commitments reflect their awareness of their universal connectedness: a middle-aged widow who spends all her time crocheting blankets for the orphaned babies who die of AIDS so that their precious little bodies won't be wrapped in plastic when they are buried by the state; a young professional who has moved to Haiti and dedicated herself to bringing hope and leadership skills to the earthquake victims in that country; an elderly Bernadine nun who has left all the comforts of her mother house in Pennsylvania to serve the poor in the favelas of Brazil. We find these people everywhere, and they inspire us. Revealing the Eternal Absolute in their lives, they, too, stir our souls.

At other times, a stirring occurs that is so profound that it leads to actions that benefit all of society. One such stirring occurred in 1993, when Tom Cousins, a philanthropist and real estate developer in Atlanta, Georgia, read a newspaper article which reported that seventy percent of the prison population in New York State came from only eight neighborhoods. Speaking with the Atlanta Chief of Police, Cousins learned that Georgia had even fewer neighborhoods contributing to the majority of criminals in prison and that the East Lake housing project in Atlanta was one of the worst. Cousins visited East Lake, and appalled by its deplorable conditions, he determined to do something. Seeing hundreds of children hanging around this neighborhood, where crime was rampant and drugs were openly sold on the street, he commented: "They had nothing to say about where they were born. They were born there. I thought to myself, had I been born there, I'd probably be one of those people in jail."[29]

In 1995, a year before he retired, Cousins began the East Lake Foundation, an organization that revitalized the East Lake community. Basing his model on the holistic plan he had read about in Joseph Girzone's *Joshua and*

> *When in the self of a discerning man,*
> *his very self has become all beings,*
> *What bewilderment, what sorrow can there be,*
> *regarding that self of him who sees this oneness.*
>
> Isa Upanishad 1.7

the City, and working with existing community residents, local government, educational, and social service organizations, and other business leaders in the area, Cousins built a new community that includes educational, recreational, and self-development programs for the residents. Today, the cycle of poverty in the East Lake community has been broken, and people at various income levels are attracted to living in this unique and vital neighborhood.[30]

East Lake also became a national model for community redevelopment, and, in 2009, Cousins joined with two other business leaders and philanthropists, Warren Buffett and Alex Robertson, to create Purpose Built Communities, a nonprofit organization dedicated to battling intergenerational poverty by transforming dysfunctional, crime-ridden neighborhoods into safe and thriving communities. Member foundations have already been set up in New York, Indiana, North Carolina, Tennessee, Mississippi, and Louisiana.[31]

> *The wise man, trusting in goodness,*
> *always saves men – none is an outcast to him.*
> *Trusting in goodness, he saves all things – nothing is worthless to him.*
> *He recognizes hidden values.*
>
> Tao Te Ching 27

Generating Chaos

Stirring our souls to action, the Christ inevitably generates chaos in society, as people are inspired to change the status quo and evolve. We can see this phenomenon unfolding all around us, with religious and political pandemonium breaking out across the globe, and with natural disasters that are erupting everywhere

> *First of all things was Chaos.*
>
> Theogony
> Hesiod[32]

> *Nature is sensitive to good and evil.... Nature reacts and creates havoc, generating turmoil and confusion that shakes up the souls and hearts of men.... Be patient, a new earth and a renewed kingdom of God is in the process of being born.*
>
> Joseph F. Girzone[33]

with increasing frequency and ferocity. We can also look into the past and see how the stirring of human souls has generated chaos since the beginning of human history. Many ancient civilizations, in fact, saw chaos as the primal beginning of life; and in ways we can recognize today, chaos always marks the beginning of new social structures and new stages of human consciousness.

In Exodus, we can see how chaos sweeps through Egypt each time that Pharaoh refuses Moses' request to free the enslaved people of Israel: "And the locusts came up over all the land of Egypt, and settled on the whole country of Egypt...so the land was darkened... not a green thing remained" (Exodus 10:14-15). As Pharaoh continues to refuse to free the slaves, even greater upheaval occurs: "At midnight the Lord smote all the first-born in the land of Egypt, from the first-born of Pharaoh...and the first-born of the cattle....And the Egyptians were urgent with the people, to send them out of the land in haste" (Exodus 12:29-33).

Shortly afterward, learning that Pharaoh has decided to pursue them and return them to slavery, the Israelites, themselves, collapse into chaos and confusion, and they attack Moses: "Is it because there are no graves in Egypt that you have taken us away to die in the wilderness? What have you done to us, in bringing us out of Egypt" (Exodus 14:11). And they remind Moses that they were reluctant to leave the dependable routines of their enslaved existence in Egypt in the first place: "Is this not what we said to you in Egypt, 'Let us alone and let us serve the Egyptians'? For it would have been better for us to serve the Egyptians than to die in the wilderness" (Exodus 14:12).

How very human the Israelites were! This gripping fear of discomfort and change keeps people in all cultures and in all times enslaved in untenable circumstances and in harsh psychological prisons that define their reality. Preferring to perpetuate their misery than to take the risk of trusting God and responding to the stirrings in their souls, they move from birth to grave in a state of enslavement that they, themselves, have devised. For the chaos that the Christ generates disturbs not only a society but also each individual in that society.

In the course of the forty years that the Israelites wander in the Sinai desert, they experience many miracles that continue to awe them and keep them safe, but each time they become frightened, they crumble again into chaos. When Pharaoh's chariots pursue the Israelites to the banks of the Red Sea, "the Lord drove the sea back by a strong east wind all night, and made the sea dry land, and the waters were divided. And the people of Israel went into the midst of the sea on dry ground" (Exodus 14:21-22). And when the Egyptians pressed on into the dry bed of the Red Sea to capture the escaping Israelites, "when the horses of Pharoah with his chariots and his horsemen went into the sea, the Lord brought back the waters of the sea upon them; but the people of Israel walked on dry ground in the midst of the sea" (Exodus 15:19). But these miracles are not enough to quiet the overwhelming fear and distrust of the Israelites and keep them peaceful.

Although they praise God for these miracles, the people of Israel continue to succumb to fear and deteriorate into hostility and anarchy, and "on the fifteenth day of the second month after they had departed from the land of Egypt" (Exodus 16:1), they again attack Moses: "Would that we had died...in the land of Egypt, when we sat by the fleshpots and ate bread to the full; for you have brought us out into this wilderness to kill this whole assembly with hunger" (Exodus 16:3). Sating their hunger with quails in the morning and manna in the evening, God quiets their fears (Exodus 16:9-12), but shortly after, the people become thirsty and, again, they become angry and frenzied and attack Moses: "Why did you bring us up out of Egypt, to kill us and our children and our cattle with thirst" (Exodus 17:3). And they question God's presence: "Is the Lord among us or not" (Exodus 17:7).

These "stiff-necked people" (Exodus 32:9) continue to be impatient with Moses and with God, and when Moses does not return from Mount Sinai for "forty days and forty nights" (Exodus 24:18), they fear he will never return, and they disintegrate into an unruly mob, reverting to idol worship and pagan sexual orgies.[34] Fashioning a golden calf out of their jewelry, "they rose up early on the morrow, and offered burnt offerings and brought peace offerings; and the people sat down to eat and drink, and rose up to play" (Exodus 32:6).

Observing the idol worship and depravity of the Israelites, God determines to let his "wrath...burn hot against them and...consume them" (Exodus 32:10), but Moses intervenes and convinces God that such action against them could cause the Egyptians to believe that God's intent in freeing the people of Israel was evil (Exodus 32:12). God relents, and Moses returns to the Israelites. Angered by the idolatry and wantonness he witnesses, Moses punishes the Israelites severely for their behavior: shattering, burning, and grinding the Golden Calf into powder, and scattering it upon the water, he forces the people of Israel to drink the polluted water. To dramatize the point that the people of Israel had broken their covenant with God, Moses smashes the tablets on which the Ten Commandments had been written, and he demands to know "Who is on the Lord's side? Come to me" (Exodus 32:19-26). Moses then orders the sons of Levi who came forward to go through the camp and "slay every man his brother, and every man his companion, and every man his neighbor" (Exodus 32:27). When they had done his bidding, and about three thousand men had been killed in retribution for their sins, Moses declares: "Today you have ordained yourselves for the service of the Lord, each one at the cost of his son and of his brother" (Exodus 32:28-29).

Deprived of their familiar, enslaved life in Egypt, the Israelites continue to wander through the desert like fearful, distrustful, and disgruntled victims for a total of forty years. Not any of God's miracles, which saved them from Pharaoh, starvation, and thirst, not even the retribution they suffered at Mount Sinai, was enough to erase the behaviors and the perceptions the Israelites had developed during some four hundred years in Egyptian captivity. Nor did God's patience with them, or even God's willingness to inscribe new commandment tablets to replace the ones Moses had broken in anger, convince the Israelites to trust the one God. They continue to disobey and distrust God and to "murmur" against Him (Numbers 14:27). Although "slow to anger, and abounding in steadfast love" (Numbers 14:8), God resolves that only the descendents of the Israelites who were under twenty years of age, along with two of the original group, would survive and enter the Promised Land: "...surely this I will do to all this wicked congregation that are gathered together against me: in this wilderness they shall come to a full end, and there they shall die" (Numbers 14:35).

Ultimately, only a new generation of Israelites could embrace God's commandments and bring forth a new order. For the former Egyptian slaves remain in bondage to their past experiences and never transcend their ingrained habits. They never come to trust the one God who was leading them to the land "...which flows with milk and honey" (Numbers 14-8). Two among them, Simon and Caleb, do realize a transformation. They are "...of a different spirit..." than the others, and they are allowed to enter the Promised Land along with the new generation of Israelites (Numbers 14:24).

> *In living systems the order arising from nonequilibrium is ...manifest in the richness, diversity, and beauty of life all around us. Throughout the living world chaos is transformed into order.*
>
> The Web of Life
> Fritjof Capra[35]

Because he had displeased God by taking credit for God's miracle when water poured forth from a rock in the desert (Numbers: 20:11-12), even Moses was not allowed to go into the Promised Land:

> And the Lord said to him, "This is the land of which I swore to Abraham, to Isaac, and to Jacob, 'I will give it to your descendants.' I have let you see it with your eyes, but you shall not go over there." (Deuteronomy 34:4)

From the forty years that Moses and the Israelites roam in the desert, a clear message emerges: whether master or slave, prophet or disciple, enduring freedom and change emanate from one's internal transformation and one's union with the Eternal Absolute. While the Christ may stir our souls and generate chaos, evolution depends upon individual conversion, not the conversion of governments or nations.

We see this some fourteen hundred years later, when chaos is again generated among the Israelites by the birth, life, death, and Resurrection of Jesus. Born under the tyrannical rule of the Roman Emperor Octavian, Jesus brings a way of redemption and unity to the distracted and suffering people of Israel. As Moses had delivered the people of Israel from bondage in Egypt and brought them the Ten Commandments, so Jesus offers the people of Israel deliverance from spiritual bondage to Pharisaic law and from physical bondage to Roman tyranny, and he shows them a new way to live in accord with God and his creation. The chaos that is generated by Jesus proves to be so threatening to the existing powers, both in the Sanhedrin and in Rome, that they conspire to crucify Jesus under the tyrannical rule of the Roman Emperor Tiberius.

Chaos is looming in the Roman Empire even before Jesus is born:

> In those days a decree went out from Caesar Augustus that all the world should be enrolled.... And all went to be enrolled, each to his own city. And Joseph also went up from Galilee, from the city of Nazareth, to Judea, to the city of David, which is called Bethlehem, because he was of the house and lineage of David, to be enrolled with Mary, his betrothed, who was with child. (Luke 2:1-5)

Soon after reaching Bethlehem, where their names would be added to the roster of taxpayers, Mary and Joseph seek lodging for the imminent birth of their son. Able to find only a cave where animals are sheltered, Mary gives birth to Jesus and cradles him in a feeding trough. But this humble birth does little to obscure the arrival of this descendent of Abraham, this king, this Messiah. The baby Jesus immediately stirs human souls and generates chaos throughout the Roman Empire and as far away as Syria and Persia, then part of the powerful Parthian Empire:[36] "wise men from the East came to Jerusalem, saying, 'Where is he who has been born king of the Jews? For we have seen his star in the East, and have come to worship him'" (Matthew 2:2). Learning that Jesus is being recognized as king of the Jews by the Magi, King Herod, the Roman ruler of Judea, responds with desperate measures, telling the wise men to, "search diliegently for the child" and to bring the child to him, under the guise of wanting to worhip him (Matthew 2:8). Warned in a dream that King Herod was planning to search for Jesus and kill him, Joseph takes his wife and child and flees to Egypt, where they remain until Herod's death, several years later (Matthew 2:13-15).

Upon the death of the oppressive King Herod in 4 B.C., the underlying discontent and turmoil among the people of Israel comes to a head, and insurrection breaks out throughout the land. Rome responds by rooting out, imprisoning, and crucifying some two thousand rebels. Although Rome brutally suppresses their political rebellion, the Israelites continue to dream "of a Davidic messiah who would shake off the hated foreigners and restore the fortunes of Israel."[37]

In the midst of this unrest, Joseph and his family return to Israel and settle in the village of Nazareth, in Galilee, a bustling province with a diverse and fluid population of Judean, Greek, Roman, and other Gentile inhabitants, traveling merchants, and businessmen. Here Jesus learns to be a craftsman like his father and lives the ordinary life of a young Nazarene.[38] Although his public ministry does not begin until he is about thirty years old (Luke 3:23), when Jesus turns twelve, he determines that his place is in his "father's house" (Luke 2:49). So at Passover, when his parents return to Nazareth, believing

> *Behold, my covenant is with you, and you shall be a father of a multitude of nations....your name shall be Abraham.... and I will make nations of you, and kings shall come forth from you.*
>
> Genesis 17:4-6

he is with their party, he remains in the temple in Jerusalem "sitting among the teachers, listening to them, and asking them questions; and all who heard him were amazed at his understanding and his answers" (Luke 2:46-47).

Some twenty years later, now ready to begin his ministry, Jesus is baptized in the Jordan River by his cousin John, who announces that Jesus is "the Lamb of God, who takes away the sin of the world...the Son of God" (John 1:29-34). In preparation for this ministry, Jesus spends forty days and nights fasting and praying in the desert.[39] Overcoming each of Satan's temptations, he establishes a significant contrast to the behavior of the defiant Israelites during their forty-year journey in the Sinai.

On his journey back from the Judean wilderness to Nazareth, Jesus begins to reveal his divine powers, performing his first miracle at the wedding in Cana, where, at his mother's request, he replenishes the dwindling wine reserves by turning six thirty-gallon stone jars of water into wine (John 2:1-10). Several who had heard John the Baptist proclaim Jesus as the Messiah had joined Jesus, including Philip, Andrew, and Simon Peter, and they bore witness to the miracles he performed (John 1:43-44).

Reaching Jerusalem for Passover, Jesus becomes incensed at seeing merchants and money changers doing business in the temple: "And making a whip of cords, he drove them all, with the sheep and oxen, out of the temple; and he poured out the coins of the money-changers and overturned their tables" (John 2:15). One night, while he is still in Jerusalem, the Pharisee, Nicodemus, seeks Jesus out and questions him. When Jesus proclaims to Nicodemus that "unless one is born anew....born of water and the Spirit, he cannot enter the kingdom of God" (John 3:3-5), the Pharisee responds with disbelief: "How can this be" (John 3:3).

On his way from Jerusalem to Nazareth, Jesus' disciples baptize those in the town of Judea who have come to accept Jesus as the Messiah (John 3:22); and when Jesus reaches Samaria, where many of the locals believe in him, he reveals his identity to a woman who is drawing water from Jacob's well: "The woman said to him, 'I know that Messiah is coming (he who is called Christ); when he comes, he will show us all things.' Jesus said to her, 'I who speak to you am he'" (John 4:25-26).

Jesus continues to perform miracles and to teach those who eagerly seek him out as he makes his way home. When he finally reaches Nazareth, his reputation has preceded him: "And Jesus returned in the power of the Spirit into Galilee, and a report concerning him went out through all the surrounding country. And he taught in their synagogues, being glorified by all" (Luke 4:14-15).

Now home, Jesus appears in the synagogue in Nazareth on the Sabbath, surrounded by those he grew up with, and reveals that he is the Messiah: "And all spoke well of him, and wondered at the gracious words which proceeded out of his mouth; and they said, 'Is not this Joseph's son'" (Luke 4:22). But the harmony is short lived. As Jesus starts teaching those assembled, he encounters open hostility and rejection:

> When they heard this, all in the synagogue were filled with wrath. And they rose up and put him out of the city, and led him to the brow of the hill...that they might throw him down headlong. (Luke 4:28)

What was Jesus teaching that so incensed his neighbors, people he had known all his life? Were they enraged by his words about their unwillingness to accept new ideas from someone they were so familiar with, a "prophet...in his own country" (Luke 4:24)? Were they angered because his words unveiled their unspoken suspicions about the miracles he had performed: "Doubtless you will quote to me this proverb, 'Physician heal yourself; what we heard you did at Capernaum, do here also in your own country'" (Luke 4:23)? Were they upset because the stories he told about the widows and lepers exposed the Israelis' lack of faith in God: "there were many widows in Israel...and Elijah was sent to none of them....And there were many lepers in Israel...and none of them was cleansed" (Luke 4:25-27)? What in Jesus' words could have caused so much antagonism toward him that his neighbors not only ran him out of his hometown but also attempted to do him physical harm?

If they did not want to accept Jesus as the Messiah, they could have just scoffed at him or walked

---

[He] renewed his acquaintance with his home town, and it was a disconcerting experience....they wanted but one thing - that he should depart out of their sight....He knew that he was obliterated from their lives more completely than if he had died.

You Can't Go Home Again
Thomas Wolfe[40]

away from him. After all, he was not the figure of the powerful military leader who many envisioned as their Messiah, a king who would rule over them, defend them against oppressors, and return Israel to the glorious days of King David (Jeremiah 23:5). He was only a carpenter's son, steady, soft spoken, and humble. If they were uneasy with his reputation for performing miracles and healing people, they could have simply dismissed him in their minds as just another itinerant miracle worker, not any different from many others who roamed the countryside.[41] Clearly, the stories Jesus told could have been an unwelcome reminder of the Israelites' lack of faith and idol worship from their years in the Sinai Desert and beyond: "To this day they do according to the former manner. They do not fear the Lord, and they do not follow the statutes or the ordinances or the law or the commandment which the Lord commanded" (2 Kings 17:34). But, even if the Nazarenes were irritated by those stories, they could have just ignored Jesus and disregarded his words.

What really did happen that day in the synagogue in Nazareth that incited such hostility, and how did it foreshadow the antagonism and violence Jesus would encounter throughout his ministry from the Pharisees, the Sanhedrin, and the Romans? Certainly disappointment, disbelief, and irritation are not sufficient provocations for such hostile reactions. What provoked the violence that Jesus encountered in Nazareth, and throughout his ministry, was much more fundamental: a deep-rooted fear of the chaos that he was generating in their routine, rigid, and familiar lives. Every lesson he taught, every miracle he performed, his friendships, his lifestyle, his very demeanor threatened to change the way people lived, worshiped, and perceived their reality, and this threat struck terror in the hearts of those who felt that their personal and political survival depended on things remaining the same. When people fear that their survival is being threatened by change, no matter how unfounded that fear is, they become antagonistic toward the catalyst of that change and want to destroy that catalyst at all costs.

This rigid adherence to familiar traditions and laws was considered critical by the Israelites who had endured living under foreign domination for centuries, as they were now doing in Rome. Especially after the Babylonian destruction of the temple, clinging to their traditions and laws was the only control they had for maintaining their identity as a separate nation.[42] Although continually disobeying God's first two commandments (Exodus 20:2-4) and resisting a loving relationship with God, the Israelites began to change their focus after they were exiled in Babylon. They began to transfer their devotion from the idols they had been worshiping to the Mosaic laws, and those laws became their new idols: "And the word of the Lord came to me: 'these men have taken their idols into their hearts....I the Lord will...lay hold of the hearts of the house of Israel, who are all estranged from me through their idols.'" And God orders the Israelites: "Repent and turn away from your idols" (Ezekiel 14:2-6).

By the time Jesus is born, the Great Sanhedrin is firmly entrenched in the temple in Jerusalem, and by the time he is eighteen years old, Caiaphas, who will condemn him to be crucified, has begun his nineteen-year reign as high priest. Surrounded by Roman authority and concerned primarily with protecting the temple, Caiaphas had quickly learned how to negotiate with the Romans in order to maintain order, and he "instinctively knew where the boundaries lay between what was acceptable and what was unacceptable to Rome."[43] Like those Jesus encounters in the synagogue at Nazareth, Pontius Pilate and the high priest Caiaphas had one overriding concern, maintaining the status quo at all costs.

Avoiding the violence intended by the Nazarenes, Jesus continues his ministry, and his every word and action threatens the status quo and generates chaos in Israel. The Pharisees are at a loss to stop him, and they scheme to discredit him with a public challenge: "Teacher which is the great commandment in the law" (Matthew 22:36). Indirectly attacking the Pharisees for their idolatrous worship of the law and their arrogant indifference toward God and God's children, Jesus replies:

In very truth, it is God, and God alone, whose Spirit stirs up the whole mass of the universe in ferment.

Pierre Teilhard de Chardin[44]

> You shall love the Lord your God with all your heart, and with all your soul, and with all your mind. This is the great and first commandment. And a second is like it, You shall love your neighbor as yourself. On these two commandments depend all the law and the prophets. (Matthew 22:37-40)

Then Jesus directly accuses the Pharisees of their uncaring, uninspired, and exacting enforcement of the six hundred and thirteen Mosaic laws: "Woe to you, scribes and Pharisees, hypocrites! for you tithe mint and dill and cumin, and have neglected the weightier matters of the law, justice and mercy and faith; these you ought to have done, without neglecting the others" (Matthew 23:23-24). And he accuses them of using their fastidious enforcement of the law to keep their flock from building a relationship with God, a relationship they also avoid: "But woe to you, scribes and Pharisees, hypocrites! because you shut the kingdom of heaven against men; for you neither enter yourselves, nor allow those who would enter to go in" (Matthew 23:13).

In so barren a spiritual climate as that produced by the temple cult of the Pharisees, where the high priests are "full of hypocrisy and iniquity" (Matthew 23:28), and "preach, but do not practice" (Matthew 23:3), the flock is without a shepherd, until the appearance of Jesus "the good shepherd [who] lays down his life for the sheep" (John 10:11). For this forsaken flock, Jesus is "a spring of water welling up to eternal life" (John 4:14), "the way, and the truth, and the life" (John 14:6), the gateway to the kingdom of heaven denied to them by Pharisaic theology. And at the Last Supper, knowing that the Pharisees and Romans would try, although in vain, to diminish his influence and regain their equilibrium by accusing him, condemning him, and crucifying him, Jesus establishes a new commandment, a permanent sign that would forever identify his followers: "love one another; even as I have loved you, that you also love one another. By this all men will know that you are my disciples, if you have love for one another" (John 13:34-35).

With the Crucifixion of Jesus, what the Nazarenes and the High Priests fear most, the destruction of the status quo, comes to pass. For at the exact moment of Jesus' death on the Cross, the curtain that separated the Holy of Holies in the Temple, believed to be the dwelling place of God on earth, is "torn in two, from top to bottom" (Mark 15:38). Now, for the first time in the history of Israel, everyone has access to God, and the temple hierarchy is dismantled in one stroke. No longer will the High Priest, who offers sacrifices for himself and his people once a year on the Day of Atonement, be the only living person allowed behind the curtain, face-to-face with God.[45] This event is so compelling that even the Roman centurion understands its significance: "When the centurion and those who were with him, keeping watch over Jesus' tomb, saw... what took place, they were filled with awe, and said, 'Truly this was a son of god'" (Matthew 27:54).

In the next forty days, the risen Jesus appears to many of his followers, and as he had prepared himself during his forty days in the desert to begin his ministry, he prepares his disciples to carry on their ministry, confirming what they had witnessed, promising that they would be "clothed with power from on high," and directing them to preach in his name "to all nations,

> *In living a true life a [person] must submit to the natural way of things, the constant cyclic interplay between chaos and the re-creation of the world.*
>
> Myth and Meaning
> in Early Taoism
> N. J. Girardot[46]

beginning from Jerusalem" (Luke 24:45-52). And as he had strengthened himself during his forty days in the desert in preparation for his ministry, Jesus, in the forty days before he ascends to heaven, also strengthens the ranks of his followers, converting many by his appearance, including the zealous Pharisee and persecutor of Christians, Saul of Tarsus (Acts 22:2-16). During his twenty-four years of bringing "the good news" to the Gentiles, the apostle Paul would stir souls and generate chaos from one end of the Mediterranean Sea to the other and as far south as Arabia, and he would be credited with contributing thirteen of the twenty-seven books to the New Testament.

Ten days after Jesus ascends to heaven, as he had promised, the disciples are "filled with the Holy Spirit.... Then they that gladly received his word were baptized: and the same day, there were added unto them about three thousand souls" (Acts 2:1-41).

In his life, death, and Resurrection, Jesus the Christ generates a timeless, universal state of chaos in the human heart which can transform our ingrained fear of change into an unrelenting thirst to grow continuously closer to God, to experience the ecstasy of our indwelling divinity, and to manifest our love for God in all our thoughts, words, and actions. This state of chaos, which excites every corner of the globe, every vibration in the universe, propels our evolution and shapes our future.

In the city of Mecca, in Arabia, some six hundred years after the birth of Jesus, a prophet is born who

> *We can all ... let the ego die for a while and touch the chaotic ground from which forms and order are constantly bubbling up.*
>
> Seven Life Lessons of Chaos
> John Briggs and F. David Peat[47]

will generate life-altering chaos throughout the Arab world and beyond. The year of his birth, 571 A.D., is "a confused and lawless time," filled with fierce tribal conflicts, economic upheaval, and "an uncivilized people, worshiping idols, eating carrion, committing abominations, breaking natural ties, ill-treating guests, and the strong devouring [the] weak."[48] While small communities of Jews and Christians have already settled there, Mecca remains a polytheistic society, surrounded by a Christianized Abyssinia that had invaded southern Arabia and the Christian Byzantine Empire in the north.

Although exposed to monotheism, Muhammad ibn Abdullah and his family, members of the influential Quraysh tribe, continue to worship at Ka'ba, the central temple in Mecca, paying tribute to a multitude of gods, but especially honoring "the Creator, Allah, the father and king of the other gods."[49] The three hundred and sixty idols of the gods and goddesses enshrined at Ka'ba are regarded with terror and awe, and nomadic tribes from all over Arabia make an annual pilgrimage to Mecca to worship them and seek their protection.[50]

Muhammad's father had died before his birth in 570, and until he is seven, he is raised by his mother and his paternal grandfather. After his mother's death, and his grandfather's death a few years later, his paternal uncle Abu Talib becomes the young boy's guardian. It is from this uncle that Muhammad learns how to earn a living as a businessman and a trader.[51] Muhammad leads a modest life until, at age twenty-five, he marries

Khadija, a wealthy widow for whom he worked.⁵² After the marriage, Muhammad's fortunes improve, but until he is almost forty years old, there is "little outward indication that he was a remarkable person."⁵³

All this changes in the year 610 when Muhammad goes on a month-long retreat with his family to Mount Hira during Ramadan, a customary practice of his Quraysh tribe. One night while there, he is visited in a dream by the Archangel Gabriel who asks him to recite the following lines:

> Recite: In the name of the Lord who created, created man from clots of blood,
> Recite! Your Lord is the Most Bountiful One, who by the pen taught man what he did not know.⁵⁴

On awakening, Muhammad cannot forget these words, and he is deeply distressed by his dream:

> Now none of God's creatures was more hateful to me than an (ecstatic) poet or a man possessed; I could not even bear to look at them. I thought, "Woe is me – poet or possessed. Never shall Quraysh say that of me! I will go to the top of the mountain and throw myself down that I may kill myself and gain rest."⁵⁵

Halfway up the mountain, Muhammad again hears the voice of the Angel Gabriel addressing him: "O Muhammad! Thou art the Apostle of God and I am Gabriel." This distresses Muhammad further, and he stands fixated on the mountain.⁵⁶

Now the word of the Lord came to me saying, "Before I formed you in the womb I knew you, and before you were born I consecrated you; I appointed you as a prophet to the nations."

Jeremiah 1:4-5

Muhammad's distress proves to be well-founded. The prominent Quraysh tribe, to which he belongs, is the custodian of the Ka'ba shrine at Mecca, and their wealth derives both from the annual pilgrimages of nomadic tribes to the shrine and from ongoing trade with these heathen worshipers. In the years to come, as Muhammad pursues his calling and proclaims that there is only one God and that Islam is the only true religion, the Quraysh, fearful that his ideas will alienate the visiting tribes, escalate their opposition to him and his followers with severe, ruthless persecution.[57]

Convinced by his experience on the mountain and the subsequent affirmations of his first converts, his wife, Khadija, and her Christian uncle, Waraqa, that he is the chosen apostle of the one true God, Muhammad begins to share the revelations he receives and to convert those closest to him. In his teachings, Muhammad proclaims that, because the prophets of Israel did not stay true to the word of God, he is the one true prophet of the God of Abraham, and that Islam, derived from an Arabic word meaning obedience and submission, is the one true Abrahamic religion:

> God made a covenant with the Israelites and raised among them twelve chieftains. God said: "I shall be with you. If you attend to your prayers and render the alms levy; if you believe in My apostles and assist them and give God a generous loan, I shall forgive you your sins and admit you to gardens watered by running streams. But he that hereafter

> denies Me shall stray from the right path."
> But because they broke their covenant We laid on them Our curse and hardened their hearts. They have tampered with words out of their context and forgotten much of what they were enjoined. (The Koran 5:12-14)

Christians, Muhammad declares, have also broken their covenant with God:

> They do blaspheme, that say: "God is the Messiah, the son of Mary." For the Messiah himself said: "Children of Israel, serve God, my Lord and your Lord." He that worships other deities besides God, God will deny him Paradise, and the Fire shall be his home....
>
> They do blaspheme, that say: "God is one of three." There is but one God. If they do not desist from so saying, those of them that disbelieve shall be sternly punished. (The Koran 5:72-73)

Muhammad, according to Islamic tradition, is illiterate and never writes down these revelations, which he continues to discern and teach throughout his life. The Koran, the sacred book of Islam, includes a collection of these revelations which were recorded and later compiled by those who heard the prophet speak.[58]

Three years after his experience on Mount Hira, Muhammad begins to bring his message into the public forum, and as he attracts increasing numbers of converts, his ministry alarms the Quraysh establishment. While he is under the protection of his guardian, his uncle Abu Talib, head of the Banu Hashim clan in the Quraysh tribe and a powerful political figure in Mecca, Muhammad is able to continue spreading his message of the one true God, Allah, with little direct interference.[59] This changes dramatically after his uncle's death in 619, and soon Muhammad and his followers are being overtly and viciously assaulted in Mecca. Another uncle, Abu Lahab, who replaces Abu Talib as the new leader of the Banu Hashim clan, becomes one of Muhammad's worst adversaries. So offensive is his hostility toward his nephew that he is named and openly cursed in the Koran (111:1-5):

Al – Lahab

In the name of God the compassionate, the Merciful

May the hands of Abu-Lahab perish! May he himself perish! Nothing shall his wealth and gains avail him. He shall be burnt in a flaming fire, and his wife, laden with firewood, shall have a rope of fibre round her neck!

Because the city lacks a central political body, the social, political, and economic structure of Mecca depends upon carefully maintaining tribal affiliations and loyalties and strictly enforcing adherence to tribal authority and customs.[60] As the devoted followers who are rapidly increasing around Muhammad transfer their allegiances from their tribes to the burgeoning Islamic

> *Do not think that I have come to bring peace on earth; I have not come to bring peace, but a sword.... For I have come to set a man against his father....and a man's foes will be those of his own household.*
>
> Matthew 10:36

community, they represent a substantial threat to the existing tribal authority in Mecca. Muhammad and his followers also pose a threat to the volatile, yet lucrative trading relationships that newly affluent members of the Quraysh tribe are building with nomadic merchants, who regularly come to worship their gods at the Ka'ba shrine.

The tribal leaders, determined to maintain the existing social and political structure and to protect their flourishing mercantile interests, respond to the threat posed by Muhammad and his supporters with harassment and unrelenting brutality and torture. At first, the prophet and his converts are shunned by their tribes and cut off from doing business or interacting with them, but as the Quraysh opposition becomes more violent, Muhammad is forced to find safe havens for himself and his followers.

In 622, three years after he lost the protection of his uncle, Abu Talib, and after he had sent some of his followers to Abyssinia, where they were protected by the Negus, Muhammad learns of a plot to assassinate him. On July 16, 622, the date that marks the beginning of the Muslim era, Muhammad and his converts devise a plan to flee from Mecca and head north to the city of Medina.[61] The hand of God in these pivotal events is recorded in the Koran (8:30): "Remember how the unbelievers plotted against you. They sought to take you captive or to have you slain or banished. They schemed – but God also schemed. God is most profound in His machinations."

> *A prophet is not without honor except in his own country and in his own house.*
> Matthew 13:57

In Medina, Muhammad's influence spreads rapidly, and Islam becomes fully established as a religion with fixed times for prayer, an alms tax, official periods of fasting, defined legal punishments, and prohibited and acceptable behaviors identified.[62] While there is initial cooperation between Muhammad and the monotheistic Jewish tribes living in Medina, as Islam becomes an established religion and Muhammad seeks to convert them, the Jewish tribes resist. Subsequently, suspected of plotting against Muhammad and his mission, they are either killed or banished from the city.[63]

With increased numbers of organized converts, Muhammad is able to lead a series of victorious battles against the Quraysh in Mecca, and in 630, the Prophet wins a decisive battle against the enemies from whom he had to flee only seven years earlier. After Muhammad smashes the three hundred and sixty idols at Ka'ba, the pagan cults throughout Arabia continue to convert to Islam, and the Prophet returns to Medina: "The quarreling tribes had been united in one nation...and in Medina, at least, where he ruled as beloved patriarch, judge, lawgiver, commander in chief and intercessor with God, his community was well established."[64]

The unity among the nomadic tribes of Arabia and their loyalty to Medina and Muhammad begin to dwindle soon after the Prophet's death in 632, and the ensuing years of fierce tribal conflict threaten to tear down all he had built.[65] Eventually, Muhammad's closest friends and successors, Abu Bakr, who had helped him

And the city and all that is within it shall be devoted to the Lord for destruction.

Joshua 6:17

> *There was something chaotic yet complete Which existed before the creation of heaven and earth.... It can be regarded then as the mother of the world.*
>
> Tao Te Ching 25

escape from Mecca in 622, and Umar ibn al-Khattab, are able to bring the warring tribes together again to fight in a wide-ranging military campaign. By 642, these disparate tribes, united by their commitment to the One God, conquer Mesopotamia, Syria, Palestine, Egypt, and Persia. By 711, a continuing surge of Muslim armies also conquers North Africa and Spain, and after each conquest, emerging from the chaos generated by these fervent believers in the One God, multitudes convert to Islam.[66] Today, 1.6 billion people, 23.4 percent of the world's population, follow the teachings of the Prophet Muhammad, contributing their rich history, culture, and beliefs to the diverse global societies in which they live.[67]

Shaping the Future

From the dynamic state of perpetual chaos that is continuously being generated by the Eternal Absolute, boundless inspiration bursts forth for shaping the future. Arousing a desire in us to transform ourselves and the world in which we live, this inspiration ignites our deepest hopes and our most exalted beliefs. We experience this repeatedly in times of personal turmoil, when we are catapulted beyond our daily comings and goings into extraordinary and, often, heroic behavior; and we witness this in others in times of social turmoil, when great leaders emerge, as if from nowhere, and change the course of nations.

On a bus in Montgomery, Alabama, on December 1, 1955, such a great leader emerges, and her resolve starts a movement that shapes the future of race relations in the United States and beyond. At the time, segregation laws were being strictly enforced on buses, as they were in all public places throughout the South:

> ....the front four rows of seats were always reserved for white customers....behind the reserved-for-whites section was a middle section where African Americans could sit if the seats were not needed by white customers. If just one white customer, however, needed a seat in this center section, all those already seated had to move....Even getting on the bus was an elaborate process for black people. They would pay their fare in the front, exit, and then reboard the bus at the back.[68]

Rosa Parks recalls the course of events on that historic December day:

> I took a seat that was just back of where the white people were sitting, in fact, the last seat. A man was next to the window, and I took an aisle seat and there were two women across. We went on undisturbed until about the second or third stop when some white people boarded the bus and left one man standing. And when the driver noticed him standing, he told us to stand up and let him have those seats....And when the other three people – after some hesitancy – stood up, he wanted to know if I was going to stand

up, and I told him I was not. And he told me he would have me arrested. And I told him he may do that. And of course, he did."[69]

Forty-two years old when this occurred, Rosa Parks was no stranger to intimidation and violence. While a strong, supportive family and an abiding relationship with God strengthen her throughout her lifetime, her memories are riddled with the brutalities she encountered: "It was just a matter of survival... existing from one day to the next. I remember going to sleep as a girl hearing the Klan ride at night and hearing a lynching and being afraid the house would burn down."[70] Rosa's grandfather, who had grown up in slavery, harbored deep hostility toward white people and always kept a loaded gun at the ready in case the Klan decided to make him and his family its next target. Rosa acknowledges the effect this had on her: "I think I inherited his hostility...my mother and I both learned not to let anyone mistreat us. It was passed down almost in our genes."[72]

For twelve years before her arrest, Rosa had been working with the National Association for the Advancement of Colored People (NAACP), first as a secretary of the Montgomery chapter and, later, as an advisor to the Youth Council.[73] She recounts that her work there exposed her to an even greater awareness of the "discrimination and acts of violence against blacks.... And the more I learned about these incidents, the more I felt I could no longer passively sit by and accept the Jim Crow laws. A better day had to come."[74] So when

---

History, despite its wrenching pain,
Cannot be unlived,
and if faced with courage,
Need not be lived again.
Lift up your eyes upon
The day breaking for you.
Give birth again
To the dream.

On the Pulse of Morning
Maya Angelou[71]

the Montgomery police arrest her for not yielding her seat on the bus to a white man and take her to jail, then fingerprint her and permit her to make just one phone call, she places that call to Edgar Nixon, the president of the local NAACP.

Rosa vividly remembers what it was like spending the night behind bars: "I felt as if the world had forgotten me. But I felt God's presence with me in the jail cell."[75]

The next day, Nixon and Clifford Durr, a white lawyer who supports NAACP objectives, arrive at the jail to bail her out. Nixon, having consulted with other civil rights advocates, suggests to Rosa that, with their backing, she should appeal her case as a challenge to Alabama's segregation ordinances.[76] Weighing the support as well as the misgivings of her husband and her mother, Rosa agrees: "I felt the Lord would give me the strength to endure whatever I had to face. God did away with all my fear."[78]

To build a strong coalition for his agenda, Nixon unites several major civic organizations and churches under the umbrella of a newly formed Montgomery Improvement Association (MIA). Among the founding members are Ralph Abernathy, pastor of the First Baptist Church, and the twenty-six-year-old pastor of the Dexter Avenue Baptist Church, Dr. Martin Luther King, Jr. Elected president of MIA, King is appointed to spearhead their first protest, the Montgomery bus boycott.[79]

Soon after the start of the boycott, King's home is fire-bombed, and on February 23, he is arrested for

We need to be the change we wish to see in the world.

Mahatma Gandhi[77]

his part in the non-violent protest.[80] At about the same time, because of her involvement in the boycott, Rosa is fired from her job as a seamstress at the Montgomery Fair Department Store, and, subsequently, her husband Raymond loses his job as well. During the next year, Rosa and her husband are also constantly threatened with intimidating phone calls and letters.[81]

Finally, on December 21, 1956, three hundred and eighty-one days after it began, the boycott comes to an end when the United States Supreme Court declares that segregation on public transportation is unconstitutional.

Unable to find a job in Montgomery, Rosa and her husband are forced to move to Detroit in 1957 to seek employment.[82] Rosa reflects on that time in her life and finds that what troubled her most was not her arrest or losing her job or the intimidation she had to endure: "[It] was that we waited so long to make this protest and to let it be known wherever we go that all of us should be free and equal and have all opportunities that others should have....it was not right to be deprived of freedom."[84] Evaluating the impact of her arrest and the subsequent boycott, she concludes:

> ...my arrest brought about the protests for more than a year. And in doing so, Dr. Martin Luther King became prominent because he was the leader of our protests along with many other people. And I'm very glad that this experience I had then brought about a movement that triggered across the United States and in other places.[85]

There is no right place, and no event too humdrum to start from....Any action, anywhere, can trigger a chain of events that crosses space and time, to end (perhaps) clear across the world.

The Pinball Effect
James Burke[83]

Rosa first met Reverend King in August 1955, just four months before she was arrested, when he was a guest speaker at the Montgomery chapter of the NAACP. She remembers being impressed with his speaking ability and with his commitment "to work and do whatever he could in the community for the church to make a difference in the way of life we had at that time." And she was equally impressed "by his leadership, because he seemed to be a very genuine and very concerned person, and, I thought, a real Christian."[86]

King, equally inspired by Rosa, predicts that "the protest sparked by Rosa Park's arrest would have lasting historical significance," and he goes on to clarify her place in history:

> Mrs. Parks' refusal to move back was her intrepid affirmation that she had had enough. It was an individual expression of a timeless longing for human dignity and freedom.... She was anchored to that seat by the accumulated indignities of days gone by and the boundless aspirations of generations yet unborn. She was a victim of both the forces of history and the forces of destiny. She has been tracked down by the *Zeitgeist* – the spirit of the time.[87]

The friendship between Rosa and King strengthens over the years after the boycott, and Rosa continues her active support of the civil rights movement. She is one of only five women to be introduced to a crowd of over two hundred thousand people in Washington, D.C., on

August 28, 1963, when King delivers his inspirational "I Have a Dream" speech;[88] and from March 17 to 25 1965, Rosa joins King and some twenty-five thousand others in a protest march, resulting in the passage, on August 6, of the Voting Rights Act. The march, which begins in Selma, Alabama, ends in Montgomery, where the atrocities of racial discrimination first stirred Rosa to take a stand against injustice.[89]

Inspired by the harsh, chaotic realities of her childhood in the segregated South, Rosa Parks is able to shape the future not only of the civil rights movement in America but also of the human fight for freedom across the globe. In turn, her actions inspire others, including her contemporary and hero, Nelson Mandela. Reflecting on the significance of Rosa's impact on his own struggles to end apartheid in South Africa, Mandela asserts: "Before King there was Rosa Parks. She is who inspired us...to be fearless when facing our oppressors."[90]

On June 20, 1990, just four months and nine days after his release from Victor Verster Prison, the last of three prisons in which he had been incarcerated for high treason for a total of twenty-seven years, Mandela arrives in New York City for an eight-city tour. His itinerary includes a ticker-tape parade through the financial district, an address to the United Nations General Assembly, and a meeting with President George H. W. Bush in Washington, D.C. And on June 27, Mandela travels to Atlanta, Georgia, where he places a memorial wreath at the grave of the Reverend Dr. Martin Luther

King, Jr.[91] The next day, his Freedom Tour heads for Detroit, Michigan. Alighting from the plane at Detroit Metropolitan Airport, Mandela is greeted by a cheering crowd of admirers and local dignitaries, among them the seventy-seven-year-old Rosa Parks. Seeing her in the crowd, the seventy-one-year-old Mandela exuberantly cries out: "Rosa Parks! Rosa Parks!" Then, warmly embracing her, Mandela tells Rosa: "You sustained me while I was in prison all those years."[92]

Unifying Time

The boundless inspiration that arises out of perpetual chaos and shapes the future connects all mankind and unifies the past and future with the present, as down through the ages, we each pursue a timeless yearning to evolve and become one with Christ, the Eternal Absolute. No matter how fleeting our thoughts or how seemingly insignificant our actions, they are influenced by those who have come before us for the past two and a half million years and they are contributing to those who will come after us for countless more millions of years. All those who have come before us are here, now, in our collective experience; and all those who will come after us are here, now, in our life force.

Stating that "every part of the universe is related to every other part but in different degrees," quantum physicist David Bohm explains: "At any given

Look ahead! See how they have gone,
those who have gone before us!
Look back! So will they go,
those who will come after us.

Katha Upanishad 1.6

moment we feel the presence of all the past and also the anticipated future. It's all present and active.... Ultimately, all moments are really one. Therefore now is eternity."[93] Consequently, when we cook our hot dogs over an open campfire, we are sharing in one of the major civilizing experiences of *Homo habilis* and *Homo erectus*, our earliest ancestors;[94] and when we dump millions of gallons of water containing radioactive iodine-131 and caesium-137 into the Pacific Ocean, following a nuclear plant disaster in Japan, we are irreversibly destroying an immeasurable portion of the human and marine food chain for centuries to come.

Like the Christ, we exist in the now, beyond measured time, and our energy is eternal. When we separate past, present, and future in our perception of reality, we are avoiding the truth of our interconnectedness with others and we are avoiding responsibility for the lasting consequences of our thoughts, our words, and our actions. We are, fundamentally, avoiding responsibility for the lasting consequences of our very being, and in doing so, we are unconsciously creating an unintended barrier between ourselves and the Eternal Absolute.

When we drop the illusion of finite time, we become part of a universal community that knows no boundaries, and we can begin to find our way back to the unity we seek with the Eternal Absolute. As Jesus was born in the "fullness of time" (Galatians 4:4) to do the work that had to be done, so we each are born in the "fullness of time" to fulfill a specific purpose. When we

> *...history is always the present past or the present future.*
>
> Social Systems
> Niklas Luhmann[95]

discern our connectedness to the timeless continuum of life, we understand the times into which we are born and the contributions that we are here to make.

Without this discernment, we are destined to live as if we had no responsibility to the past or to the future, and we are doomed by our narrow view of reality to live without benefit of the collected wisdom of the past and without concern for those who are coming after us. We will continue to develop new technologies, amass data and calculate short-term gains while we continue to ignore the long-range consequences of our actions and our decisions. We will continue to resolve problems by reaching for the solutions that promise quick results and immediate gratification while we continue to ignore the implications of everything we do, from turning a blind eye to the alarming rise in AIDS orphans and global starvation to waging unjustifiable wars and inflating the national debt beyond our capacity to regain economic equilibrium. We will continue to rush headlong into new applications of genetic engineering, nanotechnology, and robotics while we ignore the ethical conflicts and imminent dangers these technologies embody.

In his article, "Why the Future Doesn't Need Us," Bill Joy, cofounder and former chief scientist of Sun Microsystems, expresses concern about unrestrained technology development and asks:

> Given the incredible power of these new technologies, shouldn't we be asking how we can best coexist with them? And if our

Behold, now is the acceptable time; behold, now is the day of salvation.

2 Corinthians 6:2

own extinction is a likely, or even possible, outcome of our technological development, shouldn't we proceed with great caution?[96]

Confronting the possibility that "we will gradually replace ourselves with our robotic technology, achieving near immortality by downloading our consciousness," Joy poses another question: "But if we are downloaded into our technology, what are the chances that we will thereafter be ourselves or even human"? He continues: "It seems to me far more likely that a robotic existence would not be like a human one in any sense that we understand ... that on this path our humanity may well be lost."[97]

Along with our humanity being lost, Joy cautions that genetic engineering will "challenge all our notions of what life is" and because of its potential value to the military and to terrorists, "an immediate consequence of the Faustian bargain in obtaining the great power of nanotechnology is that we run a grave risk – the risk that we might destroy the biosphere on which all life depends."[98]

Such unprecedented challenges to the survival of life as we recognize it cannot be met if we continue to perceive an artificial separation between the past, the present, and the future. No matter how much data we accumulate with our advanced technologies, we will not be able to convert that data into solutions that will sustain human life until we consciously and actively accept the reality of our interconnection and interdependence. The

Austrian physicist, Fritjof Capra, speaks of the need for this new paradigm shift, for "an awareness of global interdependence," at a time when "there is an actual possibility of annihilating ourselves if we don't shift." He warns: "The paradigm shift is now really a question of survival for the human race."[99]

While such a shift in consciousness may seem daunting, there are many, over the centuries, who have already made that shift and have fulfilled their unique purpose in the timeless chain of human experience. In the last century, we can look at the lives of exceptional individuals like Mahatma Gandhi, Mother Teresa, and Mikhail Gorbachev to see this new paradigm in action. These people are the avant-garde of human evolution, and each one of them has helped to clear the path for the rest of us and has shown us, by their example, our own potential for transformation. We can also look at people closer to home, unknown heroes whose inspiration and commitment vibrate far beyond the scope and span of their own personal lives, far beyond their own imaginings, and far beyond their own expectations. Such people have moved beyond the limitations of finite time toward unity with the Eternal Absolute. If we seek them out, they will be our guides to a new, evolved consciousness.

He is best qualified to be and to act who... feels each day, each hour, is precious in itself as belonging to the vast sweep of eternity.

Living Words
Edwin Hubbell Chapin[100]

2

CONSCIOUSNESS AND THE SOUL

> *We are conscious automata.*
>
> Collected Essays
> Thomas Huxley[3]

Human consciousness embodies the wisdom of all human experience and the promise of all human progress, personal and collective. Yet, to most neuroscientists, it is simply the result of "the activity of specific neural substrates,"[1] with "the capability to be conscious of being conscious."[2] While there are several theories of exactly how this works, Julian Jaynes, the American psychologist, favors the explanation that this neural substrate is lodged in the connecting neurons, the reticular formation, located in the brainstem, with "direct lines of command to half a dozen major areas of the cortex and probably all the nuclei of the brainstem, as well as sending fibers down the spinal cord where it influences the peripheral sensory and motor system."[4]

Seeing consciousness as simply a function of neural interactions in the brain, Francis Crick, the co-discoverer with James Watson of the structure of DNA, concluded: "'You,' your joys and your sorrows, your memories and your ambitions, your sense of personal identity and free will, are in fact no more than the behavior of a vast assembly of nerve cells and their associated molecules."[5] Going a step further, Crick declares: "the seat of the Will has been discovered!" And he continues: "Free Will is located in or near the anterior cingulated sulcus."[6]

The existence of a "collective unconscious," proposed by the Swiss psychoanalyst Carl Jung, adds yet another dimension to understanding human consciousness and free will. According to Jung, there is a layer of unconsciousness which shapes our responses that is inborn and universal: "The contents of the collective unconscious...are known as *archetypes*... archaic...primordial types, that is, with universal images that have existed since the remotest times."[7] While we cannot free ourselves or be fully conscious of these inherent *archetypes*, Jung suggests that it is important to identify them and understand how they influence our dreams, our myths, our perceptions, and our drives. And he stresses that attempts to deny or disassociate from these embedded, universal *archetypes* can lead to psychosis.[8]

If, as Crick maintains, our free will is located somewhere on a brain fold in the middle wall of the cerebral cortex, and if, as Jung suggests, our perceptions and drives are being influenced by our collective unconscious, where in this configuration of interacting neurons and archetypes can we find our individual souls?

Crick states with certainty: "A modern neurobiologist sees no need for the religious concept of a soul to explain the behavior of humans and other animals."[9] But not all of Crick's colleagues are as adamant on this point. While Nobel Laureate and neuroscientist Gerald Edelman and neurobiologist Giulio Tonini warn us not to "search for the mystical here," they concede: "each mind is unique, not fully exhaustible by scientific means and not a machine," and they allow that not "all meaningful relations at the level of consciousness constitute objects for scientific study." Edelman and Tonini cite as an example "poetic exchanges as they are enacted by sentient humans....To grasp their meaning requires both the unique phenomenal experience and the historically based culture of each participating individual."[10]

Finding that scientific research has failed to explain our persistent sense of self, of personal identity and individuality, neuroscientist and Nobel Prize winner Sir John Eccles offers a more definitive point of view, insisting that any theory that describes the "human mystery...in terms of patterns of neuronal activity... must be classified as a superstition." He elaborates: "neither the genetic uniqueness with its fantastically impossible lottery nor the environmental differentiations, which do not determine one's uniqueness but merely modify it," provide an explanation for "our experienced uniqueness." Further, Eccles contends that, in any comparison of the body and brain to "a superb computer built by genetic coding, which has been created by the wonderful process of biological evolution..., the Soul or Self is the programmer of the computer." He continues: "Each of us as a programmer is born with our computer in its initial embryonic state. We develop it throughout life. It is our lifelong intimate companion in all transactions." Eccles emphatically states: "we are spiritual beings with souls existing in a spiritual world as well as material beings with bodies and brains existing in a material world." And he concludes: "the coming to be of each of us as a unique self-conscious being...is a miracle for ever beyond science."[11]

Like Eccles, Jung also recognizes that his scientific discipline, analytical psychology, has its limitations, particularly when analyzing God and the soul: "The ideas of the moral order and of God belong to the ineradicable substrate of the human soul...what God is in himself remains a question outside the competence of all psychology." Viewing the soul as "underlying all philosophies and all religions," Jung posits: "the facts of the human soul...may ultimately be the arbiters of truth and error."[13]

To date, it would seem that our consciousness and our souls are surviving the scrutiny of the scientific laboratories and the advancement of technology, but we cannot assume their continued survival or the continued survival of our basic human values or our current way

> *...the soul of the universe, the animating principle of nature, the universal spirit...which breathes life into matter....is the source of consciousness.*
>
> Hindu Philosophy
> Theos Bernard[12]

of life. Consider, for example, a paper presented at the IEEE (Institute of Electrical and Electronics Engineers) International Conference on Robotics and Automation in Shanghai, China, on the morning of May 10, 2011. The paper, *Lingodroids: Studies in Spatial Cognition and Language,* written by Ruth Schultz and her team of researchers from the University of Queensland and Queensland University of Technology in Australia, introduced some fifteen hundred conference participants from the international academic and business community to a pair of robots, Lingodroids, who could use language to communicate orally like human beings. Not limited to a programmed set of words, these robots can create new words and teach these words to one another with an unlimited capacity to expand their vocabulary. Schultz and her research team anticipate that this innovative technology will help robots to communicate more effectively with each other and, eventually, to communicate more effectively with human beings. While the ability of the Lingodroids to communicate currently focuses on simple tasks like giving directions and agreeing on names for places they find on a map, the researchers hope that the robots will eventually learn to use language to communicate more abstract and complex concepts.[14]

If millions of years of interaction with our environment led to neural changes that supported our ability to create language, and if our ability to create language led, in turn, to our ability to interact more effectively with each other, which, in turn, accelerated the development of our higher order of consciousness,[15] what might the impact of this latest breakthrough in technology be on our lives? Could robots become so adept at expanding their ability to develop language, communicate orally, and process information and abstract ideas that they will be able to surpass our slowly evolved semantic abilities and create a culture of their own, perhaps even a culture that can live harmoniously, without personal and tribal conflicts? And if, as Ludwig Wittgenstein suggests, language and culture are so inextricably intertwined that even "if a lion could talk, we wouldn't be able to understand it,"[16] could humans find themselves left in the evolutionary dust as a Lingodroid culture evolves faster than we can comprehend or control?

With robots now having the potential to evolve with a speed that is alien to human experience, the time has come for us to reevaluate our own developmental process, how we have come to this juncture in evolution and how we will go forward from here. If we are interested in the survival of human life as we define it, then it is vital for us to make an intentional effort to understand the role that consciousness plays in our survival and to engage purposefully in our own evolutionary process. And it is critical for us to define clearly those values that we want to preserve and reinforce in our culture as we are being catapulted into our own twenty-first century version of Aldous Huxley's *Brave New World*.[18]

> *...if computers do not have the advantage over brains already, then they will certainly have it before too long.*
>
> Shadows of the Mind
> Roger Penrose[17]

Consciousness and Survival: Primal Beginnings

> *Consciousness has emerged during the course of evolution because its advent gave great survival advantage.*
>
> The Primordial Emotions: The Dawning of Consciousness
> Derek Denton[19]

However we may define human consciousness, it is clear that our consciousness is linked to our survival. This is most evident when we consider the development of our conscious awareness of ourselves and the environment in which we live, our prevailing adaptations to that environment over many millions of years, and our continuing ability to change both our environment and ourselves. While it is impossible to verify, with certainty, why one species prevails while another species fades into history, to date, human consciousness, and the behaviors and adaptations that are connected to it, proves to be a key factor in distinguishing *Homo sapiens* from all other species on earth.

The conscious experiences of the earliest hominids, like those of a newborn infant, are stressful and driven by the basic ordeals of survival: being hungry, thirsty, and cold. These ordeals determine all activity, including the way they perceive themselves, one another, and the environment. Whether quadrupeds sleeping in trees at night to protect themselves from animals or bipeds living in caves, these primal hominids, like newborns, sense little distinction between themselves and the world around them. Sensations and emotions are all experienced in the moment, and, without language, communication is limited to instinctive facial expressions and repetitive sounds that, as Darwin proposes, become recognized and understood within a given tribe or species and help them to survive.[20]

Nearly two million years ago, still fully absorbed with immediate survival, *Homo habilis* begins to control and use fire to ward off predators at night, to keep warm, and to cook raw food. This relationship with fire, in time, gives rise to the development of *Homo erectus*, a species with more human characteristics. No longer needed to help them climb into trees at night for protection, their arms grow shorter, and their legs and feet become adapted to walking upright. Now able to rely on fire to keep warm, many venture forth from Africa and migrate to colder climates in glacial regions of Europe and Asia.[21] Their stomachs, no longer an organ used solely for digesting raw food, begin to get smaller, and the energy they need to eat raw food is now utilized for the development of a brain that grows to nearly double the size of their predecessors and closer to the size of our brains today.[22] A social creature, a group of *Homo erectus* may even sit together around the fire at night, although aside from uttering familiar sounds used for indicating immediate survival, mating, and routine needs, there are no campfire stories being told. Language, which permanently separates humans from all other animals, has not yet developed,[24] and consciousness remains primal and instinctive.

Until the emergence of *Homo sapiens*, around 200,000 B.C., communication among hominids continues to be limited, although there is evidence that they are

FIRE
- the power behind all
  works of hands -
he stole it, he gave it away
to human beings.
That's his crime, and
the Gods demand
  he pay for it.

Prometheus Bound
Aeschylus[23]

able to make increasingly sophisticated tools.[25] And while theories abound about exactly when the ability to develop language appears, there is no conclusive evidence to support any one theory. Addressing those theories that point to the larger brain size of *Homo sapiens* in determining the time that language first appeared, biological anthropologist and linguist Terrence Deacon cautions: "the relevant anatomical information, the internal microarchitecture of these brains, has left no fossil trail. With respect to fossil brains, we will never find the 'smoking gun' – the first brain capable of language."[26] We will also never be able to say for sure how early in our history language actually began to develop. Pointing to the earliest hominids with a brain size "within the normal range of modern humans," linguist Derek Bickerton suggests that language had "an early start coupled with painfully slow development."[27] But linguist Guy Deutscher pokes fun at any attempt to determine when language began: "Failing the discovery of a camcorder left behind by careless aliens on a previous visit, it is...difficult to see how the first emergence of speech in hominids can ever be much more than the stuff of fantasy."[28]

Accepting that the question of when speech first emerges remains unanswered, perhaps we can try to understand how it emerges, and here, too, conflicting theories abound. In addition to brain size, language development is also attributed to other vital physical characteristics which may also play a vital role, such as the position of the larynx or the size of the tongue or hyoid bone.[29] Another theory put forth by linguist Noam Chomsky proposes that humans have a "genetic program that provides for the growth of the capacity for language and the particular forms that it assumes."[30] Whether genetically hardwired or a physical structure, or a combination of both, the ability to develop complex language is so unique to humans, and to no other species in the evolutionary chain, that even Darwin found it problematic to explain its existence and, therefore, he concluded: "language is an art….It differs from all ordinary arts, for man has an instinctive tendency to speak…it has been slowly and unconsciously developed by many steps."[31]

Given the limitations of current fossil research, we may find clues to how and why language developed by observing the stages of language development in an infant. In its primal stage of development, a newborn is unconsciously stimulated by basic physical needs. He does not distinguish himself from the people and objects in his environment, nor does he have any understanding of how the people and objects in his environment are meeting his needs.[32] A steady flow between the newborn's initial use of sounds and facial expressions and the responses to those sounds and facial expressions from those in his environment constitute the full extent of the newborn's interactions. As in the interactions of primal hominids, the newborn's sounds are a tool for survival.[33]

Continually experimenting with sounds, the growing infant eventually learns to imitate the sounds he hears, and before he is a year old, he begins to babble, producing single syllables using consonants and vowels. It is at this stage that parents often misinterpret the babbling of "da-da" or "ma-ma" as the infant's first words.[34] By the time the infant reaches his first birthday, his babbling becomes more extensive and the sounds produced become clearer and more distinct and more and more like words, but he is still unable to make sounds that involve two or more adjoining consonants.[35] Although he is more responsive to the words he hears and can point to the correct object when he hears a sound that identifies that object, the one-year old is still not producing words or sentences.

The shift to using actual words, to naming things, and to speaking in sentences begins around twenty-four months, when the toddler, continuing to learn about himself through sensory and motor activities, starts to develop self-consciousness. This growing awareness of the separation between himself and all the objects and people in his environment stimulates the toddler to explore new ways to adapt to his environment.[36] A social being by nature, as the toddler becomes increasingly conscious of the disconnection between himself and his surroundings, he soon experiences an urgent need to reconnect with others, and he meets that need with words. He now identifies himself as "me" and claims his possessions by declaring them as "mine." Asking for

> *Language is a big part of what makes humans distinctive.... human language acquisition is...a consequence of the human drive to communicate.*
>
> Psychiatry and the Human Condition
> Bruce G. Charlton[37]

what he needs and wants with words, instead of merely pointing or crying, the toddler's speech exhibits such a marked difference from the babbling sounds he made as an infant that it appears he has actually lost the ability to make sounds.[38] As the infant continues to perceive that he is separate from his environment, his sense of self and his language skills continue to expand. It is at this point, with the appearance of self-consciousness and language, that human development fundamentally splits from the development of all other living species. This split is reflected clearly in the Indo-European root word for consciousness, *skei,* meaning *cut, split, divide, part.*[39]

One of the toddler's initial adaptations, before learning to combine words and form complex sentences, is the use of simple words to name objects and to identify actions. When the environment has not provided a word, the toddler will often make up a word or use an existing, unrelated word to name an object or an action. Often, these new words and new applications of old words become part of the nuclear family's permanent vocabulary and continue to evoke delightful memories that the family cherishes well after the toddler has grown into an adult.

While we often find the toddler's word creation amusing, it is not in any way different from what adults do when faced with new experiences and new technologies. Now in its twenty-fifth edition, Harry Newton's best-selling *Telecom Dictionary,* first published in 1997 as a *Glossary of Computer Terms,* contains over a thousand new words and new word meanings that arose out of the need to name new technologies and processes for which no words had existed before.[40] Bytes, megabytes, gigabits, modems, hypertext, internet, ethernet, freeware, shareware, and software all found their way into our daily vocabulary. And new meanings for old words appeared: a virus became more than a microbe that made you ill; hardware became more than hammers and nails; and a crash became more than something that happened in a car or on the stock market. Like the toddler, we find ourselves still connecting to our environment by creating words to name objects and actions.

As the toddler continues to grow and as his world becomes increasingly complex, his language also becomes more complex, and, in turn, as his language becomes more complex, it facilitates the expansion of his perceptions and ideas, leading to the use of still more complex language. By the time the child is four years old, he is capable of using language as a symbol for abstract concepts.[41] A constant feedback loop between the child's emerging consciousness and his developing symbolic language abilities opens the way to his limitless expansion in a world not bounded by time or space and "not bounded within a mind or body."[42]

Recognizing the importance of language in human evolution, Derek Bickerton asserts: "it wasn't a 'highly developed brain' that gave us language…and abstract thought, but language that gave us abstract thought and a highly developed brain."[43] While we may never know for certain which came first in the evolutionary development of human beings, a 'highly developed brain,' self-consciousness, or language, there is overwhelming evidence that language is irrevocably linked to human thought and behavior and that, according to Lev Vygotsky, "Thought and speech turn out to be the key to the nature of human consciousness." He elaborates: "Consciousness is reflected in a word as the sun in a drop of water. A word relates to consciousness as a living cell relates to a whole organism, as an atom relates to the universe." And he concludes: "A word is a microcosm of human consciousness."[45]

> *And the light shone in the darkness and*
> *Against the Word the unstilled world still whirled*
> *About the center of the silent Word.*
>
> — *Ash-Wednesday*
> T.S. Eliot[44]

Ingenuity and Emerging Consciousness

If there is one word in the Indo-European lexicon that best reflects Vygotsky's view that words reflect human consciousness, that word is *ingenuity.* Evolving over a period of some four thousand years and finding its way into the language of almost fifty percent of the earth's population,[46] the dynamic Indo-European root from which the word *ingenuity* sprang is *GN.* Pronounced with resonance, this root word is powerful and fertile, with countless derivations in a wide range of languages, from German, Greek, and Latin to Old English and Sanskrit.[47] In its original form, *GN* has two meanings, *to know* and *to beget*; and its derivations, too numerous to list, include *generation, gene, generate, germinate, engine, engineer, genius, genie, ignite*, and, of course, *ingenuity*.[48] The original meaning, *to know*, through the Greek derivation, *gnosis*, means "higher knowledge of spiritual things," as in the Gnostic Gospels; and through the Sanskrit derivation, *yoni*, the word becomes associated with the worship and contemplation of Vishnu and the creative force in the universe.[49]

In its long etymology, *ingenuity* does not diverge far from its original meaning, as many other words in the English language do.[50] This can be attributed to the fact that the original root word, *GN, to know* and *to beget*, continues to be relevant as our ingenuity continues to drive and support the evolution of what we know and create. For more than a million years, at its most primitive level, the application of human ingenuity to solve problems and survive includes the development of various tools that humans make to hunt and kill, including clubs, rounded stones, and spears.[51] At this level, ingenuity is shared with other animal species who can be observed today making simple tools and who, like elephants and orangutans, can be seen using their ingenuity to pick locks and free themselves of shackles.[52]

It is very recently in archeological terms, some sixty to thirty thousand years ago, that *Homo sapiens sapiens* begins to exhibit the uniquely human aspect of its ingenuity by producing art, religious objects, and intricate technologies. Coming more than a million years after the first significant expansion in the brain size of hominids, and about a half million years after the second expansion,[53] this upsurge in creative activity suggests that the tools of ingenuity, not the size of the human brain, are the source of human progress and innovation, empowering us to survive our contemporaries, the *Homo neanderthalensis*, and move forward into the future.

Diagram A
The Dynamics of Human Ingenuity and Perception

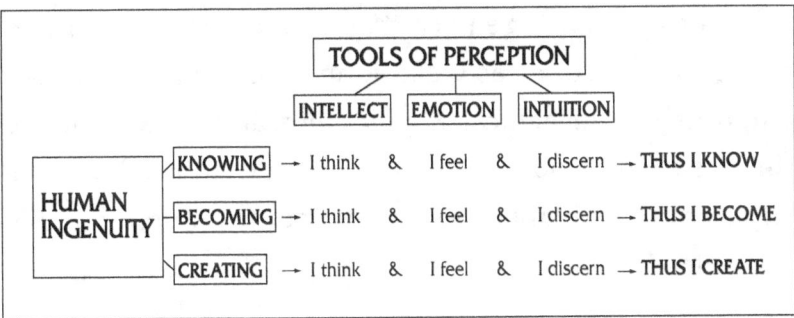

As we continue to evolve as conscious beings with increasingly complex language and social structures, our ingenuity also evolves far beyond its fundamental sense of knowing and begetting. No longer a linear, mechanical response to basic survival challenges, ingenuity becomes a complex human technology that we use for knowing about ourselves and our potential, for being who we are and becoming everything we can become, and for creating and re-creating ourselves and our world. As illustrated in Diagram A, integrating our ingenuity with our distinctively human range of intellectual, emotional, and intuitive tools of perception, we continually transform, with each perceptual tool

> *It's perception that all the gods*
> *Venerate as the foremost Brahman.*
> *'Brahman is perception.'*
>
> Taittiriya Upanishad 2.5

contributing to a balanced, comprehensive perspective for solving existing problems and for setting short-term and long-term goals that will determine what we will know, how we will evolve, and what we will create.

All the technologies that we create are an expression of our ingenuity, and throughout our history, we have come to rely on our ingenuity to develop new technologies that will meet both our existing and emerging needs. In addition to scientific technologies, it is our applied ingenuity that creates new social and economic structures as well. John H. Lienhard, Professor Emeritus of Mechanical Engineering and History at the University of Houston, eloquently describes how the application of human ingenuity led to America being "invented":

> America was not discovered, it was invented. Its name was invented; its machines were invented; its way of life was invented. America was an adventure of the mind. America sprang from the minds of that unlikely breed of people who were able to pack up a few belongings and step into a great unknown. That step into the expanse of a new continent unleashed astonishing creative energy.
>
> The land seemed to reach into infinity, and minds opened to fill it. The colonists...were poorly equipped, but they were freedom-driven and freedom-shaped. They were free of method and free of tradition. They were free to create a new life.[54]

The process of exercising our ingenuity and the new technologies that emerge are so alluring to us that, without considering the consequences, we often use the new technologies we create as an opportunity to exercise our ingenuity again and again to create more and more new technologies. This uninterrupted attraction between our ingenuity and our successive innovations has a life of its own and often spins out of control, leaving us surprised and perplexed that our careless indulgence in exercising our ingenuity has left us with unanticipated and, possibly, lasting problems. Although we often fail to consider this in advance, every technology we create is a potential catalyst for political, social, economic, demographic, and scientific change, generating new needs and new dilemmas that we have not anticipated and are often not prepared to handle. Referring to the dangers of our fascination with our ingenuity, Leinhard comments: "Human ingenuity creates new human appetites, which are eventually met by new ingenuity[56]....The terrifying fact [is] that human ingenuity will do more than we dare dream to meet frivolous wants as well as real needs."[57] And he adds: "The true mother of invention is a powerful, driving internal need to invent."[58]

Our lives are replete with examples of ingenuity spinning out of control. Infatuated with the potential of nuclear energy, we rushed headlong into building nuclear facilities across the globe, motivated not only by our excitement with this new technology but also

> *...for tens of thousands of years we've depended for our survival on our own inventions, on our own creation.*
>
> *Evolution of the Mind*
> Steven Pinker[55]

by our anticipation of new industrial profits. Today, in addition to the well-publicized disasters at Chernobyl and Fukushima that have so far been responsible for millions of deaths and irreversible damage to the environment, we are still faced with the dilemma of disposing of hundreds of thousands of tons of atomic waste precariously stored in nuclear facilities across the globe, with the quantities of spent fuel rods increasing yearly. And in China and India, where the potential of ultrasound technology has been exploited for decades for gender selection, serious population imbalances now exist. With its preference for aborting girl fetuses at the rate of one million a year for the past decade, China now faces a surplus of more than twenty million young males left without any hope for marriage because there simply are not enough females in the population to marry, and it is projected that this imbalance will continue to increase over the next two decades.[59] Beijing's People's University Professor Zhai Zhenwu projects that this imbalance will lead to increased crime and prostitution and "will destabilize China."[60] A similar imbalance exists in India where over twelve million girls were aborted over the last thirty years. Because they can afford the expense of ultrasound testing, India's more affluent, more educated families are responsible for the majority of these abortions.[61]

On a less critical level, we see ingenuity running amok in the availability of a wide range of trivial products. While we could not have imagined needing a microwave prior to 1970 or an Internet connection prior to the early 1980s, these products of our ingenuity have proven to be very valuable and useful. But what about other products: an alarm clock that makes no noise but uses light that slowly gets brighter to gently stir you into awakening each morning; or a watch that talks, reporting the time, day, and date, and chiming at the start of each hour; or a bulb in a battery-operated case that will kill germs on your toothbrush?

Diagram B
The Evolution of Ingenuity and Consciousness

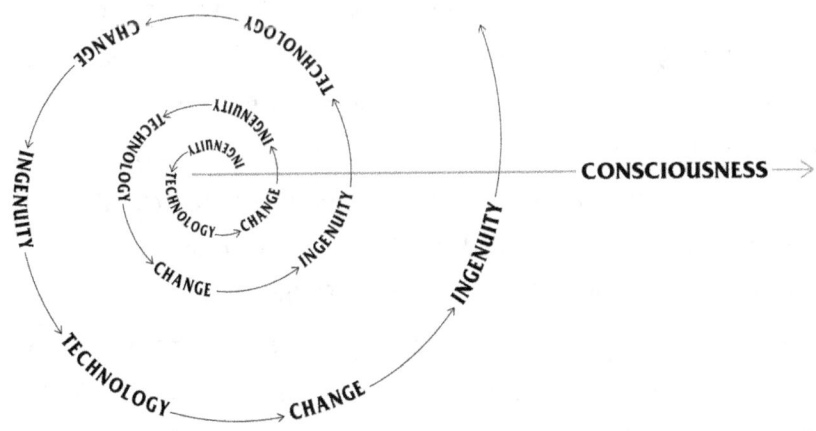

From generating the disastrous to the ridiculous, we seem to have lost touch with how our ingenuity works and with how we can integrate our intellectual, emotional, and intuitive perceptions to ensure that this essential human power is directed toward developing technologies and creating changes that advance our emerging consciousness. See Diagram B above.

> *Thought is always trying to claim that it knows everything.... It has that tendency in it and...this is a very dangerous tendency that leads to self-deception. It doesn't leave open the unknown. It doesn't leave open that the thought is only a representation.*
>
> Thought as a System
> David Bohm[64]

In its current limited definition as "the generation of good ideas and their implementation within society,"[62] ingenuity has become reduced to a quantitative, intellectual application of this essential, driving force of human development. Just how this happened, just why we began to disregard and marginalize the emotional and intuitive perceptions that we need to balance our pursuit of knowing, of becoming, and of creating is explained by Daniel O'Leary, in his book, *Escaping the Progress Trap*: "When humans embrace knowledge in order to mitigate being at the mercy of nature, there inevitably follows an overexploitation of that knowledge."[63] Tracing the history of this propensity for relying on purely rational thought in western industrialized societies, O'Leary points first to "early churchmen, in particular Loyola's Jesuits and their practice of 'mental restriction'....This talent for restrictive rationalization is a latent flaw in human behavior, when used over a long period of time, and results in systemic alienation from reality." O'Leary goes on to explain: "Pure unemotional thought evolved as a useful mechanism for responding urgently to life-threatening dangers. But for everyday purposes, pure intellect is not very useful since it excludes long-term emotional, spiritual, and instinctive knowledge."[65] O'Leary also indicts the scientists, beginning in the Renaissance, who maintained that "quantifiable factors were the only reality," and he explains the political motivations behind their position:

> Their rejection of the un-measurable was not a monument to high standards so much as insurance that the opposition, religion and artistic culture, would no longer set the agenda in worldly affairs....Francis Bacon, Galileo, Newton, and Descartes were followed by a host of thinkers, Hobbes, Locke, Mill and later Hegel and Marx, who helped entrench material empiricism as the *modus operandi* of administrators, educators, industrialists and economists, to the present day.[66]

And O'Leary attacks the myth that science is based solely on objective, rational thought: "The truth is that curiosity, coincidence, intuition, the subconscious, accident and necessity all play a part in it, and have done so since intelligence began."[67]

Initially a political scheme to mitigate tensions between science and religion, this schism between rational thought, emotion, and intuition set the stage for centuries of imbalance in the way we perceive our world, solve our problems, set our goals, and educate our children. Ironically, after more than four hundred years of focusing all our energies on controlling our environment with our ability to think, to be rational, to measure, and to quantify, while disregarding the value of our ability to feel and discern, we now have less control over ourselves and our environment than ever before in our long history on this planet. Never before now, in fact, have we had to come face to face with the reality that we have the capacity for abruptly and irreversibly destroying our world.

Concerned that, in using this exclusively rational approach, we will not be able to keep pace with our unbridled technological advances, Thomas Homer-Dixon, Centre for International Governance Innovation chair of Global Systems at the Balsillie School of International Affairs in Canada, suggests "that reason by itself is not – cannot be – our ultimate salvation, and that we must instead call on our uniquely human capacity to integrate emotion and reason." Dixon also suggests that we "create within ourselves a sense of the ineffable, and achieve a measured awareness of our place in the universe." These steps, he believes, will help us "root out some of our arrogance about our capacity to understand and control the complex systems around us."[68]

What might our world look like today if we had not been so arrogant and if we had not relied on pure intellect to try to control our world and "set the agenda in worldly affairs"[69] for over four hundred years. What might our prospects be today if, before moving forward with the development of new technologies, we had stopped to consider how we felt about the potential impact of new social, economic, and scientific technologies on the way we live? What might our outlook for the future be if we had taken the time to use our intuition to discern whether or not these technologies and the consequences of their development and applications aligned with our values and the evolution of our consciousness?

While four hundred years after the fact these questions can yield only hypothetical answers, they are questions we can begin to ask as we move into the future. And we can resolve to use our emotional and intuitive perceptions, along with our intellect, to formulate future goals and solve future problems. We can access the information provided by our emotions in any given situation and assess proposed solutions and goals in light of our emotional responses. Whether primal emotions, like "thirst, hunger for air….pain, desire to sleep following deprivation," or "scenario-induced emotions," such as "anger, hate, love, and fear,"[70] and whether conscious or subconscious, emotions can have a powerful influence on the decisions we make, on our physical and mental well-being, and, ultimately, on our survival. While it is obvious that making the decision to drink water when we feel the primal emotion of thirst is critical to our survival, more subtle interactions between our emotions and the environment can also have an impact on our well-being. We find an intriguing example of this in several scientific experiments that have shown that "scenario-induced" emotions can actually affect the chemistry of water,[72] which makes up eighty-three percent of our blood, seventy-five percent of our brain,[73] and seventy percent of the earth's surface.[74]

Unlike intellectual and emotional perceptions, which receive and respond to specific internal and external stimuli used to negotiate human survival in a defined environment, our intuitive perceptions function

Feelings, along with the emotions they come from, are not a luxury. They serve as internal guides, and they help us communicate to others signals that can also guide them.

Descartes' Error: Emotion, Reason, and the Human Brain
Antonio Damasio[71]

> *Be still, and know that I am God.*
>
> Psalm 46:10

primarily as open receptors of stimuli from the boundless space of the external world, stimuli that connect us with our inherent universal truths and arouse our collective consciousness of infinite possibilities.[75] From its Indo-European root word *teu*, meaning *consider*, *regard*, through its derivation in Sanskrit, *intuition* means *contemplation*,[76] a very different activity from the objective measurements of the intellect and the random responses of the emotions.

St. Teresa of Avila, in her discussion of what she calls the "Prayer of Quiet," uses the metaphor of an artesian well to describe intuitive perception:

> Let us suppose that we are looking at two fountains, the basins of which can be filled with water....These two large basins can be filled with water in different ways: the water in one comes from a long distance, by means of numerous conduits and through human skill; but the other has been constructed at the very source of the water and fills without making any noise. If the flow of water is abundant, as in the case we are speaking of, a great stream still runs from it after it has been filled; no skill is necessary here, and no conduits have to be made, for the water is flowing all the time. The difference between this and the carrying of the water by means of conduits is, I think, as follows. The latter corresponds to the spiritual sweetness which, as I say, is produced by meditation. It reaches us byway of the thoughts; we meditate upon created things and fatigue the

understanding; and when at last, by means of our own efforts, it comes, the satisfaction which it brings to the soul fills the basin, but in doing so makes a noise, as I have said.

To the other fountain the water comes direct from its source, which is God....I cannot say where it arises or how....For it is not a thing that we can fancy, nor, however hard we strive, can we acquire it, and from that very fact it is clear that it is a thing made, not of human metal, but of the purest gold of Divine wisdom....I mean that, however much we may practice meditation,...we cannot produce this water....it is given...often when the soul is not thinking of it at all.[77]

Explaining how intuition functions in science, transpersonal psychologist Frances Vaughan states: "Most mathematicians who have made significant discoveries in their field avoid the use of mental words, algebraic or other precise signs, and rely on the use of vague images in the process of invention." And Vaughan emphasizes the importance of utilizing all our perceptions: "The stabilization of intuitive insights, and their usefulness to humanity, are subsequently determined by careful, logical examination and validation, but the original vision or insight is intuitive."[78]

If we compare our perceptions to a roaring campfire, then our intellect and emotions are the tangible, solid logs, and our intuition is the empty space between the logs that makes the fire burn. In that empty space,

What makes a fire burn is the space between the logs.

"Fire"
Judy Brown[79]

all the wisdom within ourselves and within the universe becomes accessible. Through that open doorway which is our intuition, we receive insights into our potential which are beyond our ability to imagine,[80] and we touch the timeless, limitless infinity that we are a part of. When we integrate our intuitive discernment with our intellectual ability to know and our emotional ability to feel, we transform our ingenuity into a tool for shaping the direction and pace of our conscious evolution.

Evolving Consciously

Because we are evolving only as fast as our biological and cultural adaptations allow, it has taken us some seven million years to reach our current stage of consciousness. While around 40,000 B.C., with the development of language, we do begin to communicate information to one another and engage in the social interactions that speed up our evolutionary process, any significant change in the way we think and live still takes at least a generation to become established. Observing this in the scientific community, theoretical biologist Lynn Margulis comments: "The only way behavior changes in science is that certain people die and differently behaving people take their place."[82]

Today, with the explosion of information technology, our ability to communicate anywhere on the globe, at any time of the day or night, exponentially

---

We know what we know and we see what we see because we are who we are.

Exodus III
Orest Bedrij[81]

increases our ability for rapid change, and a new generation of "differently behaving people" appear to be utilizing this technology to incite political change. We are witnessing this phenomenon in grass-roots uprisings across the globe, where the ability to communicate instantaneously is changing the face of nations. Referring to the role of social media and its influence on the revolutions in the Middle East in 2011, Purdue professor Glenn Sparks noted, "You have this technology creating large virtual communities where information can be communicated at the speed of light." And, referring to the youth who sparked and supported these movements, his colleague Sorin Matei adds: "The technology wasn't just dropped in their lap and made them do crazy things....There is a whole generation of 20 year olds who have grown with this technology." Looking toward the future, Matei predicts: "We are now at the threshold at seeing a global society emerging, where people are far more similar across borders than ever before."[83]

While these breakthroughs in the application of information technology for political change inspire us and show us what is possible, we still have a very long way to go in changing the ingrained behaviors and familiar perspectives that determine the way we interact with each other and with our environment. On one side of the equation, new technologies and information are available to support a rapid evolution in our human consciousness; on the other side, we are handicapped by our reluctance to change. Stating that information technology will have an "intellectual impact...possibly greater than anything since the invention of language," theoretical physicist James Bailey points out a significant advantage that computers have over humans: "Electronic circuits have a delete key that works. No matter how much effort it has expended to memorize information, electronic memory can let go of it all in an instant and start afresh. Human memory cannot."[84] He explains: "As poor as we are in remembering, we are even worse at forgetting." And he defines the problem further: "We are very resistant to having our familiar rules unsettled. When faced with fundamental change...we can feel its presence, but until we delete some old prejudices, we cannot come to grips with it."[85]

Just as our unyielding ideas and behaviors keep us from moving forward, the way we use language also chains us to the past and to our familiar views of reality. In his classic work, *Language in Thought and Action*, S. I. Hayakawa explains that our words and the way we use and perceive them "largely shape [our] beliefs... prejudices... ideals... aspirations."[86] He further maintains that our use of words often obscures reality: "Words persist when the reality that lay behind them has changed. It is inherent in our intellectual activity that we seek to imprison reality in our description of it." And he warns, "Soon, long before we realize it, it is we who become the prisoners of the description."[87]

If we look at the economic, social, and political challenges we are facing, we can easily identify ourselves as prisoners not only of the words we use that no longer represent reality but also of the ideas and behaviors that have become obsolete. As if the world's resources were unlimited, both emerging industrialized nations and post-industrial western cultures continue to ignore critical realities in their unbridled and insatiable drive to acquire goods and services. Concurrent with this global expansion of industry and consumerism, basic resources of water, food, and energy are rapidly diminishing. Almost one-fifth of the earth's population does not have sufficient water to drink and nearly forty percent are without enough water to maintain minimal sanitation and hygiene. Not taking into account increasing pollution from chemical pesticides and nuclear disasters that are destroying marine life, fifty percent of the fishing areas in the world have been nearly depleted, exacerbated by widespread commercial fishing.[89] While the dwindling supply of easily accessible oil remains an ongoing global challenge,[90] since 1980 the consumption of oil in the United States has increased twenty-seven percent, and China's growing need for oil will require her to import three-quarters of her supply by the year 2020.[91]

Overwhelmed by a population that nearly doubled in the last half of the twentieth century to over six and a half billion people,[92] more than the sum of all the people who have ever lived on the earth,[93] these diminishing resources leave half the children in the world without adequate nutrition, water, sanitation, health, shelter, and education, and a staggering four thousand children die

> *The universe does not exist 'out there,' independent of us. We are inescapably involved in bringing about that which appears to be happening. We are not only observers. We are participators.*
>
> John Wheeler[88]

every day because of dirty water or poor sanitation.[94] As ten percent of the world's population that is labeled "affluent" persists in devouring over seventy-five percent of the earth's resources,[95] an estimated one billion people in the world suffer from obesity, while an equal number of people remain underfed and undernourished.[96] In India, alone, the population continues to increase by sixteen million annually, although the yearly rate of this increase is less than one and a half percent of the current Indian population.[97]

Warning that "the very mechanisms that have allowed *Homo sapiens* to reach high levels of population density are at or near exhaustion," financial analyst Harun Ibrahim maintains: "We are at peak everything: peak oil; peak food; peak water; peak industrialism; peak credit; but not peak population."[98] And Thomas Homer-Dixon paints a graphic picture of the potential for worldwide epidemics faced by this population: "Humankind now makes up one of the largest bodies of genetically identical biomasses on Earth: all of us, taken together, weigh nearly a third of a billion tons." He continues: "Combined with our proximity in enormous cities, and our constant travel back and forth across the globe, we're now a rich environment – just like a huge Petri dish brimming with nutrients – for the emergence and spread of disease."[99]

As we persist in trying to maintain a global status quo that is no longer working and that is clearly unsustainable, to any objective observer, we must look like Nero fiddling while Rome burns, and like Nero, it is we who have set the fire. And it is we who continue to imprison reality in descriptions of our circumstances that are inaccurate and obsolete; and it is we who continue to resist making fundamental changes in our approach to each other and to our global environment.

Throughout history, wars have been fought to secure resources for the victors.[100] As our global resources continue to shrink, are we inevitably headed for a devastating third world war with superpowers vying for control of water, food, and oil? Or, are we headed for "a series of major economic and environmental catastrophes that lead to the fall of Western civilization," as theoretical physicist and experimental psychologist Peter Russell suggests, leaving "pockets of indigenous peoples who survived, and who might well eventually give birth to future civilizations – hopefully wiser than ours"?[101] Will we succumb to what our collective human experience tells us is inevitable, namely, war and the disappearance of entire societies; or, with the extraordinary potential of the technologies we are developing, do we now have another choice? Could we be, as Russell proposes, "on the threshold of great changes in the realm of consciousness"?[102]

If, as most anthropologists have concluded, human adaptations are a response to environmental pressures,[103] then current and imminent threats of population explosion and depletion of resources, coupled with the technologies we are developing,

> *The time has come to take our own evolution into our hands and create a new evolutionary process....We need to replace our old minds with new ones.*
>
> *New World New Mind*
> Robert Ornstein
> and Paul Ehrlich[104]

provide a significant opportunity for us to engage in our own conscious evolution. And unlike the biological and social adaptations we have experienced in the past, which took tens of thousands of years to develop, be communicated, and become manifested in widespread new behaviors, with technology, we can experience an evolution in consciousness that can be manifested in a new behavior in one remote corner of the world and then, in a nanosecond, be communicated and replicated across the globe.

Requiring a shift in awareness and perception that is no more complicated than turning the cylinder of a kaleidoscope and discovering infinite reflected patterns of color and light,[105] evolving consciously requires only that we look inside ourselves, focus on our souls, that *"dimensionless point"*[106] of pure awareness and "quantum potentialities,"[107] and begin to perceive our infinite potential for discovering new perspectives and creating new patterns of interaction. Like the colored pieces of glass placed at the end of the kaleidoscope,[108] all the pieces we need to create a new awareness of reality are already within us. With a few turns of the cylinder, those pieces form countless new patterns, and we discover countless new ways to regard ourselves and our relationship to others. And like looking through the opening of a kaleidoscope, we cannot be distracted but, rather, we must look directly through the opening in order to see the new patterns clearly.[109] Above all, we must be willing to relinquish familiar patterns that will disappear once we turn the cylinder, let in the light, and begin to see and experience new possibilities.

Evolving consciously, daring to turn the cylinder and relinquish the patterns we have come to accept as our only reality, we have the potential to see ourselves and our world with entirely new eyes. We have the opportunity to discover an alternative to our dualistic, perceptions of wealth and poverty, success and failure, abundance and scarcity, *us* and *them*. And we have the opportunity to move away from the competitive violence that is the inevitable result of these perceptions.

Although we persist in our oppositional behavior and our dualistic view of the world, we are being told unequivocally by the scientific community, which began a paradigm shift from Newtonian physics to quantum physics in the 1920s,[110] that all existence is interrelated. Echoing the words of the Kausitaki Upanishad (1.2), "Who am I? I am you!", physicist Richard Feynman explains: "all the world is made of the same atoms…the stars are of the same stuff as ourselves.…no matter what you look at, if you look at it closely enough, you are involved in the entire universe."[111] And stating that "the laws of physics that we have found on our tiny, insignificant planet are the same as the laws found everywhere else in the universe,"[112] theoretical physicist Michio Kaku echoes the Gospel of Mary: "All things, all creatures, all forms exist within, and in relationship to, each other."[113]

Like our tonsils and other vestigial organs, any perception that we continue to maintain of ourselves as disconnected from others is a useless remnant of the past. Any attempt to reinforce a dualistic perception by continuing to live as if our individual intentions and actions do not leave an imprint on others and on every vibration in the universe simply delays the evolutionary leap we must take – that leap into conscious awareness that we are our brother's keeper because we are our brother within the universal body of the Eternal Absolute. Rene Girard warns of the dangers of delaying this leap: "The more people think that they are realizing the Utopias dreamed up by their desire...the more they will in fact be working to reinforce the competitive world that is stifling them."[114] And he adds: "We must place our bets either on the total disappearance of the human race or on our arriving at forms of freedom and awareness that we can hardly imagine."[115]

Survival is not guaranteed to any species. *Homo erectus* and *Homo neanderthalensis*, our closest evolutionary relatives, no longer walk the planet. We are surviving, so far, because we make adaptations that help us to survive. Of those adaptations, none is more beneficial than the continual development of our consciousness. The only species on earth capable of contemplating itself and its place in the world,[117] we are able to examine our thoughts and our behavior, and using our ingenuity and our tools of perception, together with the technologies we have created, we are fully equipped to evolve consciously. We can, at any time we choose, engage in a purposeful, spontaneous, and rapid

> *Our problems are plainly growing beyond conventional human control and consciousness has no choice but to enlarge itself to meet them.*
>
> The Savage and Beautiful Country
> Alan McGlashan[116]

transformation that will lead us to an awareness of an implicit universal order[118] that we now only read about in our sacred literature and in the reports of quantum physicists, an awareness that offers us the possibility of fulfilling our yearning to become reunited with the Eternal Absolute.

Empowering the Soul

From the dawn of our existence as *Homo sapiens,* our history reflects our dualistic perception of each other, the world around us, and the gods we worship. In our nuclear families, we see siblings compete against each other for approval and birthrights. In our clans, we observe families compete against each other for position and property. In our nations, we watch as political factions compete against each other for power and control. And in our world, we become drawn into one war after another as our nations compete against each other for domination over resources and peoples.

The ancient Greeks believed that even their gods were competing against each other, bickering among themselves and inciting and manipulating human conflicts. Homer's *Iliad* provides a glimpse into this Olympian world of petty resentments and violent retaliations, unfolding a story of how Eris, the goddess of discord, instigates the Trojan War by contriving a beauty contest among the three most powerful goddesses:

Hera, the queen of the gods; Athena, the goddess of wisdom and war; and Aphrodite, the goddess of beauty and love. Paris, son of Priam, king of Troy, agrees to judge the contest. Trying to influence his decision, Hera promises Paris power, Athena promises him wealth, and Aphrodite promises him Helen, the beautiful wife of Menelaus, king of Sparta. Choosing Aphrodite as the fairest of the three, Paris soon sets sail for Sparta, abducts Helen, and carries her back to Troy, where they marry. And so the Trojan War begins, as Menelaus seeks to avenge his loss and reclaim his beautiful wife. Resenting their defeat in the beauty contest, Hera and Athena intervene on the side of the Greeks, competing for victory against Aphrodite and the Trojans, until, after ten years of fighting, Troy is burned to the ground and nearly all the Trojans and Greeks are brutally slaughtered. During the war, Zeus, the king of the gods, remains neutral.[119]

In all our earliest relationships with the Eternal Absolute, it is our primal terror of the forces that are beyond our control, both in ourselves and in nature, which is reflected in the many gods and goddesses who represent these forces and in the widespread rituals of human and animal sacrifice we use to appease these deities. Whether worshiping the many gods and goddesses of ancient Greece and Rome, or engaging in prescribed rituals for obeying the more than six hundred Mosaic laws of Yahweh, the one God of the Israelites, fear pervades every aspect of our earliest relationships with the Divine. And the Divine is always perceived as a force outside of us, alien to us, detached from our suffering, and oblivious to our longing for unity.

It is into this world of fear and duality, of squabbling gods and goddesses and Pharisaic laws, that Jesus of Nazareth brings the good news of God's plan for us, "made known to us in all wisdom and insight the mystery of his will,...for the fullness of time, to unite all things in him, things in heaven and things on earth" (Ephesians 1:9-10). And he promises us that we need not live in fear, that God is not oblivious to our sufferings and our longings: "I tell you, do not be anxious about your life....Look at the birds of the air: they neither sow nor reap nor gather into barns, and yet your heavenly Father feeds them. Are you not of more value than they" (Matthew 6:25-26)?

Psychologist Julian Jaynes suggests that Jesus' message signifies a gradual transformation in human consciousness, from the dualistic perceptions of a less evolved, bicameral mind to a more evolved, subjective consciousness.[120] And he parallels this to a similar shift in other religions, in Hinduism, for example, which "hurtles from the bicameral Veda into the ultra subjective Upanishads." This shift, Jaynes explains further, requires us to change our behavior "from within the new consciousness rather than from Mosaic laws carving behavior from without."[121]

Concurring that it is a transformation in human consciousness that changed our relationship with God

> *All things that attain unity have life. And the highest unity is that which produces unity.*
>
> Tao Te Ching 39

from a dualistic alienation, fueled by fear and external laws, to an intimate union based on unconditional love, Richard Rohr, O.F.M., writes:

> The New Testament is sometimes called the New Covenant, signifying a new relationship between humanity and God. Yet...it was not God who changed. It was not as if God decided to let people get along with an old-model covenant until he was good and ready to give them a new one. Rather, it was human beings that changed. The people of Israel had to grow in their understanding of God and the salvation God promised them. Human faith had to develop to the point where people could enter into a new relationship, a new covenant with the God who had always loved them unconditionally. The New Testament is the story of that new relationship.[122]

The connection between human consciousness and the new covenant with God is also addressed by Carl Jung. Through the Incarnation, Jung maintains that "man – that is, his ego – is inwardly replaced by 'God', and God becomes outwardly man."[123] He explains further: "The unconscious wholeness penetrated into the psychic realm of inner experience, and humankind was made aware of all that entered into its configuration." Jung continues: "This was a decisive step, not only for humankind, but also for the Creator – Who, in the eyes of those who had been delivered from darkness, cast off His dark qualities and became the *summum bonum*."[124]

With this new image of God, we embrace our souls, and we come to experience our inherent oneness with God and with all creation.

Regrettably, according to Jung, this "sense of wholeness" that is achieved through the Incarnation begins to deteriorate in the early eleventh century. A period sometimes referred to as the "reign of the Anti-Christ,"[125] this century sees tensions increase between Christians and Muslims, the beginning of the Crusades, which will continue for two hundred years, and the rise of disquieting premonitions about the forces of good and evil and the fate of mankind. Typical of these premonitions, in 1036, in an Armenian kingdom in eastern Turkey, a holy man interprets a concurrent eclipse and earthquake, "something beyond the ken of ordinary men," as a sign of "the release of Satan from the confinement in which Christ's Crucifixion had placed him; the end of the world was at hand."[126] This time of upheaval and confusion, according to Jung, triggers a rise in "symptoms of unrest and doubt," culminating in "a universal catastrophe," and by the beginning of the twentieth century, any perception of unity with God is completely lost in a "hubris of consciousness: 'nothing is greater than man and his deeds.'" Jung proposes that now "humankind's task is to heal the metaphysical divide in the psychic cosmos."[128] Agreeing with Jung, Jaynes laments that "Christianity does not and cannot remain true to its originator," and he notes that the Church "returns again and again to this same longing

> *I laugh when I hear that the fish in the water is thirsty:*
> *You do not see that the Real is in your home, and you wander from forest to forest listlessly!*
> *Here is the truth! Go where you will...; if you do not find your soul, the world is unreal to you.*
>
> *The Songs of Kabir*[127]

> *Do you not yet perceive or understand? Are your hearts hardened? Having eyes do you not see, and having ears do you not hear? And do you not remember?*
>
> Mark 8:17-18

for bicameral absolutes, away from the difficult inner kingdoms of *agape* to an external hierarchy reaching through a cloud of miracles and infallibility to an archaic authorization in an extended heaven."[129]

Why do we not remain true to our new "sense of wholeness," our new consciousness, and our beloved souls? Now more than two thousand years since the beginning of the new covenant began, why do we still revert to an ancient, oppositional, and dualistic relationship with God and, thus, with each other? And why, as Jaynes describes, is the "inner kingdom of *agape*" so "difficult" to sustain? Is it that our faith is so fragile that our fears can easily overcome our faith whenever external forces threaten, causing us to abandon ourselves and our intuitive wisdom to these fears? Or is it our original sin, our hubris, our insistence on preserving an illusion of control that keeps tripping us up? Do we still want to go on living like Adam, separated and alienated from the divine guidance of the Eternal Absolute and, consequently, separated and alienated from each other, from ourselves, from our indwelling divinity, and from our timeless souls?

In *Interior Castle,* St. Teresa of Avila writes: "there are souls so infirm and so accustomed to busying themselves with outside affairs that nothing can be done for them, and it seems as though they are incapable of entering within themselves at all."[130] Is it possible that some people are actually "incapable" of doing this, those for whom "nothing can be done"? And what is the nature of this infirmity in our souls? Could it be that the infirmity in our souls is related to our fragile faith, our fears, and our excessive pride; and could these frailties, in turn, be related to an inability to trust ourselves, trust others, and trust God?

Caryll Houselander, in her book, *A Rocking Horse Catholic*, vividly describes just how fragile human trust is and how easily it can be broken:

> Emotionally children identify their parents with God. They stand for the things that the idea of God stands for to the human race as a whole – security, home, refuge, food and warmth and light, things taken for granted as unquestioningly as the love which provides them is taken for granted, and with the same innocent egoism of childhood. On the day that a young child learns that his trust in father and mother was misplaced…emotionally if not consciously his trust in God is shattered. He will not, of course, reflect that circumstances may have overcome his parents; he looked to them for the invulnerability, the unchanging love that belongs only to God.[131]

Perhaps, if we admit to ourselves just how vulnerable and fragile we really are, floating around in the universe on this infinitesimally tiny blue dot called Earth, we can begin to accept our frailties and we can begin to value ourselves and value each other. We can begin to embrace our need to reunite with the Eternal Absolute and to reawaken that consciousness that, over two thousand years ago, made it possible for us to empower our souls and enter into a new covenant and a more intimate relationship with God. And we can begin, at long last, to do our part to "heal the metaphysical divide in the psychic cosmos."[132]

Acknowledging and accepting our frailties — our fragile trust, our fears, and our hubris — requires both courage and humility, the kind of courage and humility that Jesus reveals to us on the Cross when he cries out in anguish: "My God, my God, why hast thou forsaken me" (Matthew 27:46)? It is at this moment that we can see our most primal fear reflected most clearly in Jesus' suffering: our deep-seated fear of being alone in the universe, abandoned and forsaken. It is this basic human fear that shakes and shatters our trust in our souls and in God, that makes us depend only on those things we can measure with our minds, touch with our hands, and see with our eyes. It is this basic human fear that compels us to clutch tightly to our illusion of control and revert to our most primitive, dualistic perception of our relationship to each other and to the Eternal Absolute. And it is to avoid this primal fear, this personal suffering on the Cross, that we avoid introspection and contemplation, that we busy ourselves with distractions, and that we abandon ourselves, our evolved consciousness, and our empowered souls.

Although we persist in this response to our most deep-seated fear, Jesus offers us an alternative response. Before breathing his last breath on the Cross,

> *...the soul is interior to the mind; it is not inside the mind - the only thing inside the mind is thoughts... introspecting the mind never reveals the soul. As thoughts quiet down, however, the soul emerges... and therefore can transcend the mind, see beyond it, escape it.*
>
> Transformation of Consciousness
> Ken Wilber[133]

Jesus affirms his trust in his Father and cries out: "Father, into thy hands I commit my spirit" (Luke 23:46). If we are to experience being freed from this primal fear of abandonment that is our human cross, then we, too, must have the courage and humility to confront and accept this fear instead of avoiding it. Suspending our intellectual pursuit of the illusion of control and relying upon our intuitive wisdom, we, too, must affirm our trust in the Eternal Absolute, instead of abandoning that trust to our fears.

Through engaging in this process of suffering and affirmation of faith that Jesus reveals to us in his Crucifixion and Resurrection, we can evolve consciously and we can empower our souls. We can become united with the Eternal Absolute, and we can begin to manifest our indwelling divinity in the world.

Therefore, if any one is in Christ, he is a new creation; the old has passed away, behold, the new has come.

2 Corinthians 5:17

3

LEADERSHIP AT A CROSSROAD

We worship in the temple of cutthroat competition.

Desmond M. Tutu[1]

Leadership is a longstanding, universal survival mechanism utilized by groups, no matter how small or large, to provide a competitive advantage. The rank of leadership establishes a pecking order within a group, defining the social, economic, and political duties and status of its members and positioning the group to engage in oppositional encounters with other groups. Except for the smallest nomadic groups, those with between five and eighty members, most related to one another, and tribal groups, settled into a territory and consisting of several hundred members from more than one clan,[2] leadership is generally determined by heredity, as in ancient Egypt and modern Saudi Arabia, or by an official political process, such as popular elections. In the smaller nomadic and tribal groups, the leader is chosen by group selection of their smartest and strongest member, that member who can make the best decisions and ensure the group the best chances of victory in battles with other groups.[3]

With the exception of constitutional republics, like the United States, and constitutional monarchies, like the United Kingdom, the role of the leader in most larger groups establishes a strict chain of command, characterized by a single chief or political bloc that has decisive, centralized control over the entire group. In a constitutional republic like the United States, the leader's role is limited by an intentionally structured balance of power so that no one centralized chief or political bloc can assume total control. This leadership structure also guards against the inherent tyranny of majority rule,[4] so that not even a majority of the citizens can gain total control over the national decision-making process. Only the people's elected representatives have a mandate to make the laws that govern the country. This limitation on popular rule by the majority also applies to presidential elections, which are determined by the votes cast by electors representing the population in each state. Each state is allotted the same number of electors as the number of representatives it has in Congress, plus two additional electors for its two senators. States with larger populations have more Congressional representatives and, consequently, have more electoral votes. For example, a state with ten Congressional representatives and two senators has twelve electors, each casting one vote in the presidential elections. As can happen under this system, over the years, four candidates who win a majority of the popular vote do lose the election because they fail to win a majority of Electoral College votes.[5]

Further ensuring a balance of power in the leadership structure of the United States, each state maintains individual authority over specific responsibilities, and the federal government, itself, is divided into three equally accountable branches, executive, legislative, and judicial, each with specified responsibilities. While subject to interpretation by the Supreme Court, the laws in the Constitution of the United States are the only absolute, recognized authority in the country. If anyone in the nation, including the president of the United States, breaks a constitutional law, that person can be accused, tried, and prosecuted.

The balance of power in this carefully structured constitutional republic extends even to a presidential executive order, one of the only provisions for a president to act without the approval of Congress. If Congress opposes an executive order, it can pass a bill that cancels or changes that order. If the president then vetoes the opposing bill, Congress can vote to override the veto. Presidential executive orders are also subject to the interpretation of the Supreme Court, which can decide that an executive order is unconstitutional.

Unfortunately, history reveals that even in a carefully structured constitutional republic like the United

States, political and special interest power blocs do emerge, gaining enough centralized authority to engage in civil and international wars, perpetuate human rights violations, and influence social policy.

At the farthest end of the spectrum of centralized power structures, we find oppressive totalitarian leaders like Adolf Hitler, chancellor of Nazi Germany, and Mao Zedong, chairman of the People's Republic of China, leaders who not only have total, consolidated authority and control but also tolerate no opposition to their ideas and actions. And oppressive totalitarian leaders are not limited to large national governments. They are also found in smaller, nomadic and tribal groups, in social groups, and even in families. They are found in corporate and non-profit companies, in churches, and in educational and legal institutions. Wherever groups of any size seek a dominant authority to provide them with a survival advantage, they are exposed to the danger of being controlled by oppressive leaders.

Between these two extremes, we find a variety of leadership structures, all designed to help the group fulfill its survival needs and prevail. Addressing the wide spectrum of leadership behaviors in centralized societies, Jared Diamond, author of *Guns, Germs, and Steel: The Fates of Human Societies,* suggests: "At best, [chiefdoms] do good by providing expensive services impossible to contract for on an individual basis. At worst, they function unabashedly as kleptocracies, transferring net wealth from commoners to upper classes." He further suggests

> *The art of leadership, as displayed by really great leaders in all ages, consists in consolidating the attention of the people against a single adversary and taking care that nothing will split up that attention.*
>
> *Mein Kampf*
> Adolf Hitler[6]

that most governments are a combination of both of these functions, that "the difference between a kleptocrat and a wise statesman, between a robber baron and a public benefactor, is merely one of degree." Diamond explains that a society will remain stable depending on "just how large a percentage of tribute extracted from producers is retained by the elite, and how much the commoners like the public uses to which the distributed tribute is put." A kleptocracy, according to Diamond, will always "run the risk of being overthrown" if the "producers," whose creativity and hard work generate the wealth in a society, object to the percentage of money that is being extracted from them or if they disagree with the way that money is being used.[7] Both the French and American revolutions in the late eighteenth century are classic examples of "producers" overthrowing entrenched kleptocracies. More recent popular uprisings against incumbent kleptocrats include the overthrow of Idi Amin in Uganda in 1979, the deposing of "Baby Doc" Duvalier in Haiti in 1986, and, in that same year, the removal and exile of President Ferdinand Marcos in the Philippines.

Diamond also points out that a disgruntled populace sets the stage for a kleptocracy to be overthrown by "upstart would-be replacement kleptocrats seeking public support by promising a higher ratio of services rendered to fruits stolen."[8] The little known island nation of Comoros, located off the east coast of Africa, stands out as the best example on the globe of how an unrestrained assault of "upstart would-be replacement kleptocrats" can destabilize a country for more than thirty-five years. Considered the world's most politically volatile country, Comoros has suffered from at least twenty coups and attempted coups since 1975, when it gained its independence from France.[9]

While every variation of centralized, hierarchical leadership, including a wide assortment of republics, continues to present problems that lead to violations of human rights, revolutions, and, often, genocide, it still remains the prevailing group structure in human history. And while we continue to experience major revolutionary shifts in the way we live and work in western societies, from hunting and gathering to agriculture, which developed very slowly over ten thousand years ago, to the Industrial Age, which began less than three hundred years ago, to the emerging Interactive Age,[10] we still cling to the same, entrenched leadership structures. Even the word *chief*, to describe the positional leader at the top of the chain of command, remains the same. Like the chief in the nomadic hunter-gatherer tribes, our modern companies have a chief executive officer at the top of the leadership pyramid, and with the introduction of information technology, we have added a new chief, the chief information officer. The Indo-European root for the word *chief*, *caput*, means *head*,[11] so along with the structure of leadership remaining the same, the connotation of the root word for the head of that structure, the *chief*, continues to retain the same meaning for over five thousand years.

...it is now well established that of all the higher organisms, humans manifest the greatest resistance to change, preferring to repeat over and over behaviors that lead to results [that are] undesirable.

The Secret of the Incas
William Sullivan[12]

One could easily conclude from our unyielding attachment to this leadership structure that large groups of humans are simply incapable of living without this centralized, authoritative, hierarchy that we consistently endure, in spite of all its proven shortcomings. But we can, in fact, find evidence that we are capable of an alternative leadership structure if we go back far enough into our history to the Nhunggabarra Aborigines who lived in Australia about sixty thousand years ago. Nearly forty thousand years before modern man begins to expand into Northern Europe and forty-five thousand years before North America is settled by nomadic Indian tribes,[13] this large group of more than ten thousand people provides us with significant proof that it is possible to function without a centralized authority. Rather than choose a single leader, all the members of the Nhunggabarra society willingly assume a leadership role, as needed, based on the knowledge, experience, and skill they have for addressing a given problem. As different areas of expertise are needed for different problems that arise, the leadership roles continually shift. This ad hoc, knowledge-based leadership system ensures that no one person or bloc of people can ever seize total authority for controlling information and making vital decisions. Management professor, Karl-Erik Sveiby marvels: "This is a highly advanced form of leadership, found primarily in high-performing teams and in knowledge-intensive organizations." And Sveiby explains that it is this unique, innovative leadership system, "together with spiritual principles that emphasised the *interconnectedness* of all and everything,"[14] that accounts for the Nhunggabarra's ability to thrive peacefully for over fifty thousand years. In the end, only an external assault, a severe smallpox epidemic introduced by European explorers in the early nineteenth century, could bring about the tragic demise of this extraordinary society.[15]

Whether or not any society today would be interested in adopting the alternative ad hoc, knowledge-based leadership structure that sustained the ancient Nhunggabarra society longer than any other civilization in recorded human history, the centralized, hierarchical leadership model that we are so accustomed to is now facing essential and irreversible challenges. Those challenges are rapidly arising from a relatively new technology, the Internet. First bundled with Microsoft Windows 95 and offered free of charge in 1996, this technology is changing the world in ways we could not have imagined a decade ago and in ways we will not recognize a decade from now.

Johnny Ryan, senior researcher at the Institute of International and European Affairs, illustrates how the Internet affords a departure from traditional centralized, hierarchical leadership structures: "The defining pattern of the emerging digital age is the absence of the central dot. In its place a mesh of many points is evolving, each linked by webs and networks." And Ryan indicates the major shift in the source of leadership power that is emerging: "It is also the story about the coming power of the networked individual as the new vital unit of effective participation and creativity." This new "networked individual," according to Ryan, has the "power to challenge even the state, to compete for markets across the globe, to demand and create new types of media, to subvert a society or to elect a president."[16] Defining the Internet as "a centrifugal force, user-driven and open," Ryan observes that this technology is "freeing communities for the first time in human history from the tyranny of geography."[17]

As the Internet continues to provide anonymous individuals across the globe with unlimited access to information and to each other, it creates a level playing field on which everyone is empowered to connect with everyone else, everywhere, and to make a significant contribution in every existing sphere of influence. In addition to empowering unknown and unnamed individuals, this level playing field of information and communication is rapidly eroding a fundamental power base of traditional leaders, namely, control over the ownership, interpretation, and dissemination of information and exclusive authority to shape opinions and make decisions based on that information. And so we are witnessing a groundswell of ordinary, unidentified people demonstrating their ability to confront and overthrow governments, shape world opinion, and make decisions that are defining the future. Oblivious to the geographic boundaries of the past, these newly empowered individuals are able to

> *I know no safe depository of the ultimate powers of the society but the people themselves.*
>
> Thomas Jefferson[18]

share common interests and ideas with countless other individuals, building virtual bridges that span the globe and developing virtual communities that redefine our connection to each other.

Whether or not an untold number of newly empowered individuals or their traditional leaders are ready for such an unprecedented shift in power, from centralized, hierarchical leadership to a "mesh of many points...each linked by webs and networks," this shift is already changing the world we live in. Clearly, former Tunisian President Zine al-Abidine Ben Ali is neither ready for nor aware of the power of thousands of anonymous, digitally connected individuals when they overthrow his regime and cause him to flee the country on January 14, 2011, less than a month after their popular protest begins.[19] Although the corrupt and repressive Tunisian government had previously censored many websites, at the time of the rebellion, eighty-five percent of the ten million Tunisian citizens still own cell phones and approximately two million have Facebook accounts. In addition, another two million expatriates are able to use cell phones, Twitter, and Facebook to maintain contact with the protesters throughout the uprising.[20] One report estimates that, on the day the Ben Ali regime falls, more than fifty million Twitter users reach over twenty-six million people, posting over three hundred million messages about the events. And on that same day, at the highest point of traffic, over fifteen hundred messages are being transmitted every minute.[21]

> *As the Internet takes on an even greater role in the politics of both authoritarian and democratic states, the pressure to forget the context and start with what the Internet allows will only grow. All by itself, however, the Internet provides nothing certain.*
>
> The Net Delusion: The Dark Side of Internet Freedom
> Evgeny Morozov[23]

While this impressive exchange of information certainly does not cause the revolution, both the protesters, themselves, and the pundits assessing the Tunisian uprising agree that the availability of real-time information, before and during the coup, plays a significant role in inciting and spreading anti-government sentiment throughout the country, organizing the revolution, and communicating what is happening to the outside world. The protesters also rely heavily on mobile phones, Twitter, and other Internet communications to protect themselves against government retaliation, to dispel anti-revolutionary propaganda and false rumors, and to control the rampant chaos that erupts after the regime is toppled. During the months leading up to and following the coup, Al Jazeera satellite cable television also plays a major role, circumventing government-censored domestic television channels and broadcasting the videos that are being posted on the web to a widespread audience of older generation Tunisians who are not connected on the Internet, many of them the parents and grandparents of the young activists.[22]

Eleven days after the fall of Ben Ali in Tunisia, Egyptian President Hosni Mubarak also finds himself facing a popular uprising. Immediately following the "Day of Revolt," on January 25, 2011, the Egyptian government attempts to curtail communication among the protesters by disconnecting all Internet and mobile and landline phone services. Reports out of Egypt confirm that, within three days, the government shuts down all four of the major Internet providers, severely disrupting communication within Egypt and between Egypt and other countries. But even with this sweeping response from the government, the Egyptian populace finds a variety of local providers to work around the blackout,[24] and on February 11, only eighteen days after the protests begin, Hosni Mubarak resigns as president of Egypt.

Anticipating the impact the Internet could have on the stability of their regimes, many governments severely restrict and even ban Internet use. In Myanmar, a turbulent, repressive government in Southeast Asia, it is illegal for individual citizens even to own a modem. The consequence for disobeying this law is fifteen years in prison for "endangering the security of the state, national unity, culture, the national economy, and law and order." Similarly restricting laws are in place in many other nations, including North Korea, where only the military elite and government officials are permitted Internet access. In many other nations, such as China, Cuba, and Syria, all Internet communication is censored and under strict government surveillance. In Saudi Arabia, censorship is so severe that the government arrested a blogger for engaging in an intellectual discussion on the positive and negative aspects of being a Muslim.[25] Concerned that the Internet could provide a platform for anti-American propaganda, even the United States imposes restrictions on its Internet companies, requiring them to deny service to certain government officials and organizations in a wide range of countries, including Zimbabwe, Belarus, Cuba, North Korea, Syria, and parts of the Sudan.[26]

While it is now apparent that open access to the Internet poses a permanent challenge to governments, especially to centralized, autocratic regimes, the challenge is even greater for the billions of individuals worldwide who are now more empowered to influence the future than ever before in the history of mankind. The question that each of us, as cyberspace citizens, must now face is how we are going to prepare ourselves to use our expanding power in a way that will bring about the greatest benefit for the evolution and survival of humanity.

Leading into the Unknown

...if you want to test a man's character, give him power.

Abraham Lincoln[27]

In this digitally interconnected world, where each of our thoughts, words, and actions has a potentially significant impact on the course of human events, we are, by virtue of our interconnectedness, accountable for ourselves in ways that are unparalleled in our human experience. For the first time in human history, several billion random individuals are now able to communicate randomly with other billions of random, unknown individuals, in real time, and influence them in ways that are completely unpredictable. Since we cannot track all the possible receivers of our digital communications or estimate the influence we are having on them, recognizing and accepting our personal responsibility for the potential power of our thoughts, words, and actions in this random, unpredictable, digital environment presents an incomparable challenge for each of us.

Defining a random sequence of events, Edward Lorenz, MIT meteorologist and one of the principal architects of chaos theory, explains that "a *random* sequence is simply one in which any one of several things can happen next, even though not necessarily *anything* that can ever happen can happen next. What actually is possible next will depend on what has just happened."[28] Since we cannot control or track "what has just happened" in cyberspace and since we transmit millions of messages from one nanosecond to another, we each bear ultimate responsibility for "what can happen next."

Before 1996, when the Internet becomes more widely accessible, the majority of messages are sent from one individual to another in a deterministic sequence, that is, according to Lorenz, "one in which only one thing can happen next because its evolution is governed by precise rules."[29] By contrast, the randomness of Internet communication has no precise rules governing it or determining what can happen next. Likewise, to use Lorenz's metaphor for chaos, "if a single flap of a butterfly's wings can be instrumental in generating a tornado, so also can the flaps of the wings of millions of other butterflies."[30] And, in digital terms, if a single

Internet tweet can be responsible for inciting a revolution, so also can the millions of tweets that are transmitted every day. The messages we send, like the flapping of a butterfly's wings, can become a powerful new force for advancing global understanding and unity, or they can be used to reinforce our centuries-old habits of opposition and hostility; and each of us, not our positional leaders, has the ultimate responsibility for deciding which path we will take.

Historically divided into two roles, informed, authoritative leaders and law-abiding followers, most people never have to concern themselves with any direct responsibility for influencing the policies and procedures of their society, or for forming opinions about those policies and procedures. Centralized, dominant leaders, with nearly total control over access to vital information and over what information they want to communicate, can maneuver that information to get the responses they want from their followers, and the followers, more often than not, respond as expected. But, today, the traditional lines separating positional leaders and their followers are becoming blurred, as hierarchical leaders are finding that they have less exclusive control over the information they want to communicate and over the responses they try to regulate, and as ordinary people, with universal access to information, are emerging, ad hoc, from everywhere within and outside of a society, to assume leadership responsibilities and fill unanticipated needs as they arise.

> *I believe that the capacity that any organisation needs is for leadership to appear anywhere it is needed, when it is needed.*
>
> Margaret J. Wheatley[31]

More akin to the knowledge-based leadership structure that characterizes the Nhunggabarra Aborigines than to traditional centralized leadership, this new spontaneous leadership behavior can be identified in many of the stories reported during the political uprisings of 2011. One such story illustrates how quickly the role of an ordinary citizen can change from activist to prisoner to government official and then back to ordinary citizen in less than five months. On January 6, Slim Amamou, a thirty-three-year-old computer programmer and Tunisian protester uses his Twitter to inform his friends that the police had arrested him and accused him of "destroying government sites."[32] Seven days later, on January 13, he again uses his Twitter to announce his freedom, and four days later, he sends a message informing his friends that he had accepted the position of Minister of Youth and Sports in Tunisia's interim government so that he could "watch and report and be part of the decisions."[33] Amamou also reports that various members of the interim government who were left over from the old regime are upset that he did not wear a tie to his first meeting.[34] Resigning from his position in the interim government only four months later, on May 25, 2011, Amamou explains: "I agreed to be part of this government with the idea of influencing the decisions. I came out of it because we have defined a clear political agenda." Recognizing Amamou's contribution to the cause of improving democracy in Tunisia, the Friedrich-Ebert Foundation awards Amamou its 2011 human rights prize.[35]

While both traditional and spontaneous leaders are facing uncharted territory in the digital world, the Internet is just one of many dynamic, interrelated driving forces for change that are continually reshaping the landscape and contributing to an uncertain and unknown future. Rapidly shifting social, political, economic, demographic, and scientific realities are eroding all attempts to conduct business as usual, since there is little that is usual about anything that is happening anywhere in the world. Today, every internationally mobile worker is competing against every other worker for every available job on the globe, and enterprising nations are competing against each other to entice long-established local companies, who are looking for the most economical place to do business, not only to export jobs offshore but also to relocate their entire corporate headquarters onto foreign soil. With technology continuing to displace millions of traditional Industrial Age factory and management jobs, with attempts to retrain workers lagging behind demand, and with companies continuing to invest more money in purchasing smart machines than in hiring new workers,[36] we find ourselves knowing what we are losing but painfully uncertain about what we will be gaining.

In the middle of this upheaval in how we work and where we work, nearly eighty percent of college graduates in America are unable to find work equivalent to their education and skill level,[37] and it is estimated that by 2015, more than three million American service jobs will be lost to offshore workers, primarily in the information technology field.[38] At the same time that nearly seventeen million American college graduates find themselves taking jobs below their level of ability and training, including over five thousand with doctoral and professional degrees who are working as janitors,[39] the tuition in both private and public colleges continues to rise, more than doubling the cost of an undergraduate education in the past twenty years.[40] Along with rising tuitions and global competition for jobs, the quality of education in America is declining, and employees report that recent college graduates are deficient in writing English, in written communication, and in leadership, and only adequately prepared with the skills needed for appropriate entry level jobs.[41]

With world markets becoming increasingly interconnected, their economic stability also becomes increasingly interdependent. Since emerging industrialized nations are primarily dependent upon the consumers in the post-industrialized countries to purchase the majority of their manufactured goods, any downturn in purchasing power among the consumer nations has an immediately negative impact on the economy of the emerging nations. At the same time, any downturn in the economy of the emerging nations has a negative impact on the trading opportunities for the developed nations. Contributing further to this ever-increasing interdependence is the degree to which emerging nations are dependent on established economies for energy, grain, and metals.[42] This unprecedented degree of interdependence, providing millions on the globe with expanding opportunities for economic growth, also creates unprecedented problems which can only be resolved with unprecedented solutions; and any traditional perceptions or political and fiscal policies that we have relied on in the past are clearly not adequate for resolving these problems.[43]

The inadequacy of past perceptions and solutions for addressing emerging problems is extending into every aspect of our human experience, as even our birth rates threaten to affect our interdependent economic stability. In China, for example, the one-child policy, while controlling population growth, will lead to a twenty percent drop in both the workforce and consumers in the next forty years. Also, as the population in China ages over the next twenty-five years, another twenty percent of the population will drop out of the workforce.[44] At the same time, reports out of Britain are showing that sixteen percent fewer married couples are having children,[45] and, in America, only seventeen percent of high school females think that a woman's role is in the home.[46] With the rapid expansion of emerging markets fueling the global economy, it is not clear how a diminished workforce and consumer base in any one nation may affect the economic stability of other nations, nor is it clear how, or if, we will begin to address these forecasts.

While this global interaction and interdependence is unparalleled in our human history, so is the pace of this transition from a protected, industrialized society to an increasingly open, worldwide marketplace. Fueled by technologies that facilitate seamless communication across international time zones, at any time and from any place, post-industrial western societies are being propelled into an interconnected global economy five times faster than the last major transition from an agricultural to an industrial economy, which took two hundred years. And supported by modern technology, countries whose gross domestic product was based primarily on agriculture only thirty-five years ago are becoming industrialized at the same breakneck pace and are facing the same dilemmas and the same unknown future.[47]

Not confined exclusively to post-industrial western societies, leading into an unknown future at an unprecedented pace of continuous change presents a dilemma for everyone on the globe, and nothing in our collective human experience has prepared us for this. We may be prepared by past experiences to manage a localized status quo and deal with a few intermittent disruptions, but today's status quo lasts only as long as the next unanticipated disturbance in the weather destroys a rice crop in Indonesia or another breakthrough technology displaces half of the auto workers in Detroit.[48] We are not prepared to lead without being able to forecast outcomes in the distant future, and we are not prepared to make decisions based on information that changes nanosecond to nanosecond. Trying to adjust to this dynamic, interconnected global environment,

There is always something we, here and now, being what we are and where we are, cannot know.

Evolution as Revelation
Jacob Kohn[49]

we use computer forecasting to project scenarios that give us a glimpse into what may occur in the future, but we are reluctant to restructure our mental maps to *not know,* to lead the way into the unknown future by being intuitive, receptive, spontaneous, and free. Reminiscent of the American settlers in the first doomed Jamestown colony, we may have neither the disposition nor the will to change how we think, how we function, or how we are motivated, and like these first ill-fated settlers, we may prefer to die than to change.[50]

Freedom and the Ability to Lead

This persistent reluctance to change, from day to day and from generation to generation, even when our survival depends on our changing, appears to be irrational, and it is. It is as irrational as our fear of the unknown, of losing the illusion of control over the world as we understand it, as irrational as our fear of separating from the lessons and habits of our parents and grandparents, from the attitudes and traditions of our tribe. In our fear, we convince ourselves that we are safer if everything in our environment remains familiar and fixed, if we follow the lessons and habits we learned as children in our families, our schools, and our churches, and if we can predict, with certainty, that by avoiding change in the way we think and function, tomorrow will be just like yesterday. And we cling to the past, to what is familiar, without questioning or reflecting on whether that past is filled with idyllic joys or abusive nightmares, whether that past is providing us with a foundation for lifelong growth or is paralyzing us and holding us back from fulfilling our personal destiny. As long as we can hold on to the familiarity of what we have experienced in the past, we feel safe.

Psychoanalyst Erich Fromm, in his classic book, *Escape from Freedom*, explains how this fear of change begins in childhood, as "the child becomes more free to develop and express his own individual self unhampered by those ties which were limiting it. But the child also becomes more free *from* a world which gave it security and reassurance." Fromm goes on to describe how this freedom to individuate, and the corresponding separation from the people and ideas that are familiar and comforting, often leads to "an isolation that has the quality of desolation and creates intense anxiety and insecurity." If, on the other hand, the child's ability to individuate and separate were balanced by a "corresponding growth of self," this freedom can lead to the child developing a "new kind of relatedness to the world." Unfortunately, according to Fromm, "This does not occur. While the process of individuation takes place automatically, the growth of the self is hampered for a number of individual and social reasons." Fromm concludes: "The lag between these two trends results in an unbearable feeling of isolation and powerlessness, and this in its turn leads to psychic...*mechanisms of escape.*"[52]

> *So, first of all, let me assert my firm belief that the only thing we have to fear is fear itself - nameless, unreasoning, unjustified terror which paralyzes needed efforts to convert retreat into advance.*
>
> Franklin Delano Roosevelt[51]

Armed with these unresolved childhood fears of separation, fears of being free *from* what is familiar and makes us feel safe, we resist any departure from customary procedures and thoughts. Yet, no matter how desperately we may try to resist, the world still continues to change, technologically, demographically, and economically, and rather than acknowledge our fears and our inability to separate from the past, we blame our discomfort on these changes. To the extent that we are threatened by these changes, we become obsessed with undermining and opposing anyone or anything that is an agent of change, with a range of destructive behaviors from passive aggression to open hostility and violence. Such violence marks the opposition of the infamous Theodore Kaczynski to the industrial and technological advancements of the twentieth century that he considers a threat to his well-being. Labeled "the Unabomber" by the FBI because the initial targets of his violence were people connected with universities and airlines,[53] he spends nearly two decades sending parcel bombs to his victims, killing three people and injuring twenty-nine others, and inspiring future terrorists with his ideas.[54] Only a few weeks before his arrest on April 3, 1996, Kaczynski, a Harvard alumnus, writes: "My opposition to the technological society now is less a matter of bitter and sullen revenge than formerly. I now have more of a sense of mission."[55] According to the court-appointed forensic psychiatrist who examines him at the time of his trial, Kaczynski "has intertwined his two belief systems, that society is bad and he should rebel against it and his intense anger at his family for his perceived injustices."[56]

Opposing the continual threat of change in an increasingly diverse and culturally integrated world, various religious groups across the globe are also engaged in violent activities to maintain their most fundamental, age-old traditions, believing that such violent behavior is justified by their devotion to preserving a familiar and conventional way of life. As the world moves toward becoming more open and interconnected, with people discovering common ground across diverse cultures, the fear that these new connections will generate change and threaten traditions escalates, and as the fear escalates, so does the violence.

On a daily basis, our fear of change is also expressed in more socially acceptable, yet equally destructive behaviors. Whether in our families, our communities, or the workplace, we are always on guard, ready at the least sign of change, to defend the status quo and protect our fragile sense of security, and this fear of change, of being free *from* our familiar and comforting alliances and patterns, in turn, motivates all our thoughts and actions. In our families and in our communities, we anxiously align ourselves with others who reinforce our fears, and in the workplace, we oppose any innovation or person who threatens to change the prevailing culture.

This fear of change can bring about disastrous consequences for an entire industry, as futurist and author Joel Barker illustrates in his discussion of how the

The reasonings of mortals are unsure and our intentions unstable.

Wisdom 9:14[57]

Swiss watchmakers, who dominate the watch industry in 1968, find themselves with only ten percent of the market by 1980 because they would not accept change: "The irony...is that the Swiss watch manufacturers... invented the electronic quartz movement at their research institute in Neuchatel, Switzerland. Yet when the Swiss researchers presented this revolutionary new idea to the Swiss manufacturers in 1967, it was rejected." Because the new quartz movement watch does not have a mainspring or bearings, the Swiss manufacturers determine that it is a "useless invention," and without patenting their work, they exhibit it at the World Watch Congress. Barker writes: "Seiko took one look and the rest is history." Japan, which had only one percent of the market before 1968, now dominates the industry, leaving the Swiss watchmaking industry in ruins, with fifty thousand of sixty-two thousand workers laid off.[58]

In the last half of the twentieth century, the same avoidance of change plagues the American car industry, and in the 1950s, while European car manufacturers are introducing innovations such as disc brakes, rack-and-pinion steering, and air-cooled and diesel engines, and Japanese car manufacturers are finding new, more efficient ways to manufacture smaller cars, GM and Ford, stuck in their familiar culture, opt to focus their efforts on increasing their profits by building bigger, heavier, and more expensive cars, adding air conditioning, power steering, and enhanced sound systems. By the 1970s, when oil becomes scarce and the oil prices begin to rise,

Detroit is caught off guard as people begin to prefer the smaller, more economical cars produced in Japan, and by 1980, Japan captures nearly twenty-five percent of the American car market.[59]

More recently, the inability to anticipate and embrace change even afflicts a technology giant like IBM. In 1952, convinced that the company's future is still in IBM punch cards,[60] Thomas Watson, Sr. is "upset at the emphasis being given to computers" in his organization, and Thomas Watson, Jr. remembers that his father often expressed his basic business philosophy by saying, "Shoemaker, stick to your last." The younger Watson, who succeeded his father as chairman of IBM, observes: "Sometimes Dad stuck to his last a little too closely – we came close to missing the computer business for example."[61] Decades later, when IBM engineers present proposals for developing the personal computer to the old time IBM executives who succeed Tom Watson, Jr. as chairman, and who are blindsided by their success in the mainframe business, they could not "imagine why anyone would want a computer on his or her desk," and, this time, they do, in fact, stick to their last and completely miss the wave of the emerging personal computer market. By the time they come on board and start producing PCs in 1981, their share of the burgeoning computer market is already in serious decline, and by 1991, IBM finds itself reporting a loss of almost three billion dollars, followed by more devastating losses of five billion in 1992 and over eight billion in 1993, which sets a record for the amount of money lost by any one company in a single year.[62]

Our rejection of change, our fear of being free *from* what is familiar, and, ultimately, our fear of being separated from our earliest attachments have a negative influence not only on our business decisions but also on our political choices. Explaining our attraction for repressive, totalitarian forms of government, Erich Fromm suggests that "man...tries to escape into new bondage which is to be a substitute for the primary bonds which he has given up." Not a healthy bond that allows for "real union in the world," this new bondage comes at a price, and, according to Fromm, man gains this "new security by giving up the integrity of his self."[63] At the same time, Fromm warns that even a democratic form of government which tries to protect individual freedom does not achieve its ends unless *"we are able to have thoughts of our own."* And he adds: "freedom from external authority is a lasting goal only if the inner psychological conditions are such that we are able to establish our own individuality."[64]

Modern history provides countless examples of our aversion to authentic freedom and our attraction to political bondage, as we witness one nation after another overthrow oppressive rulers only to replace them with equally oppressive political or religious leaders. Overthrowing the tyrannical reign of the Romanovs and murdering the Tsar and his family in 1918, the Russian people replace the tyranny of monarchy with the tyranny of communism. Later in 1979, in Iran, an autocratic Shah is toppled only to be replaced by an equally autocratic religious authority. Even the fear of living in difficult economic times can motivate people to relinquish their integrity and freedom to a despotic dictator, as the German people do when they choose Nazism over freedom after prolonged years of economic depression under the Weimar Republic. And while the world applauds the popular victories over brutal dictators in recent revolutions in Tunisia, Egypt, and Libya, the citizens in those countries are now faced with the challenge of maintaining their newly won freedom and not abandoning that freedom to new political or religious despots.

On a more personal level, being afraid of being free *from* the tyrannies of familiar habits of thought and behavior, we are often driven by those familiar habits to introduce new tyrannies into our lives. Internally afraid of separation from the past, we can become enslaved by an external pursuit of safety, by a quest to accumulate wealth or amass valuable real estate and natural resources, hoping these tangible possessions will quiet our intangible insecurities. And we see entire nations engaging in this same external pursuit of safety, fighting against other nations to amass and control resources. However, as everyone on the globe becomes more interdependent and interconnected socially, politically, and economically, being afraid of being free *from* old attachments and continuing to compete with

So long as men worship the Caesars and Napoleons, Caesars and Napoleons will duly rise and make them miserable.

Ends and Means
Aldous Huxley[65]

> *One of our major problems is fear…. Where there is fear, there is aggression…. Can man be free of fear….. not only at the conscious level but also at the hidden, secret levels of his mind?… Not at the end of one's life but now?…Fear… makes everything go dark, there is no clarity, and a mind that is afraid cannot see what life is, what the real problems are….it is only in freedom that you can explore, discover.*
>
> You Are the World
> Jiddu Krishnamurti[67]

others to accumulate wealth and resources to assuage our insecurities severely undermine our ability to be collaborative and to lead into an unknown future.

Our greatest challenge in our conscious evolution, then, is finding a way to shift our motivations from being afraid to be free *from* the past to being free to move away from the past and into the future. And we can discover clues for making this shift embedded in the history of our language, in the Indo-European root word *prai,* from which both the words *free* and *afraid* derive.[66] Since both these words are derivations of the same root word, *prai,* the first clue we discover is that there is an underlying relationship between being free and being afraid. In fact, they are the antithesis of each other: if we are afraid, that fear automatically controls our thoughts, shapes our words, drives our actions, and prevents us from being free; so, if we are afraid, by definition, we cannot, at the same time, be free. And, as history repeatedly proves, if we are not free, we cannot recreate ourselves and our world; we cannot lead into the future.

The original meaning of the word *prai* – *beloved, precious, at peace* – also provides significant insight into the components of being free. If we sense that we are beloved, we feel precious and enjoy a strong sense of self worth, and, consequently, we are at peace with ourselves and the world. We are *prai, beloved, precious,* and *at peace*, and we are free. Conversely, if experiences in our lives result in our feeling unloved, we find it difficult to comprehend that we have innate human value, and, lacking a sense of self worth, we are at odds with ourselves and, consequently, with the world. We are *effrayer*, the French word derived from the Indo-European *prai* and the Latin *ex*, meaning *out of*.[68] Being without a sense that we are beloved, precious, and at peace, we are afraid.

Since few of us are ever entirely free or entirely afraid, our thoughts, words, and actions are constantly vacillating back and forth on an internal continuum between being free and being afraid. As we begin to take notice of our motivations, and especially of those shaped by our fears, we can clearly begin to see how those fears are distorting not only our perceptions of ourselves and our environment but also our ability to build a new consciousness and a new world. And the antidote to those fears is clear: we can consciously reexamine those experiences that make us feel unloved, worthless, and insecure, and we can leave those experiences in the past and seek out new experiences that will reinforce that we are beloved, we are precious, and, consequently, we can be at peace. We can be free. And we can continually be open to helping others feel beloved, precious, and at peace. We can continually help others to become free.

If we do not take this course of action, if we remain oblivious to the control our fears have over us, if we let those fears continue to distort our perceptions of ourselves and reality, and if we do not choose to change, to become free, we will keep traveling on a desperate path of fear, self-destruction, opposition, and aggression. And as Rene Girard predicts, we will continue "battling to the end" in a downward spiral where "humanity is more than ever the author of its own fall because it has become able to destroy its world."[69]

The World Awaits Its Leaders

No matter what continent we inhabit on this planet, we cannot escape the ravages of irrational human fear and the oppositional, aggressive, and violent behaviors that are its by-products. Even if we try to insulate ourselves by accumulating wealth or political position, or by taking refuge in mountain top retreats or gated communities, we cannot avoid the realities that surround us. Wherever we live, we are, in some way, affected by the relentless warfare in the Middle East, the threats of nuclear attacks from North Korea and Iran, the ruthless, persistent genocide on the African continent, the environmental abuses of local and multi-national corporations in India and China, and the global threats of terrorism on the land, on the sea, and in the sky. Even if we avoid listening to the nightly CNN newscasts or reading the Drudge reports on the Internet, we are accosted by the reality of living in a hostile environment when we board a plane for a business trip or a holiday and are subjected to body searches, and we are accosted by the reality of living in a hostile environment when we

> *The time is out of joint: O cursed spite, That ever I was born to set it right!*
>
> Hamlet 1.5
> William Shakespeare[70]

walk down Main Street in any number of our cities with surveillance cameras recording our every move. And no matter what local community or nation we are living in, most of our leaders seem to have no ability to reverse the burgeoning violence or to control their defensive and aggressive responses to it. Visiting this planet for the first time, an alien might perceive that we are all locked in a *teufelskreis* of fear, violence, and paranoid defensiveness, a devil's circle with no way out. And until we each come to terms with how our irrational fears are driving us to create an increasingly oppositional, aggressive, and violent world, in both our personal and global interactions, we *are* locked in a devil's circle, and there is no way out.

Child-development expert Joseph Chilton Pearce suggests that this devil's circle of fear and violence begins to form immediately, at birth, in the anxiety caused by the unnatural environment of hospital delivery rooms, where the natural "birthing process is disrupted, slowed, or even halted...resulting in a kind of internal chaos...and mother and infant lose on all fronts."[71] This initial interruption in the bonding of mother and child is further exacerbated if the mother is not available for the next critical nine months to nurse and hold the infant. Pearce explains: "Just as it took nature nine months to grow the infant in the mother's womb, it takes another nine months in the arms of the mother to establish that infant firmly in the matrix of its new world."[72] Pearce further maintains that this interruption in bonding leads to a variety of developmental deficits, including "impaired vision...compromised overall neural growth, a diminished sensory system and general conscious awareness," and he emphasizes that infant development is impaired when they are "separated from their mothers at birth and confined to various forms of ongoing separation thereafter (as most modern infants are through cribs, bassinets, carriages, playpens, strollers, and the lengthy separation of daycare)."[73]

Psychiatrist Clancy McKenzie and a majority of mental health and child development professionals also point out that, when a mother is temporarily upset and emotionally or physically unavailable to the baby, the trauma of perceived or actual separation from the mother is the primary cause of human anxiety and subsequent learning and personality disorders, including "schizophrenia, depression, ADHD, school violence, autism, drug and alcohol dependence...and more."[74] While the potential causes of trauma are clear, neither Pearce's ideal of natural, undisturbed childbirth and bonding nor the ideal of a mother who is always available to the child can offer a practical solution for breaking the vicious cycle of fear and violence that can escalate to the point of threatening human survival. The major obstacle to achieving such ideal conditions is that most mothers have, themselves, experienced interrupted bonding as infants and are, consequently, not emotionally stable and mature enough to provide consistent nurturing. Also, as in the past, the average mother is often distracted by social and family pressures and may find it necessary to relinquish a majority of the infant's care to others. Add to this scenario the fact that today many mothers find themselves torn away from their infants from early in the morning to late at night by economic pressures, and it becomes clear that the problem of interrupted bonding is on the increase, as are concurrent child development crises, child and adolescent suicides, and violent gang activities.

The statistics are ominous: since 1996, the rate of autism among children has doubled, with one child in a hundred now being diagnosed as autistic;[75] suicide is now the third leading cause of death among fifteen to twenty-four year olds, accounting for over twelve percent of all annual deaths among youth and young adults aged ten to twenty-four;[76] and the nation's growing number of juvenile gang members, now estimated to be over a million, are responsible, in some communities, for as much as eighty percent of all crimes.[77] While these facts are alarming, it is even more alarming to consider that parents who, themselves, continue to suffer from the post-traumatic stresses of interrupted bonding, as well as subsequent arrested development, may not be equipped to break this vicious cycle of trauma, fear, and violence that begins at birth and is repeated generation after generation.

Still more ominous are the statistics that reveal a worldwide explosion in the number of children being abused and abandoned and in the number of AIDS and

> *...whoever causes one of these little ones who believe in me to sin, it would be better for him to have a great millstone fastened round his neck and to be drowned in the depth of the sea.*
>
> Matthew 18:6

war orphans. In America, alone, abuse and neglect claim the lives of nearly five children a day, with more than a quarter of a million children known to be abused each year, the majority ranging from birth to six years of age.[78] And on city streets across the globe, an estimated one hundred million children are abandoned and struggling to keep alive, with UNICEF reporting that there are at least eleven million street children in India alone.[79] Facing death because of malnutrition, many engage in pornographic activities and, according to UNICEF, approximately one million children find their way into the international sex trade each year, which is estimated to include a population of ten million child prostitutes, ninety percent of them young girls. Adding to this staggering number of abandoned and starving children, AIDS orphans increase at the rate of one every fourteen seconds.[80]

In every society, parents have the primary responsibility for shaping the next generation, and, consequently, for shaping the future of mankind. As the world waits for them to lead the children into a future defined by harmony, trust, and love, how are they going to break the vicious, recurring cycle of trauma, fear, aggression, and violence? How are they going to heal their own childhood traumas and fears so that they can be free *from* the past and free to communicate new messages of unconditional love and acceptance to the children? Where will they find the courage and faith to face these challenges? And if they do face these challenges, who will help them in their struggle to evolve past the imprinting of the past, expand their consciousness, and create a more peaceful world?

Similarly charged with the responsibility of leading the next generation into the future, educators face their own set of challenges. Accosted by the violence we see everywhere in our society, public elementary, middle, and high school educators are increasingly becoming the victims of student violence, with thirty-nine crimes committed for every one thousand teachers, and, of these, fourteen are violent crimes.[81] In addition, during the first decade of the twenty-first century, eighty-five percent of the public schools report a total of nearly two million crimes a year, with seventy-five percent of these schools reporting acts of violence, and an average of forty-three crimes being committed for every one thousand students enrolled.[82]

Contributing further to the chaotic environment of the public schools, political demands for producing standardized results that are rewarded with local, state, and federal funding can severely inhibit educators from implementing their best pedagogical practices and customizing the curriculum to meet the diverse needs of each student. And as economies deteriorate and budgets are cut, educators are also faced with meeting student needs without school psychologists, social workers, and resource room support. In many communities, educators are also facing pressures from property owners, town finance boards, and school boards to keep costs down to protect the local property tax rate. These pressures often

A child miseducated is a child lost.

John F. Kennedy[83]

translate into outdated and inadequate equipment and learning materials in the classroom. At times impeded by their own inertia as well as by resistance from the community, educators often fall far behind the curve in providing an updated curriculum that will prepare their "digital generation" students[84] for the emerging world of work. Consequently, as students find it increasingly difficult to relate their educational experiences to the demands of the real world they live in, both their motivation and their learning suffers, and many drop out.

While the U.S. Department of Education spent nearly forty-four billion dollars in 2011, with the president's budget calling for an increase to more than sixty-eight billion dollars for 2012,[85] it is projected that, across the country, one million of the nearly four million students who start high school in 2011 will not graduate with a diploma,[86] and statistics show that of those who are graduating and going to college, less than twenty-five percent are prepared to pass freshman courses or to handle an entry-level job.[87] In fact, although we are spending far more on education than any other nation in the world, we are achieving far less. Allocating approximately two thousand dollars more per capita for the education of our children than any other country, we find our students scoring at the bottom of the achievement curve in both math and science. And while our student literacy rate is equal to the rate in Japan, that country spends four thousand dollars less than we do for the education of each child. In total, the United

States spends more than eight hundred billion dollars on education, nearly twenty times the amount spent for education in Australia, and nearly twice as much as the total expenditures for education in Canada, the United Kingdom, Australia, Japan, and Russia combined.[88]

Struggling to provide relevant and stimulating learning experiences for their students, how can educators prevail over the social, political, and economic forces that impede their mission? What steps can they take to overcome their own inertia and resistance to change and help their students develop the ingenuity and competence they will need to thrive in an environment of continual change? And while the world awaits its educators to lead the students into an unknown future, who can they rely on to support their efforts?

In our interconnected, interdependent global world, the clergy of every religion also bear responsibility for leading humanity into the future, toward the Light of Christ, the Eternal Absolute, toward the highest values and beliefs that we have ever aspired to – toward embracing the unity of all existence, toward love for each other, and toward peace. It is to the clergy that we look for guidance in times of dynamic and confusing change, and it is in the clergy that we hope to find role models for building a new awareness of ourselves, our interactions with each other, and our relationship with God.

Unfortunately, our clergy are letting us down. With the exception of countless courageous men and women who are dedicated to their ministry, many clergy are politically motivated, fueling the fires of religious dissension not only between different religions but also within their own religions. Although they have established a Joint Christian Council, Catholic, Anglican, and Orthodox priests still compete in Uganda for political supremacy, while other Christian churches are entirely excluded from the Council.[89] Throughout the Arab world, Sunni and Shia Muslims engage in violent clashes to achieve political supremacy, often resulting in igniting violence against non-Muslims;[90] and in India, where Hindu philosophy and a secular state assert tolerance of religious differences, "because different faiths represent different paths to the same absolute and universal truth," that tolerance does not extend to the caste system or to gender, racial, and ethnic differences within the society.[91]

Far more destructive are the age-old wars waged by one religion against another. From the time of the Crusades, in the twelfth and thirteenth centuries, when over nine million Christians and Muslims die,[92] through the sixteenth century when the wars between French Catholics and Huguenots claim between two and four million lives,[93] and into the twenty-first century when Muslim fundamentalists, declaring a holy war against non-believers, continue to murder thousands of innocent people in random terrorist attacks, religion is reduced to violent, oppositional conflicts that fail to reflect the teachings of the Eternal Absolute in any culture.

Even from the pulpit, opposition, not unity, is often preached. In temples, churches, and mosques

---

Civilisation must be judged and prized, not by the amount of power it has developed, but by how much it has evolved and given expression to, by its laws and institutions, the love of humanity.

Sadhana -
The Realization of Life
Rabindranath Tagore[94]

across the world, the flock is often bombarded week after week with sermons that stress the fine points of theology and law, reinforcing the confusions and anxieties of worshipers, while they hunger for love and spiritual intimacy with God. If, upon leaving their places of worship each week without divine inspiration, the flock returns to the community and the workplace and functions oppositionally, aggressively, and carelessly, what alternative behaviors have they observed? When the majority of our corporate executives are self-serving, arrogant, aggressive, "brutally exploitative" narcissists,[95] what alternative behaviors have they been taught? And when our financial institutions and our governments engage in larceny, supported by their own self-serving legal manipulations, what alternative behaviors have been required of them?

If, in fact, all of our systems seem broken and unreliable, what alternative models are there for us to trust and emulate? If our nearly bankrupt healthcare system focuses on illness, invasive surgery, and prescription drugs rather than on wellness and healing, if our laws do not yield justice and "our prisons are filled with the indigent and poor who can't afford lawyers or who are assigned indifferent ones,"[96] where can we find alternatives to trust and emulate?

While the world is waiting for its clergy to lead the flock into a future marked by commitment to their highest good and faith in God, and by love, compassion, and charity for each other, who will support those who

> *... this is the Hour....*
> *It is time to speak your Truth.*
> *Create your community.*
> *Be good to each other.*
> *And do not look outside yourself for the leader....*
> *Gather yourselves! Banish the word struggle from your attitude and your vocabulary. All that we do now must be done in a sacred manner and in celebration.*
> *We are the ones we've been waiting for.*
>
> Prophecy from
> the Hopi Nation
> Thomas Banyacya, Sr.[98]

are trying to do this? Will they be supported by their superiors and by their fellow clergymen or will they also be victimized by those who would remain oppositional, aggressive, and violent even in the temples, churches, and mosques?

The Christ Conscious Leader

To find alternatives to the way we live, we will have to look to ourselves. If we want our systems to change, first each of us will have to change. We will have to change the way we view the world and the way we perceive our role in the world. To do this, we will have to move forward, beyond the conscious and unconscious imprinting of the past that shapes our worldview before we are old enough to speak,[97] and beyond the subsequent fears and impulses that drive us to behave oppositionally and aggressively, to an evolved awareness of our innate potential for freedom, fulfillment, and harmony.

We will have to recognize that we are all interconnected and interdependent, that we each have ultimate responsibility for the impact of our thoughts, words, and actions, and that each of us has a leadership role to fulfill: each parent, educator, minister, corporate executive, healthcare professional, lawyer, and elected official, and each universal, cyberspace citizen.

The Indo-European root word for *leader*, *kla*, means *load*. As this root word took on new connotations, it came to mean *carry your load*.⁹⁹ In the emerging reality of each of us on the globe having a leadership role, carrying our load becomes an immeasurable personal responsibility, a responsibility that we cannot possibly fulfill without developing a new consciousness, Christ consciousness.

In becoming Christ conscious, we will have to embrace the reality of our unity and connection with each other and with every vibration in the universe, a reality discovered only recently by the quantum physicists, but a reality that has been part of the wisdom of every ancient culture, from the teachings of the Aborigines to the teachings of Jesus. We will have to embrace each other as part of that unity and have the courage to separate from the cultural messages that would keep us believing that our survival depends on those oppositional, tribal allegiances that fuel our fears and promote violence against others. We will have to discover our unique talents and make lifelong commitments to use those talents for advancing our common evolution. And we will have to become active partners with the Eternal Absolute in realizing the kingdom of heaven on earth. To meet this challenge, to become Christ conscious leaders, we will each have to take whatever steps we find necessary to reveal to ourselves and to others "the mystery, which is Christ in you" (Colossians 1:27).

Now at a crossroad in our human evolution, we cannot turn away from this challenge. The consequences of doing so are unthinkable.

SECTION TWO

THE WAY
TO
CHRIST CONSCIOUS
LEADERSHIP

Ring in the valiant man and free,
The larger heart, the kindlier hand;
Ring out the darkness of the land,
Ring in the Christ that is to be.

Ring Out, Wild Bells
Alfred Lord Tennyson

4

UNITY
The First Step

Finding its way into one culture after another since the fourth century B.C.,[1] the Buddhist tale of the six blind men and the elephant[2] illustrates the recurring dilemma of humanity's blindness, of our inability to see the whole picture. As the tale is told in the Hindu tradition, "Once some blind men chanced to come near an animal that someone told them was an elephant. They were asked what the elephant was like. The blind men began to feel its body." Being blind, they each described something different, depending on which part of the elephant they touched. The blind man who touched only the elephant's leg declared: "the elephant was like a pillar." The blind man who touched only its ear described the elephant as "a winnowing-fan." And each of the others,

> *We do not know why human perception is limited to such a small sector of the real world, but it seems to be an unavoidable fact.*
>
> Hugh Everett[3]

touching other parts of the animal, "gave their different versions of the elephant." The Hindu version concludes: "Just so, a man who has seen only one aspect of God limits God to that alone. It is his conviction that God cannot be anything else."[4] Offering his nineteenth-century interpretation, poet John Godfrey Saxe draws this conclusion at the end of the tale:

> And so these men of Indostan
> Disputed loud and long,
> Each in his own opinion
> Exceeding stiff and strong,
> Though each was partly in the right,
> And all were in the wrong![5]

Why, throughout human history, are we always "in the wrong," unable to see the big picture? Why are we able to see God only through the lens of our separate tribe, our separate church, our separate culture? And why do we persist, down through the ages, in creating a duality between ourselves and God, between ourselves and all of God's creation, and between ourselves and the timeless energy of the universe? Why do we not see that God is one with the universe and that we, too, are one with God, as God is one with us?

Many attempts are made to answer these questions and to explain our perpetual oppositional, dualistic approach to each other and to God. Some claim that the problem lies in our basic covetous nature, that we always desire what others have;[6] others suggest that we are "driven to some fairly beastly behaviors by enculturation,"[7] or that we are psychologically imprinted with primal Oedipal and sibling rivalries;[8] and yet others assert that we must compete to ensure our survival.[9] Since any one of these answers can explain our violent, oppositional behavior – why Cain slew Abel, or why we crucified Christ, or why we persist in competing against each other to the brink of global annihilation – we accept them as truth. Yet, we do this as blind men. Because our forefathers have accepted these answers as truth, we continue to accept them, blindly, without considering proven alternatives and without questioning our behavior or its consequences. We do this without seeing the reality of our unity in our relationship to each other and to the Eternal Absolute.

Suggesting that we do have to question the widely accepted premise that opposition and competition are necessary for the "survival of the fittest," molecular biologist Michael Le Page maintains:"although the phrase conjures up an image of a violent struggle for survival, in reality the word 'fittest' seldom means the strongest or the most aggressive." Rather, Le Page asserts, "it can mean anything from the best camouflaged or the most fecund to the cleverest or the most cooperative," and he suggests: "Forget Rambo, think Einstein or Gandhi." Le Page goes on to explain: "Cooperation is an incredibly successful survival strategy. Indeed it has been the basis of all the most dramatic steps in the history of life," and he illustrates his point: "Complex cells evolved from cooperating simple cells.

Multicellular organisms are made up of cooperating complex cells. Superorganisms such as bee or ant colonies consist of cooperating individuals." Conversely, Le Page, points out: "When cooperation breaks down, the results can be disastrous. When cells in our bodies turn rogue, for instance, the result is cancer," and he describes how "elaborate mechanisms have evolved to maintain cooperation and suppress selfishness, such as cellular 'surveillance' programmes that trigger cell suicide if they start to turn cancerous." Alluding to our tendency to use survival of the fittest and examples in nature to promote particular political systems and to justify our oppositional behavior, he states: "the concept of the survival of the fittest could be used to justify socialism rather than *laissez-faire* capitalism. Then again, the success of social insects could be used to argue for totalitarianism." And he concludes: "it is nonsense to appeal to the 'survival of the fittest' to justify any economic or political ideology, especially on the basis that it is 'natural.'"[10]

Blind loyalty to familiar ways of thinking distorts our perceptions not only in understanding human survival but also in understanding the realities of everyday life. In "Mending Wall," poet Robert Frost sees this blindness in his neighbor who, each spring, insists on repairing the dry stone wall that lies between their properties, needlessly separating a pine grove from an apple orchard. Reflecting on his neighbor's irrational, annual routine, Frost writes:

> ...There where it is we do not need a wall:
> He is all pine and I am apple orchard.
> My apple trees will never get across
> And eat the cones under his pines, I tell him.
> He only says, "Good fences make good neighbors."
> Spring is the mischief in me, and I wonder
> If I could put a notion in his head:
> Why do they make good neighbors?...
> Before I built a wall I'd ask to know
> What I was walling in or walling out,
> And to whom I was like to give offense,
> Something there is that doesn't love a wall,
> That wants it down....I see him there
> Bringing a stone grasped firmly by the top
> In each hand, like an old-stone savage armed.
> He moves in darkness as it seems to me,
> Not of woods only and the shade of trees.
> He will not go behind his father's saying,
> And he likes having thought of it so well
> He says again, "Good fences make good neighbors."[11]

Because the cultural influences of our childhood remain so strong throughout our lives, we are all, to some extent, like Frost's neighbor, robotically repeating our "father's saying," and trapped in those perceptions and beliefs that have always given structure and meaning to the way we think about, experience, and discern our world. We are so trapped, in fact, that we rarely get a glimpse of how trapped we really are, always assuming that reality is what we have been taught it is and what we, therefore, ego-syntonically, go on believing it is. As we each grow into adulthood, if we fail to question and consider the habits and beliefs handed down to us by our families, the lessons we learn at school and at church, and the messages that we are always unconsciously absorbing from the culture we live in, we do continue to live "in darkness," unable to see the elephant, unable to recognize the truth about our inherent unity with all that exists in the universe, and unable to move forward in our evolution.

How, then, can we step away from our habitual experiences to discover more accurate realities and to evolve past our current, limited perceptions? How can we stop seeing our world, as quantum physicist David Bohm claims we do, "according to the general collective representations circulating around our society and culture"?[12] And how can we overcome the fact that, as Bohm points out, "through centuries of habit and conditioning, our prevailing tendency is now to suppose that 'basically we ourselves are all right' and that our difficulties generally have outward causes that can be treated as problems"? Explaining that "the mind... tends, for the most part, to be caught in paradoxes, and to mistake the resulting difficulties for problems," Bohm suggests that what we need is "a deep and intense awareness, going beyond the imagery and intellectual analysis of our confused process of thought, and capable of penetrating to the contradictory presuppositions and states of feeling in которых the confusion originates."[14] If we each can do this, if we each can reach beyond our confusion and perceive the wholeness and the harmony in what we now see as contradictions, paradoxes, and

> *Do I contradict myself?*
> *Very well then I contradict myself,*
> *(I am large, I contain multitudes.)*
>
> Song of Myself
> Walt Whitman[13]

problems, we will each be closer to perceiving the unity that exists in the world, closer to becoming an open, dynamic, expanding system like the universe we live in, the universe that is an intrinsic part of each of us, and closer to becoming a Christ conscious leader.

To do this, to become aware of the harmony and wholeness in our universe, requires only that we use our inherent intellectual, emotional, and intuitive perceptions to reach beyond our habitual responses: to open our minds to receive new information; to open our hearts to receive new inspiration; and to open our souls to receive new insights.

The Quantum Breakthrough: The End of Duality

More than a century ago, physicists began making discoveries that changed our understanding of ourselves and our relationship to our world and to the universe. They were discovering that we live in a universe which is part of a multiverse of parallel worlds,[15] where, according to physicist Hugh Everett, "both the observer and the object are composed of interacting atomic particles, which are represented by interacting, overlapping, superposing, *entangling* wave functions."[16] And they were discovering that "it is not possible for an observer to stand outside the quantum state that necessarily includes himself because the whole universe

People...must learn how to discard old ideas, how and when to replace them.

Future Shock
Alvin Toffler[17]

is entangled with itself."[18] As physicist Walter Heitler insists: "the separation of the world into an 'objective outside reality,' and 'us,' the self-conscious onlookers, can no longer be maintained. Object and subject are inseparable from one another."[19] And David Bohm agrees: "the classical idea of the separability of the world into distinct but interacting parts is no longer valid or relevant." Bohm explains: "we have to regard the universe as *an individual and unbroken whole*....an order that is radically different from that of Galileo and Newton – the order of *"undivided wholeness."*[20] In this *"undivided wholeness,"* Bohm adds, there is a new order, an "implicate order" that moves without restriction and is, therefore, *"undefinable and immeasurable."*[21]

If, as the quantum physicists are finding, the multiverse in which we live has no separable parts, and if, as Everett proposes, "since the beginning of time particles have been interacting, exchanging energy, entangling, cooking up reality,"[22] why do we persist in functioning as if we are separate from this interaction, separate from each other, and separate from the Divine? Why do we not enthusiastically embrace the infinite potential of a world where "there are no measurements...only correlations...two systems [that] come together, get correlated, then start to realize all their mutual possibilities"?[23] Perhaps we resist embracing these discoveries because, as Nobel prize physicist Erwin Schrodinger suggests, we would prefer to hold on to "the time-honored discrimination between subject and object," even though, as he underscores, "subject and object are only one." Or, perhaps, we want to blame and dismiss science for dismantling our old perceptions of duality, of a separation between subject and object, but Schrodinger adamantly argues: "The barrier between them cannot be said to have broken down as a result of recent experience in the physical sciences, for this barrier does not exist."[24]

Quantum physicist, Niels Bohr, offers yet another perspective of why we resist "the new situation in physics,"[25] suggesting that "we are concerned with the recognition of physical laws which lie outside the domain of our ordinary experiences and which present difficulties to our accustomed forms of perception."[26] But Bohr writes that in 1934, twelve years after he receives the Nobel Prize in Physics for his work in atomic theory. Now, nearly a hundred years later, why are we still having difficulty adjusting our perceptions and adapting our thinking and our behavior to reflect the fact that we live in a world of infinite, immeasurable, and unknown possibilities, a world that, "in spite of its obvious partitions and boundaries...in actuality is a seamless and inseparable whole"?[27] It would appear that no matter how accurate and evolutionary the newly discovered reality, we will persist in denying it if it challenges familiar perceptions, comfortable attitudes, and entrenched beliefs. We will choose to remain closed, deteriorating systems rather than being open to new evidence that disturbs our obsolete understanding

Perhaps the...reason you do not understand what I am telling you is...you just can't believe it. You can't accept it. You don't like it. A little screen comes down and you don't listen anymore. ...if you don't like it, that's going to get in the way of your understanding it.

The Strange Theory
of Light and Matter
Richard P. Feynman[28]

of our world and our place in that world – even if that evidence carries with it all our hope for transforming our consciousness and living in harmony and peace.

Denying proven reality is not a new phenomenon in human history. Over two thousand years ago, finding ourselves facing an equally startling shift in our understanding of the universe in which we live, we purposefully and methodically find a way to ignore a demonstrated fact for the next nineteen hundred years. This shift in our understanding of our universe emerges in the third century B.C., in ancient Greece, when Aristarchus of Samos, a member of the Pythagorean school of mathematics, geometrically calculates that the sun and not the earth is the center of the universe and that the earth is a planet like all the other celestial bodies moving around the sun.[29] At the time, the prevailing belief, held earlier by Aristotle and later by Ptolemy, and influenced by ancient religions and the mysticism of the Orphic Mystery Cult, places the earth at the center of the universe, with all other heavenly spheres, including the sun and the moon, moving around the earth.[30]

Rejecting new and disturbing realities as systematically as we do today, the ancient and medieval worlds continue to believe that the earth is the center of the universe well into the sixteenth century, a belief that, as microbiologist Stuart Kauffman proposes, "was no mere matter of science. Rather, it was the cornerstone evidence that the entire universe revolved around us." Kauffman explains: "With God, angels, man, the beasts, and fertile plants made for our benefit, with the sun and stars wheeling overhead, we knew our place: at the center of God's creation."[31]

This place of man "at the center of God's creation" is religiously protected until nearly eighteen hundred years later when Aristarchus' ancient heliocentric calculations come to light again in Nicolaus Copernicus' *De Revolutionibus,* published just before his death in 1543. Although it defies Church and university teachings, and threatens to "dismantle the unity of a thousand-year-old tradition of duty and rights, of obligations and roles, of moral fabric,"[32] the book, written in Latin, is allowed to sit quietly on library shelves, which it does for nearly a century, almost unnoticed by anyone except a few clergymen and university scholars.[33]

A crueler fate, however, awaits Giordano Bruno, a Dominican friar, philosopher, mathematician, and astronomer, who, in 1584, forty-one years after the death of Copernicus, publishes *On the Infinite Universe and Worlds*, in which he proposes not only that we live in a heliocentric cosmos but also that the sun is one of many stars in a limitless universe that has no center.[34] To avoid prosecution by the Inquisition, Bruno moves from country to country throughout Europe, but seven years later, in 1591, he is arrested and tried for his heretical views, including his belief that the universe is composed of atoms and that there are many other worlds in the cosmos. Refusing to renounce his beliefs even under the pressure of interrogation, he remains imprisoned for eight years, and on February 16, 1600, he is stripped naked and burned at the stake during the Church's jubilee celebration.[35]

Sixteen years after Bruno's death, in 1616, Copernicus' book again comes under Church scrutiny when Galileo Galilei, a mathematics professor and astronomer, begins to openly challenge Aristotelian philosophy and cosmology and publicly support the Copernican heliocentric theories. Concerned that the outspoken Galileo will influence public opinion, Church officials now rush to denounce Copernicus' book as "absurd, devoid of philosophy, and erroneous in faith… notwithstanding the efforts made by Galileo…and other Copernicans to try to prove the contrary."[36] And on March 5, 1616, in a public decree, Rome announces that *De Revolutionibus* is "condemned by the congregation of the most Eminent Cardinals formed by his Holiness Paul V for the disposition of the Index of forbidden books." This is followed, on June 22, 1633, by a decree of the next pope, his Holiness Urban VIII, which keeps Copernicus' book on the Index.[37]

Realizing that banning Copernicus' book is not enough to stem the tide of what it considers heresy, in 1616, the Church also uses its jurisdiction over the conduct of university professors[38] to issue a papal command to Galileo not to "hold or defend" the heliocentric theory.[39] Drawing a rather fine line, the Church allows Galileo to discuss the theory, but he is strictly banned from expressing any support for it. Unfortunately, in early

1632, according to the Congregation of the Holy Office, commonly known as the Inquisition, Galileo crosses that fine line when he publishes *A Dialogue Concerning the Two Chief World Systems*, a book comparing the Copernican view of the universe with the accepted Ptolemaic view. Accusing him of defending Copernicus' hypothesis as "a potentially true description of reality," the Inquisition, in June 1632, bans all sales of the book and impounds any unsold copies, and by September, a commission appointed to evaluate the issue concludes that the book does, in fact, support a heliocentric view.[40]

Although formally charged with heresy and threatened with torture, Galileo, under interrogation by the Inquisition, continues to maintain that he had not intentionally shown support for the Copernican theory in his book. Nevertheless, in the summer of 1633, the Inquisition finds Galileo guilty of "vehemently suspected heresy," citing two specific heretical ideas: that the earth rotates on its axis every day and circles the sun over a period of one year; and "the methodological principal that one may believe and defend a probable theory contrary to the Bible."[41]

Sentenced by the Inquisition to house arrest for the rest of his life, Galileo spends his remaining nine years studying the laws of motion, carefully avoiding any specific discussion of the movement of the earth, and in 1638, four years before his death, he publishes his findings in *The Two New Sciences*. This book, which is to become a fundamental resource for physicists and engineers, also provides the basis for a later, more precise investigation into the earth's motion than anything Galileo has previously written.[42]

Although the Church can no longer control the swell of scientific inquiries and breakthroughs that are challenging the established beliefs, the ban on prohibited books related to the earth's movement around the sun is not lifted until 1664. Included on the list of once-banned books is Protestant Johannes Kepler's *Epitome of Copernican Astronomy*, first published in 1615, and, of course, Copernicus' *De Revolutionibus* and Galileo's *A Dialogue Concerning the Two Chief World Systems*. Within the next twenty-five years, Bernard le Bovier de Fortenelle's *Conversations on the Plurality of Worlds*[43] and Isaac Newton's *Mathematical Principles of Natural Philosophy* are published and become widely distributed and read throughout Europe.[44] Now, after nearly two thousand years, the world begins to awaken, and we begin to accept that the sun, and not the earth, is the center of our solar system.

Today, as we face the end of duality in our understanding of our relationship to each other, to the world we live in, and to the Eternal Absolute, we may think ourselves superior to our ancestors. We may pride ourselves on being more open to new realities and more accepting of proven facts. But are we? How quickly are we accepting the reality not only that the earth is not the center of the solar system but also that our solar system is not even the center of our galaxy, and, further, that our

---

A new scientific truth does not triumph by convincing its opponents and making them see the light, but rather because...a new generation grows up that is familiar with it.

Scientific Biography
and Other Papers
Max Planck[45]

galaxy is just one of countless galaxies in an expanding multiverse of parallel worlds? And how quickly are we embracing our place in a totally unified, undivided world and changing our behavior and attitudes toward each other to reflect the reality that we are all part of one seamless, "inseparable quantum interconnectedness"?[46] Will it, in fact, take us even longer to accept the end of duality than it took our ancestors to accept that the sun and not the earth is the center of our solar system?

Since the beginning of time, the wisdom literature of every major culture has repeatedly taught us that there is no duality, that we are connected with each other, with the world we live in, and with the Eternal Absolute; and yet, we continue, down through the ages, to live oppositionally and competitively, as if we are separate from each other, from the world, and from the Christ. Perhaps, we do not believe the lessons in the wisdom literature because believing requires faith, which requires trust, and not everyone has faith, not everyone trusts what they cannot see. But now that quantum physics has proven that the universe is "an interconnected web of physical and mental relations whose parts are defined only through their connections to the whole,"[47] we no longer have to rely purely on faith; we no longer have to trust what we cannot see. We have been shown, in one discovery after another, that there is no separation or duality anywhere in the universe.

Why then, with the scientific facts before us, are we still witnessing the escalating outbreak of violent

The self, indeed, is below; the self is above; the self is in the west; the self is in the east; the self is in the south; and the self is in the north. Indeed, the self extends over this whole world.

Chandogya Upanishad 7.25.2

tribal and religious conflict throughout the world? Should we conclude from this that there is abosolutely no hope that we will never move past our perception of *us* and *them*, past our pattern of interacting aggressively with each other? Or, could it be that this escalation in oppositional violence is actually a panic reaction against the new reality that is slowly trickling into our consciousness, very much like the panic reaction of the Inquisition to the inevitable reality of the Copernican heliocentric cosmos? Could it be that what we are witnessing is the last, desperate roar of the tribal, oppositional, dualistic past trying to hold onto itself? Director and co-founder of the Institute for Advanced Studies in Leadership at the Drucker Ito Graduate School of Management, Jean Lipman-Blumen suggests that, "while separatism, tribalism, and individual identities" are pulling in one direction, "interdependence pulls in a different direction, promoting alliances, collaboration, mutuality, and universalism," and she empahtically insists: "competitive and authoritarian leaders are destined to fail."[48]

To experience the end of duality and a future of universal harmony, it is now up to each of us to open our minds, our hearts, and our souls to embrace this new manifest reality. It is also up to each of us to ask ourselves vital questions that will help us to know ourselves, to assess our current perspectives, and to determine our willingness to evolve beyond obsolete perceptions and patterns that we cling to as if they were real.

The Individual in an Undivided Universe

While, in time, we may be able to accept intellectually that there is no duality in the universe, to open our minds and receive this newly revealed information, will we also become willing to open our hearts and accept emotionally the implications of this new reality for our individual lives? Will we become willing to accept the personal responsibility that is implicit in knowing that there is no separation between ourselves and others or between ourselves and every vibration in the universe? Will we become willing not only to change our perspective of our connection to the world but also to change our motivations and interactions with others, with the universe we live in, and with the Eternal Absolute? Or, is there something in our hearts that may prevent us from doing so? Is there something in our hearts that may keep us from being inspired to change how we view others and how we relate to them?

Motivated from the beginning of time by a perception that we had to fight "the other" for survival, can we begin to accept and experience, emotionally, that we are "the other," and that "the other" is us? Can we get beyond our culturally imbedded perception that we live in a world where we each are "not only different from others but...extremely different," and where, "because every culture entertains this feeling of difference," we "consider such 'differences' legitimate

A human being... is part of the whole called by us "universe" .... We experience ourselves, our thoughts and feelings as something separate from the rest. A kind of optical delusion of consciousness. This delusion is a kind of prison for us, restricting us to our personal desires and to affection for a few persons nearest to us. Our task must be to free ourselves from this prison.... We shall require a substantially new manner of thinking if mankind is to survive.

Albert Einstein[49]

> *...the life which is unexamined is not worth living.*
>
> Socrates[52]

and necessary"?[50] Can we emotionally mature beyond our psychologically imbedded perception that our survival is bound up with the sights, sounds, and smells that we associate with our primal family, our tribe, where we were protected during the long years of our infant and childhood dependency?[51] And can we relinquish our illusion of controlling our environment and controlling others to ensure our survival and, instead, begin to trust that we and others are interconnected observers and participators in the creation of the universe?[53] Will we, in short, get real, or will we continue to live with obsolete responses that ignore demonstrated realities?

If we do not make an effort to get real, if we fail to contribute purposefully and meaningfully to the world we create, if we continue to experience ourselves as separate and remain fixated in a narcissistic perception of ourselves as the omnipotent center of the universe, with all systems existing only for our personal survival and self-gratification, if we maintain that our primary concern is the preservation of our uniqueness and our individuality, then, we will not prevail and we will not survive, individually or collectively. Our uniqueness, our individuality, will be wasted on a fear-based pursuit of personal security rather than being applied productively to advancing our interconnected and interdependent evolution. And our narcissistic obsession with self-gratification and personal survival will be frustrated by our own unwillingness to engage in the transformation of ourselves and our world.

Trappist monk Thomas Merton paints a vivid picture of an individual's oppositional, narcissistic behavior and its consequences:

> People...whose lives are centered on themselves imagine that they can only find themselves by asserting their own desires and ambitions and appetites in a struggle with the rest of the world....They can only conceive one way of becoming real: cutting themselves off from other people and building a barrier of contrast and distinction between themselves and other men. They do not know that reality is to be sought not in division but in unity, for we are "members of one another."

Stating that "the man who lives in division is not a person but only an individual," Merton depicts the thought process behind this individual's narcissistic behavior:

> I have what you have not. I am what you are not. I have taken what you have failed to take and I have seized what you could never get. Therefore you suffer and I am happy, you are despised and I am praised, you die and I live; you are nothing and I am something, and I am all the more something because you are nothing. And thus I spend my life admiring the distance between you and me.

Merton concludes: "The man who lives in division is living in death. He cannot find himself because he is lost;

he has ceased to be a reality. The person he believes himself to be is a bad dream."[54]

This "bad dream" that Merton speaks of, when replicated by billions of others, creates a world that looks like a "bad dream," a world that is struggling on the brink to sustain its people and its economies, a world brought to the edge of annihilation by its own oppositional, unevolved, and unquestioned behavior. Understanding the importance of questioning one's thoughts and actions, poet Rainer Maria Rilke suggests: "Try to *love the questions themselves*....Don't search for the answers.... *Live* the questions. Perhaps, then, someday,...you will gradually...live your way into the answer."[55] Now, as we look over the cliff at the potential consequences we are facing, are we ready, at last, to examine our behavior, to ask the questions that may awaken us to our outdated perceptions and behaviors, questions that may inspire us to embrace new possibilities and new realities? And are we ready to live in the question as we move toward a new understanding of ourselves and our world?

To move beyond our experience of ourselves as separate, to move beyond our obsessions with self-preservation and personal gratification, to retain our uniqueness while productively applying it to creating a better world, we need to examine those perceptions, motivations, and behaviors that imprison us and deaden our hearts. And we have to reach within our souls to discern our connections with each other, with our universe, and with the Eternal Absolute.

The Oneness of Humanity and the Divine

Today, presented with scientific facts that confirm that we are one with each other, with the universe, and with the Divine, we are facing a revealing paradox. On the one hand, the sacred writings of our major cultures all describe the agony of our being separated from the Divine and our deep longing to regain paradise, and, as St. John of the Cross writes: "to unite [ourselves] perfectly through grace…in this life" with God.[56] On the other hand, both the sacred writings and the scientific community concur that we *are*, in fact, inextricably united with each other, with the universe, and with the Eternal Absolute. Now, with both science and the sacred writings verifying that separation does not exist, not in the natural world or in the spiritual world, we are left to come to only one conclusion: that this agony of separation from the Eternal Absolute is something that we must be creating.

Testimony to humanity's oneness with the Divine finds expression in our very earliest sacred writings. In the Brhadaranyaka Upanishad, dating back more than twenty-five hundred years, the seeker of unity with the Brahman, the Eternal Absolute of the Hindus, asks: "explain to me the *brahman*,…the self…that is within all." And the seeker receives this answer: "Who breathes out with the out-breath – he is the self of yours that is within all. Who breathes in with the in-breath – he is the self of yours that is within all....The self within all is this self of yours. All else besides this is grief" (Brhadaranyaka Upanishad 4). And in the Tao Te Ching, Lao Tzu, who wrote in the third century B.C., affirms: "These two things – spirit and matter – so different in nature, have the same origin. The unity of origin is the mystery of mysteries and the gateway to spirituality" (Tao Te Ching 1).

In the Abrahamic religions, we, again, find testimony to our unity with the Eternal Absolute. In the Old Testament, it is the breath of Yahweh that unites all creation and brings forth life from the dust: "then the Lord God formed man of dust from the ground, and breathed into his nostrils the breath of life; and man became a living being" (Genesis 2:7). And in Isaiah 42:5, we find this unity affirmed yet again: "Thus says God, the Lord, who created the heavens and stretched them out, who spread forth the earth and what comes from it, who gives breath to the people upon it and spirit to those who walk in it."

The unity of man and God become most evident to us in the New Testament. Both "the Christ, the Son of the Living God" (Matthew 16:16-17), and a man of "flesh and bones" (Luke 24:39), Jesus often refers to his oneness with God. With the same words that Yahweh identified himself to Moses on Mount Sinai, Jesus tells the suspicious Jews who are questioning him: "Truly, truly, I say to you, before Abraham was, I am" (John 8:58), and as the Jews continue to probe his identity, Jesus tells them: "I and the Father are one" (John 10:30).

> *Everything in heaven and earth breathes. Breath is the thread that ties creation together.... The interaction of the cosmic breath causes the flower of the spirit to bloom and bear fruit in this world.*
>
> The Art of Peace
> Morihei Ueshiba[57]

At the same time, Jesus frequently refers to himself as the Son of man. Speaking to the paralytic, he affirms: "But that you may know that the Son of man has authority on earth to forgive sins...I say to you, rise, take up your pallet and go home" (Mark 2:11). And responding to the accusations of the Pharisees, Jesus declares: "hereafter you will see the Son of man seated at the right hand of Power, and coming on the clouds of heaven" (Matthew 26:64).

Also establishing the oneness between himself and each of us, Jesus tells his disciples at the Last Supper: "the Father...will give you another Counselor, to be with you for ever...you know him, for he dwells with you, and will be in you....I will not leave you desolate; I will come to you" (John 14:16-18). And Jesus proclaims: "I am in my Father, and you in me, and I in you" (John 14:20). Praying to his Father at the Last Supper, Jesus shares his faith in the unity of all men with God: "The glory which thou hast given me I have given to them, that they may be one even as we are one, I in them and thou in me, that they may become perfectly one" (John 17:20-23).

Reminding us of this unity, the apostle Paul speaks of "the riches of the glory of this mystery, which is Christ in you" (Colossians 1:27), and, again, addressing the Corinthians, he asserts, "Now we have received...the Spirit which is from God....we have the mind of Christ" (1 Corinthians 2:12-16). But Paul also makes it clear that we each have a personal responsibility to manifest this unity in our lives: "If we live by the Spirit, let us also walk

> *There is a light within a person of light, and it lights up the whole world. If it does not shine, it is darkness.*
>
> Gospel of Thomas 24[58]

by the Spirit. Let us have no self-conceit, no provoking of one another, no envy of one another" (Galatians 5:25); "Bear one another's burdens, and so fulfill the law of Christ" (Galatians 6:2); "So then, as we have opportunity, let us do good to all men" (Galatians 6:10). And, again, when speaking to the Ephesians, Paul charges them with manifesting their unity with each other and with Christ: "I...beg you to lead a life worthy of the calling to which you have been called...eager to maintain the unity of the Spirit in the bond of peace" (Ephesians 4:1-3).

Also validating our oneness with the Eternal Absolute, Rumi, a revered thirteenth-century Islamic mystic and founder of the Mawlawi Sufi order, declares: "When thou has become living through Him, that (which thou hast become) is in sooth He; it is absolute Unity." And, like Paul, Rumi cautions that it is our personal responsibility to manifest this unity in our behavior: "Seek the explanation of this in the mirror of devotional works, for thou wilt not gain the understanding of it from speech and discourse."[59] Rumi further suggests that, in addition to devotional works, we must know ourselves and discern our dependence on God if we are to know God: "If from the Divine Essence were abstracted all the relations (i.e. the Name and Attributes), it would not be God....But what actualizes these (possible) relations (which are recognizable in the Essence) is ourselves." With insight that foreshadows the thinking of the twentieth-century quantum physicist John Wheeler, who proposes that "the observer is as essential to the creation of the universe as the universe is to the creation of the observer,"[60] Rumi explains further: "In this sense it is we who, with our own inner dependence upon the Absolute as God, turn it into a 'God.' So the Absolute cannot be known until we ourselves become known."[61]

As science and religion find common ground in their understanding of the oneness of humanity and the Divine, we each face an unavoidable dilemma: how in the face of all the evidence, scientific and spiritual, can we continue to maintain a dualistic, oppositional perception of ourselves and our relationship to each other, the world we live in, and the Divine? And what do we do now? How do we find the courage and the willingness to change the way we understand, respond to, and discern reality? How do we move toward the future, transform our perceptions and motivations, and become Christ conscious leaders?

To do this, to take the first decisive step on our way to becoming Christ conscious leaders, we must begin to recognize our blindness, to recognize that we are seeing only parts of the elephant. And we must throw away the keys that we are using to lock ourselves away in an obsolete past, opening our minds to the scientific discoveries of the last century that are validating our inseparable unity with the universe, opening our hearts to the inspiration of being one with everyone and everything in the universe, and opening our souls to discern that our long-desired unity with the Divine is - and has always been - here and now.

5

LOVE
The Second Step

> *The day will come when...we shall harness for God the energies of love. And, on that day, for the second time in the history of the world, man will have discovered fire.*
>
> Toward the Future
> Pierre Teilhard de Chardin[3]

At midnight on August 15, 1947, after more than twenty-five years of national protests against oppressive British colonial rule, India becomes an independent nation, a victory that is secured with a minimum of violence and bloodshed, a victory that, to this day, is attributed to one man, Mahatma Gandhi, and his lifelong dedication to unity, truth, and love.

Born in 1869 into a traditional Hindu family of the Bania caste[1] in Porbandar, a small seaport town on the west coast of India,[2] Gandhi, is pulled away from his roots, and from his young, pregnant wife, and sent off to London to study law just prior to his nineteenth birthday. Before leaving, he vows to his saintly, devoutly religious mother "not to touch wine, women and meat."[4]

While boarding near University College London, Gandhi meets a fellow vegetarian who urges him to read the Bible. He accepts the advice of his new Christian acquaintance and finds himself deeply moved by the New Testament. "Especially the Sermon on the Mount...went straight to my heart," he recalls in his autobiography: "The verses, 'But I say unto you, that ye resist not evil; but whosoever shall smite thee on the right cheek, turn to him the other side also. And if any man take away thy coat, let him have thy cloak too,' delighted me beyond measure." In this last verse, Gandhi hears an echo of the words of the Hindu poet Shamal Bhatt,[5] which made a lasting impression on him when he was still a painfully shy young boy in India:[6]

> For a bowl of water give a goodly meal;
> For a kindly greeting bow thou down in zeal;
> For a simple penny pay thou back in gold;
> If thy life be rescued, life do not withhold;
> Thus the words and actions of the wise regard,
> Every little service tenfold they reward.
> But the truly noble know all men as one,
> And return with gladness good for evil done.

Gandhi recounts his initial response to the poem: "[This] Gujarati didactic stanza likewise gripped my mind and heart. Its precept – returning good for evil – became my guiding principle."[7]

As he continues to mature, Gandhi's exposure to many cultures and religions, coupled with "an early grounding in toleration for all branches of Hinduism,"[8] evolves into an "inalienable love of mankind." Expressing his deep commitment to the unity of all men and to the unity of man and God, Gandhi explains: "I have known no distinction between relatives and strangers, countrymen and foreigners, white and coloured, Hindus and Indians of other faiths whether Muslims, Parsees, Christians or Jews....All men are brothers and no human being should be a stranger to another." And he insists, "The welfare of all...should be our aim. God is the common bond that unites all human beings. To break this bond even with our greatest enemy is to tear God himself to pieces."[9]

Devoted to fostering unity, seeking truth, and using the power of love to overcome tyranny, Gandhi begins his professional life in South Africa, where he is "the country's first 'coloured' lawyer to be admitted to the bar."[10] During his twenty years in South Africa, Gandhi establishes a lasting reputation for initiating non-violent actions to overturn entrenched laws that discriminate against Indians. Jailed twice in South Africa for his civil disobedience campaigns,[11] Gandhi is ultimately victorious in forcing the repeal of South Africa's biased Asiatic Registration Act of 1906 and the Immigration Act of 1907.[12] In 1914, at the age of forty-five, Gandhi returns to India, and as the leader of the Indian National Congress party, he turns his attention toward opposing British colonial rule and fostering tolerance among all social classes and religions. Imprisoned from 1922 to 1924 for his role in encouraging Indians to engage in civil disobedience against British authority, including boycotting British goods and services,[13] Gandhi, nevertheless, continues to prepare and lead non-violent campaigns against British colonial rule for the rest of his life.

Always adhering to his philosophy of non-violence, which he names *Satyagraha*, "its root meaning holding on to truth, hence truth force....love force or soul-force,"[14] Gandhi reaffirms his belief that "the force of love and pity is infinitely greater than the force of arms....I believe in it as much as I believe in two and two being four....The universe would disappear without the existence of that force." Proving his point, Gandhi asserts: "the greatest and most unimpeachable evidence of the success of this force is to be found in the fact that, in spite of the wars of the world,...it still lives on." And he concludes, "History is really a record of every interruption of the even working of the force of love."[15]

Looking at the future of mankind, Gandhi suggests: "It should be an essential of real education that a child should learn, that in the struggle of life, it can easily conquer hate by love."[16] Further, Gandhi points out that all attempts to make us contented, including "organized government and mechanical contrivances," do not work: "It does not require much thinking to know that, under the operation of the brute law of force, the modern world is pressed down with the weight of misery and affliction." And he proposes, "There seems to be no relief, unless we revert to the law of love."[18]

A man who dedicated his life to unity, truth, and love, Gandhi's last years are filled with disappointment

> *Gandhi is probably the first person in history to lift the love ethic of Jesus above mere interaction between individuals to a powerful and effective social force on a large scale. Love for Gandhi was a potent instrument for social and collective transformation.*
>
> Toward Freedom
> Martin Luther King, Jr.[17]

over the growing antagonism between Hindus and Muslims in India, an antagonism that threatens to erupt into civil war and that results, against his wishes, in the partitioning of the country into Muslim Pakistan and Hindu India.[19] Assessing the situation, he concludes that he has made a "mistake...of Himalayan magnitude," and he explains: "before a people could be fit for offering civil disobedience, they should thoroughly understand its deeper implications."[20] Those "deeper implications," for Gandhi, involve a dedication to the path of universal love, and he bemoans "our imperfect *ahisma*," the failure of the people to "substitute the law of love in society for the law of the jungle."[21] Making it clear that non-violence is not simply a political strategy and that "non-violent action without the cooperation of the head and heart cannot produce intended results,"[22] he insists: "non-violence springs from love."[23] And as he observes the ongoing conflict between the Muslims and Hindus, he concludes: "The violent energy that was generated among the masses, but was kept under check in the pursuit of a common objective, has now been let loose and is being used among and against ourselves."[24]

Maintaining his deep-rooted belief that "God is in every one of us....an unseen Power residing within us and nearer to us than finger-nails to flesh,"[25] and professing to "have no special revelation of God's will," Gandhi is, nevertheless, profoundly distressed that his vision of universal love and unity is being shattered because "we

> *The great Way is very plain,*
> *but most people prefer the bypaths.*
>
> Tao Te Ching 53

shut our ears to that 'still small voice.' We shut our eyes to the 'pillar of fire' in front of us."[26]

Distressed but still dedicated to his faith in universal love, Gandhi continues to make every effort to halt the bloodshed that explodes before and during the partitioning of India, including going on a hunger strike in Calcutta. Here, living among the Muslims who were being besieged by angry Hindus, he refuses to eat until the killing stops. Moved to shame and concern for this "aging man of principle," all parties in the conflict soon cease fighting, and Gandhi breaks his fast "as weeping rioters laid their machetes at his feet."[27] But the victory of love over hate that Gandhi achieves in Calcutta does not stop the violence that continues to rage throughout India, and, as over three million Hindus and Sikhs flee from the newly created Pakistan and nearly five million Muslims migrate into Pakistan,[28] one million people are killed in the conflict.[29]

Just four months after the partitioning of the country and the end of British rule in India, on January 30, 1948, Mahatma Gandhi is assassinated while walking to a prayer meeting. The assassin is Nathuram Godse, a Hindu extremist who believes Gandhi betrayed the Hindu cause by trying to make peace between Hindus and Muslims.[30] Disregarding Gandhi's devotion to non-violence and his staunch opposition to the death penalty, Godse and his co-conspirator, Narayan Apte, are tried, found guilty, and sentenced to death, and on March 15, 1949, they are both hanged inside the Ambala Central Jail.[31]

And then many will fall away, and betray one another, and hate one another....And because wickedness is multiplied, most men's love will grow cold.

Matthew 24:10-12

Now, more than half a century later, in the city of Porbandar, where Gandhi was born, an elaborate shrine is maintained in memory of "his sacrifices and ideals" which won India her independence from British colonial rule, and India's current leaders visit the shrine with some regularity. But as religious riots between Hindus and Muslims continue to tear the country apart, the locals put little stock in those ideals. "Non-violence got rid of the British but it will have very little effect in today's world," one resident comments. And another agrees: "The world does not recognise anything other than strength and power. Non-violence may have delivered for us in the past but it is completely useless today."[32]

As Gandhi understood throughout his life, "if love or non-violence be not the law of our being, the whole of my argument falls to pieces,"[33] and so it did. Today, seen as irrelevant, at best, Gandhi's personal devotion to unity, truth, and love, while having once inspired cohesive political action, failed, in the long run, to inspire the "intense self-examination, surrender to God and, lastly, grace"[34] that he believed could bring men "above the opposing currents of love and hatred, attachment and repulsion...to see the universal and all-pervading Spirit of Truth face to face...to love the meanest of creation as oneself."[35] And so, we find ourselves with unrelenting and violent tribal and religious conflicts raging not only in India and Pakistan but also across the globe; we find ourselves trying to prevail with seven billion people on the planet, nearly three times the number that were here during Gandhi's time; and we find ourselves with no sign that we will ever make a commitment to replacing the law of the jungle with the law of love. And, as we look out over the horizon, we see no one, outside ourselves, who can lead us away from our own destruction.

To move away from the law of the jungle and toward the law of love, we will each have to look inside ourselves and discover our indwelling divinity, our individual potential for becoming a Christ conscious leader. We will each have to come to recognize Divine Love as the Eternal Absolute and become familiar with the nature of Divine Love in God and in ourselves; we will each have to open our hearts to receive and experience Divine Love; and we will each have to become a vehicle of Divine Love for others.

Divine Love

Now faced with the overwhelming responsibility of trying to turn the tide of our destructive behavior by initiating a personal transformation in the way we relate to each other, we can take comfort in knowing that we have more than enough guidance for this task and more than enough role models to show us the way. As the Eternal Absolute is Divine Love, every word and allegory in the sacred literature of every culture provides us with the information we need for achieving our goal. And we have examples we can follow in those who have gone

> *God is love, and he who abides in love abides in God, and God abides in him.*
>
> 1 John 4:16

before us and achieved this transformation, legendary men and women like Nelson Mandela and Joan of Arc, and millions of men and women we have never heard of, men and women who quietly go about their lives, using the power of Divine Love to advance human evolution. But before we can even begin on this path of transformation, we need to become familiar with the nature of Divine Love.

Divine Love is infinite, compassionate, and unconditional. For the Hindu, it is "the joy of the Infinite ….not indeed a transient pleasure, but an eternal joy of the soul….All the universe has come from love and unto love all things return."[36] Like the higher self, "it cannot be grasped, by teachings or by intelligence, or even by great learning" (Mundaka Upanishad 2.3). In the *Bhagavad Gita,* the charioteer Krishna, who represents God incarnate, explains that it is only by love that one comes to know him: "All those who truly love me, even the lowest of the low – prostitutes, beggars, slaves – will attain the ultimate goal."[37] And Krishna promises: "I am the same to all beings; I favor none and reject none, but those who worship me live within me and I live in them."[38] Nor does it matter how the seeker finds God: "However men try to reach me, I return their love with my love; whatever path they may travel, it leads to me in the end."[39]

This infinite, compassionate, and unconditional love is found again in the Tao Te Ching. Here we are told:

> When creation began,
> the Tao became the world's mother.

> When you know your mother,
> you also know that you are her child.
> When you recognize that you are a child,
> You will stay close to your mother
> and she will keep you safe. (Tao Te Ching 52)

The mother, the symbol for unconditional love, informs the behavior of the wise man, who, living with compassionate, unconditional love for others, "has no fixed heart....The good he treats with goodness; the not-so-good he also treats with goodness" (Tao Te Ching 49).

We find further insight into God's Divine Love in the Old Testament, the sacred text of the Israelites. In Psalm 145:8-9, we are told: "The Lord is...abounding in steadfast love. The Lord is good to all, and his compassion is over all that he has made." In Nehemiah (9:17-18), we find testimony to God's unconditional love and forgiveness toward his people when they stray from his commandments during their flight from Egypt: "thou art a God ready to forgive....and didst not forsake them....Even when they had made for themselves a molten calf...and had committed great blasphemies." And we are assured that even when we do wrong, we are blessed by God's punishment: "Blessed is the man whom thou dost chasten, O Lord, and when thou dost teach out of thy law to give him respite from days of trouble" (Psalm 94:12-13).

I will put my law within them, and I will write it upon their hearts.

Jeremiah 31:33

In the New Testament, Jesus brings us "the good news" of his Father's Divine Love for us: "For God so loved the world that he gave his only Son, that whoever believes in him should not perish, but have eternal life" (John 1:16). And Jesus makes it clear that everything he teaches comes from the Father: "The words I say to you I do not speak on my own authority; but the Father who dwells in me does his works" (John 14:10).

In both his words and actions, Jesus reveals the infinite, compassionate, and unconditional nature of Divine Love. Reproached for allowing a sinner to anoint his feet while he is dining at the home of a Pharisee, Jesus responds:

> Do you see this woman? I entered your house, you gave me no water for my feet, but she has wet my feet with her tears and wiped them with her hair. You gave me no kiss, but from the time I came in she has not ceased to kiss my feet. You did not anoint my head with oil, but she has anointed my feet with ointment. Therefore, I tell you, her sins, which are many, are forgiven, for she loved much. (Luke 7:44-47)

Calling attention to our human capacity for showing unconditional love to God and to each other, Jesus identifies the two most important commandments: "The first is…'you shall love the Lord your God with all your heart, and with all your soul, and with all your mind, and with all your strength.' The second is this, 'You shall love your neighbor as yourself'" (Mark 12:29-31). And Jesus charges us to love our enemies as well as our neighbors: "Love your enemies and pray for those who persecute you, so that you may be sons of your Father who is in heaven," he instructs, "for he makes his sun rise on the evil and on the good, and sends rain on the most just and on the unjust" (Matthew 5:43-45). Always demonstrating the lessons he teaches, Jesus shows his unconditional love and forgiveness toward his persecutors, even on the Cross: "Father, forgive them; for they know not what they do" (Luke 23:34).

At the Last Supper, Jesus identifies the ultimate expression of unconditional love that we can show to each other: "Greater love has no man than this, that a man lay down his life for his friends," and calling the disciples "friends" (John 15:13-15), Jesus prepares them for his Crucifixion.

Divine Love is also revealed in the Koran, the sacred text of Islam. Here, God is always presented as "the Compassionate, the Merciful," and we are told: "God will love you and forgive you your sins. God is forgiving and merciful" (3:31). While it is clearly stated that "God loves the charitable" (2:195), "the righteous" (3:76), and those who "trust in God...that are trustful" (3:159), it is also acknowledged that those who stray from the path can always "seek forgiveness of your Lord and turn to Him in penitence. Merciful and loving is my Lord" (11:90). And in his compassion, God promises that "no soul shall bear another's burden" (35:18), for "if it were God's will to punish people for their misdeeds, not one creature would be left alive on the earth's surface" (35:45).

Down through the ages, from the Upanishads to the Koran, we find affirmation that God is Divine Love, infinitely, compassionately, and unconditionally loving us, and we find testimony acknowledging our love for God and our unity with God in that love. Yet, we seem to hit an impasse in receiving that love and expressing that love to each other. We seem, for some reason, to keep that love at arm's length as we continue to relate to each other with judgment and hostility, emotionally and physically destroying life.

As we become aware of the nature of Divine Love and continue to affirm our oneness with the Eternal Absolute, we can begin to make a conscious effort to open our hearts and receive God's infinite, compassionate, and unconditional love. And as we begin to experience Divine Love and integrate it into our lives and into our beings, we can, in time, begin to make a conscious effort to bring this love into our relationships with each other and with God.

Becoming Receptive to Divine Love

While Divine Love is infinite and always available to us, we often avoid receiving and experiencing that love, and, consequently, we remain incapable of being a vehicle of that love for others; for no matter how generous, loving, and kind-hearted we may be, it is impossible to give to others what we ourselves do not have. So we remain incapable of being a part of the flow of Divine Love in the universe, "flooded with divine waters, abounding in them like a plentiful fount overflowing on all sides,"[40] as St. John of the Cross exults. We remain incapable of knowing "that highest *brahman*" and becoming "that very *brahman*" that the Mundaka Upanishad (3.2.9) celebrates, and incapable of "true goodness" that "nurtures everything and harms nothing" that the Tao Te Ching (8) esteems. We remain incapable of being renewed in God's love (Zephaniah 3:17), and incapable of overflowing with the Holy Spirit as Jesus promises those who believe in him: "Out of his heart shall flow the rivers of living water" (John 7:38). And we remain incapable of finding our way to the "gardens watered by running streams," that is promised to the faithful in the Koran (22:14).

> *We love, because he first loved us.*
> 1 John 4:19

Although we are impoverished by our reluctance to receive and experience the compassionate and unconditional love of the Eternal Absolute, we, nevertheless, continue to do everything in our power to block that love. In doing so, we also block what Richard Rohr, O.F.M., describes as "the experience of being a beloved son (or daughter)...of living in a loving universe" where we can feel: "I am beloved, I am taken care of, I am believed in."[41] And while we continue to put up barriers against feeling beloved, we cannot deny that, at every level of our consciousness, there is a nagging sense that we need and desire this love. What is it, then, that gets in the way of our receiving this love, feeling beloved, and passing it on to others?

Is it that we are uncomfortable in the presence of Divine Love because it is so powerful that it makes us afraid, makes us feel insignificant and vulnerable? Certainly that sense of fear is repeatedly expressed, over three hundred times, in both the Old and New Testament. "Serve the Lord with fear," we are told (Psalms 2:11), and though we come to the Lord "through the abundance of [his] steadfast love," we are told that we "worship toward the holy temple in the fear of [him]" (Psalms 5:7). Yet we are also repeatedly told not to be afraid: "Fear not, little flock, for it is your Father's good pleasure to give you the kingdom," Jesus tells the crowd gathered about him (Luke 12:32). And in Proverbs (1:7), we are told, "The fear of the Lord is the beginning of knowledge."

If fear is at the heart of our reluctance to receive and experience Divine Love, can we begin to examine that fear and learn from it? Can our fear become "the beginning of knowledge" for us? And can we begin to examine the overwhelming need for love that makes us feel so vulnerable and so afraid?

While Divine Love is infinite, compassionate, and unconditional, the same cannot be said of human love. Human love is almost always limited by anxieties and needs, irrational expectations and fantasies, biases and judgments, family and cultural loyalties, and, often, by emotionally arrested, narcissistic behaviors. Except in a few extrodinary families, most of us, as we are growing up, experience only human love, and our understanding of building a relationship with God is often restricted to obedient observation of daily or weekly rituals. And because humans need to feel beloved, above all other needs, our earliest experiences often determine how we relate to being loved and loving others throughout our lives, even in our relationship with God. If our primal need to feel beloved is not met, we will do one of two things: we will continually seek that unrequited love throughout our lives, concerned only with irrational expectations and fantasies we have created of how we should be loved while, ironically, always being attracted to the same unsatisfying kind of love we knew in childhood; or we will determine that we are unlovable and avoid any interactions with others that remind us of how unlovable we have come to believe we are. And with only our past experiences defining our reality, we will also go through our lives amassing negative memories and perceptions that block our ability to receive and experience Divine Love.

    Conversely, if the need to feel beloved is met in our childhood, then we are open to receiving and experiencing Divine Love and passing that love on to everyone we meet. Unfortunately, it would appear from our interactions with each other that only a small minority of us have ever experienced the joy of receiving compassionate and unconditional love. For most of us, our need for love, as well as our ability to receive love and love others, remains a very painful subject, one that we would rather avoid than examine.

Defining love as "an attention or energy directed outward, the byproduct of which is happiness," psychiatrist Clancy McKenzie explains that love and need are conflicting forces: "When...needs are not met to our satisfaction, we respond by sending out negative energy: anger, hurt, bitterness, rage, even murderous impulses and non-forgiveness that some of us hang onto for the rest of our lives." And McKenzie notes: "It is hard to imagine the harm caused by bitterness, resentment, and non-forgiveness....Like creates like. Love creates love. Hatred creates more hatred. Bombs create more and bigger bombs. Where is the endpoint?"[42]

To gain more insight into our reluctance to receive and experience the compassionate and unconditional love of the Eternal Absolute, we can examine a very simple mechanical device that we all have in our homes, a P-trap pipe that is part of the standard plumbing under our sinks. If we are very fortunate, that pipe will always be clear and the water will always flow freely through it, but most of us can remember at least one occasion when the pipe could not take in any water because something was clogging it up. We usually try to fix the problem by using a plumbing snake to remove the blockage, or we may pour some caustic substance into the pipe to dissolve the blockage. Once the blockage is removed or dissolved, the water flows freely again through the pipe and into the plumbing system outside our homes.

Like the trap pipe, our psyches accumulate debris over a lifetime of feeling unloved, and that debris – our irrational expectations, fantasies, disappointments, angers, fears, and distrust – cuts off the flow of Divine Love to us and, then, from us to others. And while it may not be as simple to clear the debris in our psyches as it is to clear the trap pipe under the sink, the process is exactly the same – a powerful substance has to be put into our psyches to dissolve the blockage. That substance, the only substance that will work, is the infinite, compassionate, and unconditional love of the Eternal Absolute. We cannot love ourselves, others, or God until we first receive that love, until that love convinces us that we are beloved and dissolves all the debris that we have accumulated during our lifetime.

Now, if the process is so simple, as simple as dissolving a clogged trap pipe, what are we waiting for? Why do we not eagerly open ourselves to being restored by Divine Love and begin to clean out the debris that we have accumulated? Why do we not eagerly accept the invitation to abide in God's love (John 15:10)? And why do we not eagerly become part of "the well of living waters" (Song of Solomon 4:15) and experience the ultimate fulfillment of feeling beloved? What is holding us back from beginning this process of transformation, a process that will unite us with the Eternal Absolute in Divine Love?

What holds us back are the very same irrational expectations, fantasies, disappointments, angers, fears,

> *No one lives fully in Christ unless he knows how much the Lord loves him. Everything depends on the intensity of our conviction that Jesus loves us.*
>
> Agape in the New Testament
> Ceslaus Spicq, O.P.[43]

and distrust that are clogging our psyches. For before we can let in God's infinite, compassionate, and unconditional love, we have to be willing to relinquish our old expectations and fantasies of how we think we should be loved, and we have to be willing to replace our disappointments and anger with acceptance and forgiveness. We have to be willing to find the courage to face our fears of being hurt and feeling abandoned once again and to face the pain of old, deep wounds being opened again, wounds we have buried and tried to forget. And as we begin to realize that we are being infinitely, compassionately, and unconditionally loved by God, we have to endure the pain of becoming aware that we have been living our entire lives without being beloved. In short, we have to take the risk of completely trusting in Divine Love, even though that love is unfamiliar to us and makes us feel frightened and vulnerable.

That risk is so great for most of us that we would rather take the risk of climbing the icy slopes of Mount Everest than take the risk of being hurt again. We would rather take the risk of engaging an enemy on the battlefield than take the risk of facing our deepest pain and fear – even though, if we each faced that pain and fear, it would bring us closer to ending all wars, public and private. As history shows us, most of us would rather bring all of mankind to the edge of annihilation than to take the risk of being loved infinitely, compassionately, and unconditionally.

To become receptive to Divine Love, we will have to find the courage to build an intimate relationship with God, begin to learn God's way, and become accustomed to conversing with God as we would with a close friend. We will have to learn how to discern God's gentle presence with our hearts, and learn to listen to God's promptings with our souls; and, slowly, one small drop of love at a time, we will have to take the risk of experiencing God's love and replacing our old expectations, hurts, and fears with that love. And receiving one small drop of love at a time, we may find that we are slowly being transformed into a new self, into a vehicle for Divine Love.

Becoming a Vehicle for Divine Love

Divine Love has a single purpose, to bring all of humanity into its embrace, and, through the indwelling Christ in each of us, to manifest what Leo Tolstoy defines as the "the highest law that should guide us….the metaphysical principle of love."[44] That principle of love is universal and includes all of creation, imbuing us, as Yogi Paramahansa Yogananda describes, with "the power to do good…a Spirit that pervades all souls [to] extend [themselves] in love and service to God in others."[45] As we each take the risk to receive and experience Divine Love, we are transformed by that love, slowly moving from a state of alienation and loneliness, of unmet needs,

> *For them that have attained...union with God there is nothing necessary except the eye of the spirit and the lamp of intuitive faith: they have no concern with indications to guide them or with a road to travel by. Such people then become signs for others.*
>
> Mawlana Rumi[46]

fears, and self-absorption, to a state of unity with the Eternal Absolute, and it is through this unity that we are prepared to fulfill God's purpose in our lives: to see God in everyone and to serve God in everyone.

This story of transformation inspires all of humanity's sacred literature, celebrating the power of Divine Love to unite us with the Eternal Absolute and instructing us in the ways of loving and serving others. In the Chandogya Upanishad (4.1-2), we are introduced to one Janasruti Pautrayana, "a man who was totally devoted to giving and used to give a lot, a man who gave a lot of cooked food [and]...had hospices built everywhere, thinking: 'People will eat food from me everywhere.'" As the story is told, Janasruti Pautrayana hears of a humble wise man, Raikva, the gatherer, and after his steward finds him "under a cart scratching his sores," Janasruti Pautrayana offers him "six hundred cows, a gold necklace, and a carriage drawn by a she-mule," and he begs Raikva to teach him about the deity he worships. But Raikva rejects his gifts, teaching him that he has not understood how to serve others, for he has not given the food "to a man to whom it is due!" In the Taittiriya Upanishad (1.11.3), the lesson is clarified: "You should give with faith, and never without faith. You should give with dignity. You should give with modesty. You should give with trepidation. You should give with comprehension."

Again, in the Tao Te Ching (77), we are taught how to serve others: "the Tao of heaven...diminishes those who abound, and completes those who lack"; and the question is raised: "Where is the rich man who will use his wealth to serve the world?" And the lesson is presented: "The wise man earns much, but claims it not for himself."

Appearing to Ezekiel (18:4-8), the Lord God of the Old Testament instructs us: "Behold, all souls are mine....If a man is righteous...he...does not oppress anyone, but restores to the debtor his pledge...gives his bread to the hungry and covers the naked with a garment, does not lend at interest or take any increase." And appearing to Zechariah (7:10), the Lord teaches: "show kindness and mercy each to his brother, do not oppress the widow, the fatherless, the sojourner, or the poor; and let none of you devise evil against his brother in your heart."

The celebration of the power of Divine Love reaches a crescendo in the life and teachings of Jesus. Every page of the New Testament offers a lesson in seeing God in everyone and serving God in everyone: "For the Son of man also came not to be served, but to serve, and to give his life as a ransom for many" (Mark 10:45). Serving his Father's children with unwavering compassion, Jesus uses his power to heal a man who has been crippled for thirty-eight years, respectfully asking him first, "Do you want to be healed?" (John 5:1-18), and when a leper asks Jesus to make him clean, "moved with pity, he stretched out his hand and touched him...and he was made clean" (Mark 1:40-44). But Jesus also makes it clear that he is not the only vehicle for our healing, that we can be healed by the power of our faith in Divine Love. In restoring sight to the blind beggar Bartimaeus, Jesus confirms that it is not his power but the power of the beggar's faith that is responsible for his healing: "Go your way; your faith has made you well" (Mark 10:46-52). Again, in healing a woman who suffered with a hemorrhage for twelve years, Jesus confirms that it is the power of her faith that has made her well: "Take heart, daughter, your faith has made you well" (Matthew 9:20-23). And Jesus teaches the same lesson to ten lepers who ask for his help: "Rise and go your way; your faith has made you well" (Luke 17:11-19).

As receiving Divine Love can transform us and unite us with God, so it can also make us a vehicle of our own healing when our faith in that love is absolute.

Showing us the patience and understanding we need to see God in everyone and serve God in everyone, Jesus also manifests his infinite compassion and unconditional love by teaching everyone he encounters, never discouraged or derailed by their confusion or their resistance. Although the Pharisees resent him and plot against him, Jesus persists in teaching them. Emphasizing how important it is to fulfill His Father's commandments, he reproaches the Pharisees because they "leave the commandment of God, and hold fast the tradition of men" (Mark 7:8), and he accuses them of preaching but not practicing (Matthew 23:3), and of creating a hierarchy and exalting themselves over others: "But you are not to be called rabbi, for you have one teacher, and you are all brethren." And Jesus instructs them: "And call no man your father on earth, for you have one Father, who is in heaven. Neither be called masters, for you have one master, the Christ" (Matthew 23:7-12).

Always devoted to preparing his disciples for their ministry, Jesus also patiently and tirelessly teaches them, in words, actions, and parables. Asked by Peter if he should forgive his brother "as many as seven times" when he sins against him, Jesus responds: "not...seven times, but seventy times seven" (Matthew 18:21-22), and when his disciples were discussing among themselves "who was the greatest," Jesus tells them: "If any one would be first, he must be last of all and servant of all." To help them better understand that the greatest person is the one who serves others, Jesus takes a child in his arms and explains: "Whoever receives one such child in my name receives me; and whoever receives me, receives not me but him who sent me" (Mark 9:33-37). Again, patiently teaching his disciples about serving God, Jesus uses a parable of a man whose servant comes in from the field, and Jesus asks the disciples: "Will any one of you, who has a servant plowing or keeping sheep, say to him...'Come at once and sit down at the table'? Does he thank the servant because he did what was commanded?" Then Jesus brings the point home to them: "So you also, when you have done all that is commanded you, say, 'We are unworthy servants; we have only done what was our duty'" (Luke 17:7-10).

> *Therefore, be imitators of God, as beloved children. And walk in love, as Christ loved us and gave himself up for us.*
>
> Ephesians 5:1

It is at the Last Supper that we fully understand how receiving Divine Love can transform us and prepare us to see God in everyone and to serve God in everyone. After washing their feet, Jesus addresses his disciples and asks them: "Do you know what I have done to you?...I have given you an example, that you also should do as I have done to you." Then, after explaining to the disciples that "a servant is not greater than his master; nor is he who is sent greater than he who sent him" (John 13:12-16), Jesus gives them a new commandment: "A new commandment I give to you, that you love one another; even as I have loved you, that you also love one another." And Jesus reveals the reason for this new commandment: "By this all men will know that you are my disciples, if you have love for one another" (John 13:34). Preparing the disciples for his death and Resurrection, Jesus makes a promise to them, "He who has my commandments and keeps them, he it is who loves me; and he...will be loved by my Father, and I will love him and manifest myself to him" (John 14:21), and he promises again: "If a man loves me, he will keep my word, and my Father will love him, and we will come to him and make our home with him" (John 14:23).

While all others are capable of fulfilling the old commandment, to love one's neighbor as oneself, at the time of the Last Supper, only the disciples who have received and experienced Jesus' infinite compassion and unconditional love are capable of fulfilling this new commandment, to love one another as Jesus loved them.

Transformed by their intimate relationship with Jesus, by being loved by Jesus and by loving Jesus, the disciples are well prepared to be a vehicle for Divine Love: to love others as they have been loved by Jesus; to serve others as they have been served by Jesus; and patiently and tirelessly to teach others as they have been patiently and tirelessly taught by Jesus.

Echoing the teachings of the Lord God in the Old Testament, the Koran, the sacred book of the newest of the Abrahamic religions, also provides the seeker with lessons for becoming a vehicle of Divine Love, for serving God and serving others. "A kind word with forgiveness is better than charity followed by insult" (2:263) we are taught, and we are told, "If your debtor be in straits, grant him a delay until he can discharge his debt; but if you waive the sum as alms it will be better for you" (2:280). Making it clear that God approves of "those who give their wealth for the cause of God," the Koran declares that such men "can be compared to a grain of corn which brings forth seven ears, each bearing a hundred grains" (2:261).

As vehicles of God's compassion, the Koran instructs us further: "Do not give the feeble-minded the property with which God has entrusted you for their support; but maintain and clothe them with its proceeds, and speak kind words to them" (4:5). And we are warned, "Let not the rich guardian touch the property of his orphan ward; and let him who is poor use no more than a fair portion of it for his own advantage" (4:6).

The celebrations and revelations of Divine Love in humanity's sacred literature invite each of us to trust and receive God's compassionate and unconditional love and to experience the ecstasy of being united, in love, with the Eternal Absolute. Accepting that invitation is a lifelong process, one that begins with building an intimate relationship with God and allowing God's love to transform us so that, like the twelve disciples of Jesus, we are prepared to be Christ conscious leaders: we are prepared to love one another as God loves us.

To become a Christ conscious leader, to become capable of loving others as we are loved by God, we will have to be receptive to God's transforming love, and we will have to be willing to let that love separate us from any thought, behavior, or relationship that blocks our ability to be a vehicle of Divine Love for others. We will have to find the courage to detach from what is familiar and comfortable and move toward the unknown, toward our indwelling divinity and all that we could become, with only our blind trust in Divine Love to guide us.

6

DETACHMENT
The Third Step

Detachment is an essential and pivotal process for all human development. Even before we are born, at the most basic, organic stage of our lives, cell detachment and differentiation determines who we are and what we will become. With the fundamental structure of all life on the planet having a common origin, the human embryo, at conception, shares nearly ninety-nine percent of its prehistoric genes with chimpanzees,[1] ninety-two percent with mice,[2] eighty-five percent with fish,[3] and sixty percent with birds,[5] and, at certain phases in our pre-natal development, the embryo even looks the same as other living embryos, displaying similar features like tails and gill-like structures.[6] Similarities also exist between various adult species and adult humans. An intriguing

We are just very highly evolved fish!

Yehudit Bergman[4]

example is the adult fruit fly, which shares sixty percent of its genes with humans and has many behaviors that correspond to human behavior, including becoming addicted to alcohol and drugs, having cycles of waking and sleeping, and exhibiting intricate behavior patterns.[7]

The inherent challenge to distinguish ourselves from other species who share our genetic material is met primarily through a process of embryogenesis. During this process, cells detach from each other and differentiate their roles, developing from a mass of undefined cells into vital structures, such as the lungs, the spine, and the brain. As the fetus develops and various roles for each set of cells change or become unneeded, some cells actually die off, like the cells that form supportive webs between the developing fingers. All cells, once detached and differentiated, cannot "de-differentiate," and they lose the flexibility they originally had.[8] Although this process of cell detachment and differentiation is very complex, according to Sir Peter Gluckman, Distinguished Professor of Paediatric and Perinatal Biology at the University of Auckland, "the cell's performance is nearly perfect. It is quite astonishing!"[9]

Why or how the cells of the human fetus detach and differentiate from the prehistoric genes shared with other species can be viewed from a variety of perspectives. Some biologists find that a specific gene, G9a, controls the process, turning off selected genes so they can never function during the fetus's lifetime and utilizing other genes to build the structures and organs of the human body.[10] Others believe that certain genes control the timing of cell development and that timing differentiates the development of the human fetus from the development of other species.[11] Evolutionary biologist and paleontologist Stephen Jay Gould proposes that the main difference between chimpanzees and humans is the result of "alterations in the regulatory system that slow down the general rate of development in humans....an alteration in the timing of features already present."[12] Gould elaborates: "small changes in the timing of development can have manifold effects upon the final product," and he states: "I submit that we do know the nature of the regulatory changes that separate us from the chimps: they operate to slow down our general development (thereby setting our major adaptive differences from other higher primates)." Gould concludes: "Human development, in general, is retarded."[13]

This "retarded" development, which, according to Gould, produces a baby that is "as dependent a creature as we find among placental mammalian infants," is also responsible for many characteristics which distinguish hominids from other mammals: "intelligence (by enlarging the brain through prolongation of fetal growth tendencies and by providing a longer period of childhood learning) and...socialization (by cementing family units through increased parental care of slowly developing offspring)."[14] Gould suggests: "Pair-bonding must have been enhanced by this continual resupply of dependent offspring," as well as being a "primary impetus for the origin of the human family."[15]

By comparison, the nearest relative of the human child, the chimpanzee, is independent and ready to reproduce in ten years, and while chimpanzees live in groups of about thirty, those groups are "mobile... fluid and volatile," changing in composition "daily and even hourly."[16] And even though male and female chimpanzees will, at times, cooperate in foraging for food, monogamy and family structure do not evolve as a strategy for ensuring the protection and survival of the young.[17]

Other species who share a large percentage of the same genes as humans at the onset of fetal life have an even shorter period of development and even less social structure for protecting their young. After only three weeks in the womb,[18] mice are weaned between three and five weeks[19] and begin reproducing within two months of being born, giving birth to a dozen or more offspring, and reproducing several times in a year. Offspring survive, according to psychologist Delbert Thiessen, "on a roll of the environmental dice. A meal missed, a night of cold, may be the difference between life and death."[20] And for the majority of young fish larvae, which can take up to a month to hatch, life is even more precarious. Initially staying alive by absorbing the yolk of the egg from which they hatched, they slowly develop fins and begin swimming and looking for food, but, except for a few species, there is no parental protection, and less than five percent survive.[21] As for the fruit flies, Drosophila, which exhibit several behaviors that parallel human behavior, their life cycle lasts between ten days and three weeks, depending on the species,[22] and, only ten hours after emerging from the pupa, where they spend about five days, they are ready for reproduction.[23]

Of all the species known to share prehistoric genes with humans, birds are the most similar in their patterns of pair-bonding and parenting. For more than eighty percent of bird species, parental care includes protecting and incubating the eggs and feeding and teaching the offspring until they are ready to leave the nest. Robins, canaries, doves, and pigeons are among the common species of birds that receive prolonged care from both parents after hatching, while chickens, turkeys, and ducks leave the nest and follow the mother to find their own food only hours after hatching.[24] But not even helpless hatchlings stay in the nest as long as human infants do, and most are ready to take flight within four weeks.[25]

In fact, few other species are so slow to develop, so physically dependent, and so carefully protected for so long as humans. Although they share many human traits, such as long periods of gestation, age of sexual maturity, and high longevity,[26] even elephant calves stand and walk within hours of birth and forage and feed themselves by the time they are four months old.[27]

This elongated dependency of the human infant, while supporting the development of intelligence, family bonding, and socialization, also yields some challenging consequences. Unlike our physical ability for cell detachment and differentiation, which, although complex, is nearly foolproof, our ability to detach and differentiate from our tribes and our families as we mature is not so foolproof and can often lead to significant personal and social problems.

Because we are so dependent for so long on the tribe and the family, we learn to identify our primal attachments with our very survival, so that, even as we develop and become more independent, we instinctively continue to perceive any detachment from the tribe or family as a threat to our survival. Totally dependent when we emerge from the womb, our birth becomes our first traumatic experience of detachment, and according to psychotherapist Otto Rank, a protégé and contemporary of Sigmund Freud, that birth trauma expresses itself throughout our lives as "a primal fear that manifests itself now as a fear of life, another time as a fear of death."[28] Psychoanalyst Abraham Kardiner concurs and describes birth trauma as a time when "the primitive ego is abruptly torn from the mother." And he proposes that throughout our lives, any separation or loss can become "a reproduction of the birth situation," triggering the memory of that traumatic loss of maternal protection.[29]

While supportive and nurturing parenting can ease some of this "primal fear," it still remains in our memory banks ready to be activated at any time. In childhood, this separation anxiety, in its most extreme form, can manifest itself whenever the mother is separated from the child. In these cases, young children will refuse to go to school or to be alone, even at bedtime. In addition to having temper tantrums, screaming, and pleading, these children will also suffer with nightmares about abandonment and with various physical problems, such as stomach cramps or headaches.[30] By adolescence, if the anxiety is not addressed, such children become depressed, experience panic attacks, and avoid dealing with basic life problems. Often this can also affect their school performance and lead to learning difficulties.[31]

If this primal anxiety continues unchecked into adulthood, the panic attacks and avoidance behavior will persist, and, generally, parents who suffer unresolved separation anxiety disorder will transmit their anxiety to their infants, and the pattern of behavior will begin all over again in the next generation.[32] Because of their fears of separation, such parents will be possessive of their children and discourage them from becoming independent. And, because they are always anxious about harm coming to those who are closest to them,[33] these parents will also tend to be overprotective of their children. According to primatologist and psychologist Harriet J. Smith, "the sons of mothers who over-protect them during their first 3 years of life are excessively passive and dependent," and she observed that even in chimpanzees, this overprotective parental behavior leads to offspring who "get the message that they aren't

When I was a child, I spoke like a child, I thought like a child, I reasoned like a child; when I became a man, I gave up childish ways.

1 Corinthians 13:11

capable of going out on their own," and they become "reluctant to leave [their mothers] and grow up."[34]

While this clinical degree of separation anxiety occurs in only about fifteen percent of the population, the "primal fear" of detachment at birth that we all experience is compounded by a variety of cultural expectations that inhibit and, sometimes, forbid detachment from the norms of both tribe and family. In the Amish community, for example, conformity in language, dress, and attitude are required of everyone. Those who do not conform are abruptly expelled from the community.[35] Likewise, in the Hasidic community, behavior is strictly dictated, especially for women. Forbidden to go to movies, watch television, or read certain books, which, in some communities includes the Bible, Hasidic women are expected to conform to the practice of arranged marriages and to limit their education beyond high school to approved courses on Hasidic life and to approved reading, such as "Reader's Digest."[36]

Even in less strictly controlled tribes and families, spoken and unspoken norms and expectations are communicated to us from the moment of our birth, and these norms and expectations automatically become integrated, without question, into our growing perception of reality. That perception of reality remains fixed until we begin to move toward adolescence and adulthood, begin to experience, evaluate, and integrate new norms and expectations, and begin to detach from our childhood perspectives. In this process of maturation, we can begin to define a separate identity, discover our purpose in life, and build relationships outside the limits of our tribe and family.

Unfortunately, many tribes and families persist in discouraging and even forbidding detachment and differentiation, as if they were still living in the far-distant past, when survival actually did depend on everyone remaining in the tribe and carrying forth its traditions. But, in today's dynamic, global environment, detachment and differentiation become as critical to human survival as remaining in the tribe was when we were hunter-gatherers, as critical to our survival as the fundamental process of fetal cell detachment and differentiation that separates us from other species. Without this fundamental process of detachment and differentiation from tribe and family, there can be no personal growth, no social change, no evolution of the species.

How, then, do we detach when we all suffer with "primal fear" of detachment, when detachment may mean risking emotional and, possibly, physical rejection by tribe and family, when detachment may mean severing all ties with those on whom we are so totally dependent for our survival for so many years? How can we detach and encourage our children to detach when we are still laboring under the obsolete perception that our survival depends on every new generation always maintaining the same norms and expectations as previous generations? And if we fail to detach, how can we become receptive

> *...the names many tribal groups give themselves translate to "the people," as if they were the only real people in the world. This is the needed change point: our tribe, our family, our "us" needs now to become global and include all humanity.*
>
> Humanity on a Tightrope
> Paul Ehrlich and
> Robert Ornstein[37]

to Divine Love and become a vehicle for Divine Love, and how can we find our separate identity and our purpose in life?

To discover our personal identity and purpose in life, we will have to begin to recognize those emotional and social attachments that inhibit our growth and our usefulness, and we will have to separate ourselves from those attachments. We will have to endure the disquieting process of transformation as we continue to receive God's infinite, compassionate, and unconditional love, gradually move away from old perceptions of ourselves and our reality, and move toward new norms and expectations. And we will have to find the willingness to embrace these challenges on our way toward becoming Christ conscious leaders.

Detachment from the Tribe

In today's digitally connected world, every tribe is being bombarded by external influences beyond their control. Whether part of a modern, technologically advanced culture in the United States or an ancient aboriginal culture in Western Australia, most tribes can no longer fully isolate and protect themselves and their members from outside forces. Faced with this dilemma, almost every tribe on the globe finds itself torn into three factions: those who want to hold fast to fundamental tribal values and prohibit all external influences, those who want to find a moderate compromise with external influences and tribal norms, and those who want to abandon tribal norms and plunge headlong into the future. We see these factions everywhere, among Muslim tribes in the Middle East, among Christian denominations in the United States, and among Aborigines in Australia.

In an interview with Harvey Arden, author and longtime *National Geographic* staff writer, an Australian Aborigine, who refuses to give his name because "that's mine...and I'm not givin' it out to just anyone," addresses this conflict:

> The old ways aren't for me, mate. Not anymore. I was born in the bush. I remember how it used to be with the old people back then. But those days are gone. Gone for good. We can't go back. We're caught, Aboriginal people like me, caught between the old ways and Gadia's [the whitefella's] way. We don't want either one. 'Course you'll find plenty who'll disagree with me, traditional blackfellas who think we *should* go back.[38]

Asserting that "I'm an Aboriginal man and I'm bloody proud of it, but that doesn't mean I want the old Law.... It's violent, a violent law," he explains that the old Law was not originally violent, but it is coming back "in a violent way....It's violent because it has to overcome violence," the violence done to the Aborigines since the white settlers came to Australia. Now, he proposes, his people have to regain their dignity by fighting "the violence inside us."[39] And rejecting the current violence of the "old Law," this Aboriginal man declares: "the whitefella's God, this Jesus fella, all this Father and Son and Holy Ghost and all that....I liked that....There are some who'll tell you different, but that's what I think anyway."[40]

As we each struggle to find our way during this time of upheaval in each of our tribes, like this outspoken Aboriginal man, we will have to learn how to maintain respect for our roots while, at the same time, growing beyond those roots and discovering those lasting, universal values that connect us with all of mankind. But to do that, to find our own voice, our own identity, and our own purpose in life, we will also have to consider detaching from the external influences that are having an impact not only on the identity of our individual tribes but also on our personal identity as humans.

With waves of information continually inundating us through the television, the Internet, and the i-phone, we now find ourselves being influenced by ideas and values that are both tribal and global. And with all the noise that now surrounds us from these technologies, it is increasingly difficult to know which choices we are making freely and which choices are being subliminally induced by all the messages we continually absorb. It is also increasingly difficult to hear the sound of our own inner voice, the sound of God guiding us toward our identity, our purpose, and our destiny in life.

> *In order to hear the sound of God's voice, we must turn down the sound of the world.*
>
> God's Voice Within: The Ignatian Way to Discover God's Will
> Mark E. Thibodeaux, S.J.[41]

In his book, *The Metaphysics of Virtual Reality*, Michael Heim explains: "We are biologically finite in what we can attend to meaningfully. When we pay attention to the significance of something, we cannot proceed at the computer's breakneck pace. We have to ponder, reflect, and contemplate." And he warns us about the potential loss of our analytic and intuitive ability and our human identity in this cyberspace environment:

> Infomania erodes our capacity for significance. With a mind-set fixed on information, our attention span shortens. We collect fragments. We become mentally poorer in overall meaning. We get into the habit of clinging to knowledge bits and lose our feel for the wisdom behind the knowledge.[42]

Heim adds another word of caution: "Virtual worlds can threaten the integrity of human experience."[43] Pointing out that "technology enters the inmost recesses of human existence transforming the way we know and think and will,"[44] Heim poses some critical questions for us to consider: "How much can humans change and still remain humans as they enter the cyberspace of computerized realities?...[45] How may we preserve the contrast between virtual and real worlds?...What anchor can serve to keep virtual worlds virtual?" And he concludes: "Without a subconsciously familiar map, we will soon lose our way in the information wilderness."[46]

As Heim points out, our involvement in the world of cyberspace makes it more essential than ever before in our history to have an "anchor" that defines the nature of what it means to be human, an "anchor" that secures our identity and purpose in a sea of virtual information, an "anchor" that is detached from any tribal norms, values, and perceptions that might deter us from our destiny. If we enter cyberspace without this strong sense of who we are and what we are about, we can, indeed, be fragmented, swallowed up, and lost – and we will not be able to return to the comfort and familiarity of our tribes, because they, too, are being forced to redefine their role in a digitally connected world.

As cultures begin to connect, shift, and merge in cyberspace, it becomes increasingly difficult for each individual tribe to maintain its uniqueness and for its members to remain isolated and secure. And while one faction of the tribe will always persist in trying to maintain the traditions and practices of the past, other stronger forces within and outside the tribe continue to exert pressure for change. Now facing the reality that even our primal tribe is in transition, we are left without a choice – we must detach, and we must look to our relationship with the Eternal Absolute for guidance in redefining our values and discovering our purpose in life. As we strengthen that relationship, the integrity of our commitment to the Eternal Absoulute, to our values, and to our purpose, and not our tribe, will become our "anchor" and determine our destiny.

For some, the changes in their primal tribe are so threatening that, rather than seeking God's guidance and establishing a new sense of direction and purpose, they seek out a substitute tribe in a variety of cults or self-help groups where they hope to replace the stability, meaning, and structure they once enjoyed.[47] During the last fifty years, as technology and globalization generate continual social, economic, demographic, and political upheaval in tribes throughout the world, there is a corresponding expansion in the numbers of people who join cults. By 1997, there are over ten thousand cult websites on the Internet,[48] and by 2003, membership in the increasing numbers of available cults in the United States is reported to be seventeen million.[49] The majority of the people attracted to these cults are between eighteen and twenty-five years old,[50] the years when young adults naturally confront the challenge of detaching from their tribe and differentiating their identity. And finding that the cult is not helping them meet this challenge, more than ninety percent of those who join a cult leave within a few years.[51] Tragically, in a few well-publicized cases, such as Jonestown and Heaven's Gate, the attempt to find a substitute tribe and "black-and-white answers to today's toughest dilemmas"[52] comes to an end in mass suicide.

It is sometimes only after seeking substitutes for many years that we come to realize that there are no substitutes, that we must detach not only from our primal tribe but also from the illusion of replacing that tribe. And it is sometimes only after many years of

> *No one who puts his hand to the plow and looks back is fit for the kingdom of God.*
>
> Luke 9:62

searching everywhere outside ourselves that we come to realize that what we are looking for is inside ourselves, in our relationship with the Eternal Absolute, and in our relationship with our indwelling divinity. Only by strengthening those internal relationships can we hope to detach and differentiate effectively, establish our personal identity, define our personal values, and discover our life's purpose.

To detach and differentiate ourselves from our tribes, we will have to recognize and accept that we must move forward into an unknown future, honoring our traditions while, at the same time, acknowledging that many of our traditions are being uprooted, grafted, and replanted in new soil. And we will have to continue to build an intimate and lasting relationship with the Eternal Absolute, becoming increasingly receptive to Divine Love and guidance as we redefine our values and strengthen our ability to serve God's purpose in our lives.

Detachment from the Family

Detachment from the family presents an even greater challenge than detachment from the tribe. For nine months before our birth and for many years after our birth, mother is our only link to survival. By the time we are ready to leave our homes and begin pre-school, we have already developed a natural, deep-rooted connection between our survival and our relationship with our parents, and any detachment from them will always activate our primal concerns about safety and well-being. On the other hand, should that relationship be interrupted so that this natural bonding does not occur, we can become so chronically insecure and anxious about our survival that emotional detachment can become not merely challenging but psychologically impossible, even as we grow into adulthood and are more than capable of taking care of ourselves.[53]

Driven by this unmet, unresolved childhood need for security and our subsequent anxieties about survival, we can spend our entire lives seeking that security and never finding it. And, being so engrossed in this pursuit, we can find ourselves unable to detach from our family, differentiate our personal identity, or discover our life's work. At best, we may be able to go through the motions of living a separate life, but we never fully separate emotionally from the primal drama in which we are trapped.[54] Consequently, as we look at the numbers of orphaned, abused, and neglected children escalate across the globe, we are also looking at a future with increasing numbers of adults with unmet primal needs, who may be unable to define their identity and fulfill their potential for making a meaningful contribution to society.

Contributing further to the challenge of detaching from family is the fact that, while we are bonding with our parents, they are also becoming attached to us. And although this bonding is a positive and natural development in all families, the degree to which either

> *He who loves father or mother more than me is not worthy of me; and he who loves son or daughter more than me is not worthy of me; and he who does not take his cross and follow me is not worthy of me. He who finds his life will lose it, and he who loses his life for my sake will find it.*
>
> Matthew 10:37-39

or both parents have their identity attached to their child can severely inhibit the child's ability to detach and differentiate. If parents see their child as an extension of themselves, they may unconsciously, but decisively, influence the child to grow up "in [their] image, after [their] likeness" (Genesis 1:26), and they will do everything in their considerable power to direct the child to make those choices that they believe will enhance their own sense of self.

Exploring consumer behavior in his article, "Possessions and the Extended Self," Russell W. Beck concludes that "we are what we have,"[55] that we perceive our possessions as an extension of our selves. And Beck points out that we include our children high on that list of possessions: "Clearly, our laws allow us to regard our children, biological or adopted, as possessions. The embryo also legally is treated as property in cases of in vitro fertilization....and the same extended self notion enters arguments about abortion." Beck adds: "Children are also treated as possessions in divorce proceedings." Citing psychiatrist Robert J. Lifton, Beck explains the dynamics behind this desire to view children as possessions: "children and grandchildren may be as close as the average person gets to immortality. Such a living legacy is often a strongly desired extension of self." And quoting philosopher Janet Farrell Smith, he adds that parents show a "possessive attitude toward children when [they] make boastful claims about them and [they] 'give them away' in marriage."[56]

With so many social and legal sanctions in place encouraging parents to view their child as a possession, most parents are unaware that they are relating to their child as an extension of themselves. They are unaware of how powerfully they are obstructing their child's ability to detach, differentiate, and discern a unique path to personal fulfillment. And they are unaware that, no matter how diligent they are being in their child's religious education, they are getting in the way of their child's relationship with God.

Poet and philosopher Kahlil Gibran offers this wisdom to "a woman who held a babe against her bosom" and asks him to "Speak to us of Children":

> Your children are not your children.
> They are the sons and daughters of Life's longing for itself.
> They come through you but not from you,
> And though they are with you yet they belong not to you.
> You may give them your love but not your thoughts,
> For they have their own thoughts.
> You may house their bodies but not their souls,
> For their souls dwell in the house of tomorrow, which you cannot visit, not even in your dreams.
> You may strive to be like them, but seek not to make them like you.
> For life goes not backward nor tarries with yesterday.
> You are the bows from which your children as living arrows are sent forth....[57]

> *We are in childhood in a condition of dependency under someone's protection and supervision for some fourteen to twenty-one years....To evolve out of this position of psychological immaturity to the courage of self-responsibility and assurance requires a death and resurrection...leaving one condition and finding the source of life to bring you forth into a richer or mature condition.*
>
> *The Power of Myth*
> Joseph Campbell[62]

Recognizing the importance of our detaching and differentiating from the family, most cultures provide a rite of passage as we begin the process of moving into adulthood, moving from dependence on the family to dependence on self. And without exception, that rite of passage leads us toward an increasing intimacy with the Eternal Absolute and toward an increasing reliance upon Divine Love.

In Hindu society, as soon as a young boy is "mature enough to grasp the spirit, not only the letters of the mantras,"[58] he begins his initiation into the ceremonies of the sacred thread, the *upanayana*, and "invested with the sacred thread, [he is] thus endowed with a second or spiritual birth." With this "kindling of the sacred fire," the young boy studies the sacred knowledge in the Vedas and emerges from his studies to live a life inspired by the Scriptures: "He begins to discover himself and his own projection in the outside world. He finds the road to humanness now open."[59]

Likewise, in an ancient Chinese ceremony of "departure from childhood," sixteen-year-old boys and girls pass from dependence on the "Mother" goddess to being under "the authority of the gods in general."[60] And in the Buddhist tradition, Theravada monks mark the coming of age with ordination.[61] Siddhartha, Herman Hesse's fictional hero, gives us a glimpse into the challenge of detachment for a young man who seeks to leave his father's home and begin a spiritual journey. "With your permission, Father, I have come to tell you that I wish to leave your house tomorrow...I wish to become a Samarana," Siddhartha tells his father. After responding to this request with intense displeasure, warning his son that he didn't want to hear that request again, and then witnessing his son's total commitment to his chosen path, the father comes to realize that "Siddhartha could no longer remain with him at home – that he had already left."[63]

Over a period of twelve years, from 2000 to 2012, while the number of Buddhist monks and nuns doubles in China to fifty thousand, and while there is a slight increase to five thousand, two hundred and sixty Catholic priests and nuns, thirty-seven thousand Protestant ministers, and forty thousand Muslim imams in this country of one billion, three hundred million people, strict government quotas continue to be "explicitly and implicitly imposed" on the spread of religion.[64] Consequently, for the majority of young people in China, the rite of passage is marked not by a spiritual ritual leading to a deeper relationship with God, but, rather, by the stress and anxiety of competing for schooling and jobs in a country where the rate of modernization and economic growth cannot keep pace with the rising educational levels and expectations of the youth.[65] Under these conditions, suicide is now the primary cause of death for those between fifteen and thirty-four years of age, accounting for nineteen percent of all deaths in this group.[66] The intensity of this stress is reflected in the thoughts of an average Chinese ninth grader speaking about the number of suicides among his peers in his prestigious school: "I hope even more high school students commit suicide....That way, there will be fewer people competing to get into good high schools, colleges, and jobs."[67]

In stark contrast, all three Abrahamic cultures provide a rite of passage for young adolescents, inviting them to engage more fully in the life of the spiritual community and to become more fully responsible for their personal relationship with God. In addition to receiving religious instruction for this spiritual passage from childhood to adulthood, when a Judaic boy reaches thirteen years of age, he is considered *bar mitzvah*, literally translated, "the son of the commandment," and he is presumed ready to fulfill his obligations as a member of his congregation, including reading from the Torah and reciting the blessings. And the same rite of passage is provided in all but the most orthodox congregations for a Judaic girl, who is considered *bat mitzvah,* "the daughter of the commandment," at the age of twelve. Confirming the independence that this rite of passage signifies, on the first day that his child reads from the sacred scroll, the father publicly recites a prayer acknowledging his child's adult status and asking to be absolved of responsibility for any of the child's future sins.[68]

This focus on youth taking responsibility for their sins is found again in the rites of the Catholic Church. After going through a period of preparation and instruction for First Communion, girls and boys, "when they arrive at the years of discretion or the use of reason,"[69] starting at seven years old, are required, for the first time, to confess their sins to a priest before they can receive Holy Communion. As they mature into adolescence, they are then prepared for the sacrament of Confirmation, for becoming more intimately united with Christ and for developing "a more lively familiarity with the Holy Spirit – his actions, his gifts, and his biddings – in order to be more capable of assuming the apostolic responsibilities of Christian life."[70] And while Confession, Communion, and Confirmation are not part of the rite of passage in all Christian denominations, most do provide youth with religious instruction and prepare them to make a public commitment to their faith in a formal confirmation ceremony.

In the Muslim community, where children receive religious education and follow the Islamic way of life from the time they are born, the rite of passage into adulthood is a natural transition marked by taking a more active part in practicing their faith. This includes affirming their faith on a daily basis, praying five time a day, helping the poor and the needy, fasting during Ramadan, and, whenever possible, but at least once in their lifetime, going on a pilgrimage to Mecca, the birthplace of Muhammad.[71]

While almost every culture provides us with time-honored rituals to build a more intimate relationship with God as we make the transition from childhood to adulthood, the rituals, by themselves, do not secure that relationship. If they did, we would all be "mature

> *Truly, truly, I say to you, unless one is born anew, he cannot see the kingdom of God.*
>
> John 3:3

in Christ" (Colossians 1:28); we would all enjoy the consciousness of the Eternal Absolute; we would all be Christ conscious leaders. But this is not the case. Too often, we either go through these rituals without taking them seriously, because we are distracted by our own agenda, or we become habitually attached to the rituals and continue to perform them mindlessly, as mindlessly as we brush our teeth each day, as mindlessly as we go through our work routines. And, then, although we take part in the rites of passage that are provided to help us become more intimate with God, we find ourselves still unable to detach and differentiate ourselves from our tribe and family, still not free to define our separate identity and fulfill our unique purpose in life. Invited to the table to partake of the richness of a relationship with the Eternal Absolute, we put the food in our mouths but we go away hungry, often wondering why we are not satisfied, why we are not free.

To free ourselves of our childhood dependencies, to grow beyond the parameters of the family and tribe and discover our personal destiny, we will have to relinquish our old habits and perceptions and make room for a new, more intimate relationship with God and a new, more intimate relationship with ourselves. We will have to become aware of any conflict that may exist between our agenda and God's purpose for us, between our own self-will and God's will for us. And we will have to begin to trust that God's will for us is the path to personal freedom, fulfillment, and joy.

Detachment from Self-Will

Gradually detaching and beginning to assess and accept or reject the norms and expectations of both tribe and family, we now are left to consider how we will use our free will. We are left to consider our personal motivations and to become aware of those drives that shape our dreams, our expectations, and our goals. And as we become increasingly aware of our motivations, and as we continue to develop an intimate relationship with God, we may also become increasingly aware of a distinction between those dreams and goals we set for ourselves and the path that God is preparing for us. We may become increasingly aware of the difference between our self-will and God's will for us.

Because most of us live in a culture that is career-oriented, time-oriented, and bottom-line-results-oriented, we are often motivated to set specific goals that we wish to meet within a specific timeframe, with specific results. And because we restrict our expectations to these goals, we have little awareness that we may be severely limiting ourselves and our potential for growth and fulfillment. We may be confining our lives to a small slit of reality that we feel we can control, barely conscious of our untapped talents or our life's purpose. Thoroughly trained in our analytical, scientific world to dissect and examine, to measure and quantify, most of us will convince ourselves that we are doing well if we reach our goals within a desired time, if we have access

God called to the man and said to him....
"Have you eaten of the tree of which I commanded you not to eat?"
The man said, "The woman whom thou gavest to be with me, she gave me fruit of the tree, and I ate."
Genesis 3:9-12

> *The less empty of self we are, the less of blessing God can pour into us; the more of pride and self-sufficiency, the less fruit we can bear.*
>
> Names of God
> Nathan Stone[72]

to the goods and services that we are told will make us happy, and if we match the picture of success that we see on the television screen and in the magazines we read. The product of our self-will and limited vision, we will convince ourselves that we are all that we can be and that we have done all that we can do – and we will be pleased with ourselves. Like little children, we will follow the instructions as we perceive them, we will color inside the lines we set for ourselves, and we will receive our gold star.

On the other hand, if we are really fortunate in this process of meeting our self-willed goals, we may come to notice that we are not really so happy, that we are not really fulfilled, and that we are not making much of a difference in this world. We may come to notice that, beyond satisfying our unrelenting drive for instant gratification, we are lacking passion and excitement in our lives, that one day is, more or less, like the last day, one vacation, more or less, like the last one. In short, we may come to notice that, driven only by self-will and the formulas we design for ourselves, our lives lack adventure and meaning.

In Hindu belief, a self-willed person is seen as being stuck on the wheel of life forever, like a hamster in a cage, never finding a way to move beyond his own desires and his own imagination to become free, to become Brahman. The Brhadaranyaka Upanishad (4.4.6) describes such a man, attached to his will and his limited perception of reality:

A man who's attached goes with his action,
> to that very place to which
> his mind and character cling.
Reaching the end of his action,
> of whatever he has done in this world —
From that world he returns
> back to this world,
> back to action.
That is the course of a man who desires.

As we become more intimate with the Eternal Absolute, we can begin to see ourselves differently and begin to identify all the gifts we are given to fulfill our purpose in life. We can begin to discern God's will for us and to follow God's guidance, as we follow the path he is preparing for us. We can begin to leave the hamster wheel on which we are spinning and move toward the adventure of being released from the limitations of our own self-will.

Asserting that God knows us and the desires of our souls better than we can know ourselves, St. Teresa of Avila points out how misguided we are when we choose to limit ourselves to our own imagination, our own motivations, and our own goals: "if we have the union in which we resign our wills to the will of God.... this soul sees clearly that He knows what He does better than it knows itself what it desires"[73]....for His judgments surpass all that we can imagine here on earth."[74] And she explains that such a soul, "seems no longer to be itself, or even its own likeness....It is no longer bound by ties of relationship, friendship or property."[75]

And he withdrew from them...and knelt down and prayed, "Father, if thou art willing, remove this cup from me; nevertheless not my will, but thine be done."

Luke 22:41

Renaissance sculptor and painter Michelangelo echoes St. Teresa's observation in his poem, "To the Supreme Being," where he expresses his profound gratitude for God's hand in his life, in his work, and even in his ability to pray:

> The prayers I make will then be sweet indeed
> If Thou the spirit give by which I pray:
> My unassisted heart is barren clay,
> That of its native self can nothing feed:
> Of good and pious works thou art the seed,
> That quickens only where thou say'st it may.
> Unless Thou shew to us thine own true way
> No man can find it: Father! Thou must lead.
> Do Thou, then, breathe those thoughts
>   into my mind
> By which such virtue may in me be bred
> That in thy holy footsteps I may tread;
> The fetters of my tongue do Thou unbind,
> That I may have the power to sing of thee,
> And sound thy praises everlastingly.[76]

When, like Michelangelo, we can come to know the ecstasy of a life filled with God's boundless gifts and adventures, why do we continue to limit ourselves to our finite imaginations and goals? Why do we use our free will to remain on the hamster wheel, clinging to such a narrow perception of ourselves and our world? Is it simply because we want to protect the illusion that we are in control of our lives – and we delude ourselves into believing that limiting ourselves and our lives by our own imagination and our own self-will guarantees that we will be able to maintain that control? Is it that we do not yet discern that we can trust God to do a better job in guiding our lives than we can do for ourselves? Or are we afraid of the power of the love and the gifts that God will release in us? Are we afraid of the force of our own indwelling divinity?

To come to realize that we can trust God's will to guide us, we will have to continue to receive God's love, continue to experience how that love transforms us and reshapes our lives, and continue to take small steps on the path God is clearing for us. Gradually, as we experience the freedom that we gain as we detach from our own self-will and venture beyond those possibilities that we can imagine, we will come to trust God's plan for us, and we will become filled with love and gratitude for all the gifts we are receiving. And gradually, as our love and gratitude grow, we will become ready to make a commitment to serve God's purpose in our lives. We will become Christ conscious leaders.

7

COMMITMENT
The Fourth Step

Commitment is a lifelong process, a continual adventure of coming to understand God's will for us, coming to understand ourselves, and coming to understand our purpose for being here. And as we gradually detach from our tribe, our family, and our self-will and gradually deepen our relationship with the Eternal Absolute, our capacity for commitment also deepens. In this process, there are few plateaus, few comfort zones, and few places to stop and rest for a while, for this process is one of vibrant and continual change. Like the universe we live in, there appear to be no limits to how far we can expand in our commitment to God and to our life's work. The only limits are those we may impose on ourselves because of our hesitation to detach from all that is familiar and move forward into our unfolding destiny. And our hesitations are many – and they are real.

In our commitment to becoming Christ conscious leaders and to serving God's purpose in our lives, we will first have to be patient with ourselves and our progress, for this is not a fleeting or careless commitment. As we are steadily moving away from the known past toward the unknown future, we are leaving behind many of the road signs that once marked the pathway to our self-willed goals, and we may also be leaving behind many of the people who once provided a sense of security and comfort. Most of all, we are leaving behind our own sense of who we are and what we are all about. And because we have only recently begun to receive Divine Love and to build our relationship with the Eternal Absolute, we are as wobbly on our feet as newborn foals, and we feel painfully vulnerable.

It is at this juncture in our process of commitment that we may try to turn back to the past, but because our consciousness is already evolving beyond our previous sense of ourselves and our world, the past also alludes us. We find ourselves without a place to be, whether inside ourselves or outside in the world. We are no longer in the comfort of a familiar womb, and we are not yet born again. We are in the passageway of our rebirth, and we experience all the discomfort of being between two worlds. We are in what Saint John of the Cross calls "the dark night of the soul," a time of "trials, spiritual and

> *To come to enjoy what you have not you must go by a way in which you enjoy not.*
> *To come to the knowledge you have not you must go by a way in which you know not.*
> *To come to the possession you have not you must go by a way in which you possess not.*
> *To come to be what you are not you must go by a way in which you are not.*
>
> St. John of the Cross[1]

> *God is the light of the heavens and the earth....Light upon light.*
>
> The Koran 24:35

temporal," a time of transition when we often cannot even sense the presence of God in our lives."[2]

How long we remain in this passageway depends entirely upon how long it takes us to replace our past attractions and our past perceptions of reality with a new discernment of our purpose in the world and a new relationship with the Eternal Absolute. It depends, also, upon how much courage we can find for upholding our commitment as it leads us into uncharted territory, trusting that God, like a loving parent, is patiently awaiting our arrival out of the darkness and into the Light. And except for those few rare individuals who are instantly enraptured and transformed by Divine Love and passionately and abruptly vow a lifetime commitment to God's purpose, we all have to go through a process of introspection and growth before we are ready to fulfill our commitment. For while the Light is always present, and while our commitment may be sincere, we need to be prepared to live in that Light, and it is during this period of transition, this "dark night of the soul," that we are being prepared. So no matter how dark or how long this transition may be, it is a time of profound learning and growth.

The first and most important phase in our preparation is learning how to be alone with ourselves, without even sensing the comfort of God's presence, and in this aloneness, we are also learning how to be introspective. We are learning to examine our hearts and our motivations. And we are learning to examine the nature of our commitment. Is our commitment motivated by the genuine love of the Eternal Absolute and our fellow man or by love of self, by a narcissistic drive for perfection and gratification? Is it motivated by wanting to align ourselves with God's purpose and be useful to God or by wanting to be recognized by God and by society as someone who is virtuous? Is this a genuine commitment to a Christ conscious way of life or a misguided attempt to avoid facing some deep, unresolved issues? Does our commitment fill us with the joy of being useful and serving a purpose in society or does it fill us with a sense of righteousness? And depending on what we learn about ourselves, how do we proceed with our commitment? Do we abandon ourselves and our commitment if we find our motivations are not pure, or do we make a new commitment to ourselves to seek God's guidance in changing our motivations?

In learning to be introspective, we are also learning humility and gratitude; for many of us will discover that we are beset by a variety of conflicting emotions and drives and that, no matter how passionate and eager we may be, we are not yet prepared to fulfill our commitment. We will discover that we still have a long way to travel in examining and adjusting our motivations and in expanding our ability to serve God's purpose. And we will be humbled by these shortcomings and become grateful for God's guidance on this path. We will also be grateful for any small opportunity to be useful while we

The heights of the spirit can only be climbed by passing through the portals of humility.

Knowledge of the Higher Worlds and Its Attainment
Rudolf Steiner[3]

are moving along in our process of growth and spiritual maturation.

During this period of preparation, we are also learning how to be patient with ourselves and to wait, not passively, but with spirited anticipation. We can see what waiting entails in the Indo-European root word for *wait, ueg,* which means "*vigor, liveliness, watchfulness, and vigilance.*"[4] For while we are waiting to emerge from this passageway, we are vigilantly and vigorously seeking clarity and direction. We are seeking greater self-awareness and self-knowledge, and we are trying to discern God's plan for us. And we are watchful for every small sign of our transformation and our readiness to move forward into the Light.

We are also learning to be open systems, to live in the question, to empty ourselves of our expectations, and to trust that our path will unfold as we move forward. And we are learning that being open to unimagined possibilities is making us stronger, more flexible, more useful, and more prepared to evolve beyond the limits we envision for ourselves. As microbiologist Stuart Kauffman explains, "life exists at the edge of chaos. Networks in the regime near the edge of chaos,...this compromise between order and surprise,...appear best able to coordinate complex activities and best able to evolve as well." On the other hand, Kauffman points out, "adapting populations that are too methodical and timid in their explorations are likely to get stuck in the foothills, thinking they have reached as high as they can

> *A jar is formed from clay*
> *but its usefulness lies in the empty center....*
> *That is - everything that lives has a physical body,*
> *but the value of a life is measured by the soul.*
>
> Tao Te Ching 11

go."[5] Even worse, Kauffman warns: "For most cells... equilibrium corresponds to death."[6]

As we are learning to remain open to unimagined possibilities, we are also learning to use our intuition to discern God's promptings and guidance, even though we may still be so distracted by the turmoil inside ourselves that we initially discern very little. When we can quiet our thoughts and our emotions, when we can free ourselves of our preoccupations, what little we do discern begins to illuminate our life's work and purpose and our oneness with the Eternal Absolute and with all of creation. And it begins to illuminate our souls, the empty space within us where Divine Love dwells.

In learning to be open systems responsive to surprise and change, and in learning to discern God's promptings and guidance, we are also learning how to be part of the creative process of the universe, and we are building the personal courage we will need to do our work, to align ourselves with God's purpose and contibute to fullfilling God's plan. Psychologist Rollo May defines the challenge of being human and being useful in the world: "We are all called upon to do something new, to confront a no man's land, to push into the forest where there are no well-worn paths and from which no one has returned to guide us." And he asserts: "To live into the future means to leap into the unknown, and this requires a degree of courage for which there is no immediate precedent." Contrasting human growth to the automatic growth of an acorn into an oak tree, which requires no commitment, May continues: "a man or woman becomes fully human only by his or her choices and his or her commitment to them." And he concludes: "People attain worth and dignity by the multitude of decisions they make from day to day. These decisions require courage...it is essential to our being....In human beings courage is necessary to make *being* and *becoming* possible."[7]

If we are sincere in our commitment to becoming Christ conscious leaders, to serving God's purpose in our lives, we will welcome this period of preparation, and we will emerge from this passageway into the Light with a deepening understanding of our motivations, our strengths, and our limitations, and a deepening sense of humility and gratitude. We will know how to wait vigilantly for God's guidance, and we will be open to the unimagined and the unexpected, open to discerning God's plan for us. And as we endure this time of transition, we will build the courage to become a creative force, to manifest our indwelling divinity, and to contribute to the evolution of our world.

To prevail during this period of preparation, we will have to trust that the path we are on will lead to our growth and rebirth. We will have to trust that we will become useful to God and that we will find fulfillment in our deepening commitment. And we will have to continue to be receptive to God's unfolding purpose in our lives, define our gifts for fulfilling that purpose, and sustain our commitment to continual transformation.

Commitment to God's Purpose

While it may take a lifetime to discern and fulfill our commitment to God's purpose for us, God has but one abiding purpose, filling our souls with Divine Love, and through the indwelling of that Love, bringing all of humanity into conscious unity with Christ, the Eternal Absolute. When we open our souls to receive Divine Love, we become aware of our oneness with all creation and with the Eternal Absolute, and we are able to align ourselves with God's purpose. When we resist Divine Love, we are standing in the way of God's purpose, and we become alienated from the universe we live in and alienated from the Eternal Absolute. And because we are often so preoccupied in a world of our own making, no matter how strong we think our commitment to God's purpose may be, we will repeatedly find ourselves standing in God's way, resisting Divine Love, and perceiving ourselves as disconnected from others and disconnected from the Eternal Absolute.

This conflict between our commitment to God's purpose and our unyielding fascination with our own agenda is as old as recorded history. As early as 600 B.C.,[8] this persistent conflict is revealed in the Hindu teachings of the Katha Upanishad (2.1-5):

> The good is one thing, the gratifying is
>   quite another;
> their goals are different, both bind a man.
> Good things await him who picks the good;

So God created man in his own image, in the image of God he created him; male and female he created them.

Genesis 1:27

>   by choosing the gratifying, one misses one's goal.
>
> Both the good and the gratifying
>   present themselves to a man;
> The wise assess them, note their difference;
>   and choose the good over the gratifying;
> But the fool chooses the gratifying
>   rather than what is beneficial....
>
> Wallowing in ignorance, but calling
>   themselves wise,
> thinking themselves learned, the fools
>   go around,
> staggering about like a group of blind men,
>   led by a man who is himself blind.

And the Chandogya Upanishad (8.2-3) tells us that all our "real desires are masked by the unreal," and, therefore, "even when [we] pass over it time and again...[we] do not discover this world of *brahman*, for [we] are led astray by the unreal."

Still God's purpose, to bring all of humanity into conscious unity with the Eternal Absolute, remains constant. In the Byhadaranyaka Upanishad (4.4.6), we learn that when we detach from the distractions of our own egocentric concerns, we can achieve unity with the Eternal Absolute: "When they are all banished, those desires lurking in one's heart; then a mortal becomes immortal, and attains *brahman* in this world." In the Mundaka Upanishad (3.2.8), the importance of detachment is presented again: "As the rivers flow on and enter into the ocean giving up their names and appearances; so the knower, freed from name and appearance, reaches the heavenly Person, beyond the very highest." And in the Svetasvatara Upanishad (6.11), the unity of God with all humanity is affirmed: "The one God hidden in all beings, pervading the universe, the inner self of all beings,...dwelling in all beings."

The age-old conflict between our commitment to God's purpose and our ego-driven aspirations is addressed again in the Tao Te Ching (19), dated from 770 to 221 B.C.[9] Here we are told that even when we are outwardly professing commitment to God's purpose, we may be inwardly motivated by arrogance and self-centeredness. Pointing out the distinction between "True and False Religion," Lao Tzu counsels:

> Abandon the pretense of saintliness and asceticism,
> and the people will pursue virtue.
> Abandon ostentatious benevolence
> and conspicuous righteousness;
> then the people will return to the core virtues
> of love and respect.
> Abandon cleverness and greed;
> then thieves and robbers will disappear.

And the Tao Te Ching (34) also assures us that, no matter what our true motivations may be, God's purpose, to unite all creation with Divine Love, remains constant: "The great Tao is everywhere! It is on both the right hand and the left. All things rely upon it for their existence, and it sustains them....It lovingly nourishes everything."

> *My words fly up, my thoughts remain below: Words without thoughts never to heaven go.*
>
> Hamlet 3.3
> William Shakespeare[10]

Throughout the Old Testament, we also find evidence of this relentless struggle between our commitment to God's purpose and our attraction to our lofty dreams. In Jeremiah (23:23-40), the Lord firmly reproaches "prophets who prophesy lies, and who prophesy the deceit of their own heart, who think to make my people forget my name by their dreams which they tell one another." Again, in Ecclesiastes (5:4-7), the Preacher warns against disregarding our commitment to God while we run after our dreams: "When you vow a vow to God, do not delay paying it….It is better that you should not vow than that you should vow and not pay…. For when dreams increase, empty words grow many." And in Psalms (82:6), we learn the consequences of our vacilating commitment to God's purpose: "You are gods, sons of the Most High, all of you; nevertheless, you shall die like men, and fall like any prince."

Still God's purpose remains constant, and in Psalms (103:17), we are assured that "the steadfast love of the Lord is from everlasting to everlasting." In Jeremiah (7:5-7), we see God actively engaging in our lives to bring our thoughts and actions into harmony with Divine Love and vowing to keep his covenant: "if you truly amend your ways and your doings, if you truly execute justice one with another, if you do not oppress the alien, the fatherless or the widow, or shed innocent blood in this place." And in Hosea (6:6), God shows us the path to unity with Divine Love: "For I desire steadfast love and not sacrifice, the knowledge of God, rather than burnt offerings."

We can also gain valuable insight into those fears and fantasies that can restrict our commitment to God's purpose in the New Testament, as we witness Jesus rejecting temptations to which we often succumb: fear of being hungry, arrogance and distrust of God's love, and desire for instant power and wealth. Although hungry after forty days of fasting in the desert, Jesus refuses the devil's challenge to "command these stones to become loaves of bread," and affirming his faith in his Father's power to nourish him with wisdom and love, he responds: "Man shall not live by bread alone, but by every word that proceeds from the mouth of God." And when the devil tempts Jesus to throw himself down from the "pinnacle of the temple" to test God's pledge of protection in Psalms 91:11-12,[11] Jesus refuses to test his Father's love, and again affirming his faith, he quotes Moses in Deuteronomy 6:16:[12] "You shall not tempt the Lord your God." Jesus also rejects the devil's third temptation: "all the kingdoms of the world and the glory of them....if you will fall down and worship me." Again quoting Moses, in Deuteronomy 6:13,[13] Jesus remains loyal to God: "You shall worship the Lord your God and him only shall you serve" (Matthew 4:1-11).

In the devil's temptations, we have an accurate picture of those anxieties and desires that can distract us from our commitment, and in Jesus' responses, we find the ultimate ideal of absolute commitment to God's purpose.

While Jesus provides us with the perfect example of unconditional commitment, it is in the struggles of

> *God... called us with a holy calling, not in virtue of our works but in virtue of His own purpose.*
>
> 2 Timothy 1:9

Jesus' disciples that we find a true mirror of our human conflicts and limitations. Although each disciple is passionately attracted to Jesus and genuinely committed to his purpose, each one wrestles with personal shortcomings, misguided expectations, and doubts. We see James and John bring an impulsive, headstrong temperament to their commitment to Jesus and his ministry, and when they want to "bid fire come down from heaven and consume" those Samaritans who reject Jesus, "he turned and rebuked them" (Luke 9:51-56). And ambitiously seeking position in the new kingdom, these brothers request of Jesus: "Grant us to sit, one at your right hand and one at your left, in our glory" (Mark 10:37). When the other disciples hear of this request, "they began to be indignant at James and John" (Mark 10:41), for they, too, are concerned with having a privileged position.

Of all the disciples and their attraction to prestige and position, only Judas Iscariot and his attraction to money leads to a complete betrayal of his commitment. Even before betraying Jesus for "thirty pieces of silver" (Matthew 26:15), Judas, who was entrusted with managing the money the disciples collected for the poor, earns a reputation for being "a thief, and as he had the money box he used to take what was put into it" (John 12:6).

In Peter we also see human frailty. Although he earnestly declares to Jesus that he will never "fall away" from him, Jesus forewarns Peter that "this very night, before the cock crows, you will deny me three times" (Matthew 26:33-34). Then, although Peter and all the other disciples vow that they will never deny him, when Jesus is seized by the Romans, they all "forsook him and fled" (Matthew 26:56). And later, after denying Jesus three times, and after remembering Jesus' words, Peter "went out and wept bitterly" (Matthew 26:75).

At the Crucifixion, only John, who initially ran away with the others, returns to witness Jesus' suffering. And from the Cross, Jesus acknowledges John's presence and establishes a bond between his mother and "the disciple whom he loved": "He said to his mother, 'Woman, behold your son!' Then he said to the disciple, 'Behold your mother!' And from that hour the disciple took her to his own home" (John 19:26-27).

Even after Jesus' Resurrection, the disciples are still plagued with fear and doubt, and "questionings rise in [their] hearts" (Luke 24:38). Before Thomas will believe that he is risen, Jesus has to allow him to place his fingers "in the mark of the nails" and place his hand "in his side" (John 20:24-29). And before "they knew it was the Lord" (John 21:12-14), Jesus has to appear to the disciples three times.

It is in this patient and consistent relationship with his disciples that Jesus reveals God's unwavering commitment to his purpose. For, notwithstanding all of their conflicts and doubts, Jesus continues working with his disciples until the day of his ascension, "appearing to them during forty days, and speaking of the kingdom of

God" (Acts 1:3), and preparing them for their ministry, to "make disciples of all nations" (Matthew 28:19).

The challenge of this never-ending conflict between our commitment to God's purpose and our distractions appears again in the wisdom of the Koran, which questions, "Do people think that once they say: 'We are believers', they will be left alone and not be tested" (29:2). Addressing those whose actions and thoughts do not match their words, the Koran asks: "Does not God know best the thoughts of men? God well knows the true believers, and He well knows the hypocrites" (29:11). Then focusing on those dreams and desires that sidetrack us, the Koran counsels: "Those who serve other masters besides God may be compared to the spider which builds a cobweb for itself. Surely the spider's is the frailest of all dwellings, if they but knew it" (29:41). Again, we are warned against being distracted: "Believers, let neither your riches nor your children divert you from remembering God. Those who are so diverted will surely be the losers" (63:9). And we are warned against our appetites: "Have you considered the man who has made a god of his own appetite? Would you be guardian over him? Do you think most of them can hear or understand? They are but like cattle; indeed, even more misguided" (25:43-44).

Still, whether or not we stray from our commitment, God's commitment to his purpose remains constant. As we hear it expressed by the Eternal Absolute in every culture since the beginning of time, in the Koran, we again hear God affirm his purpose to be united in Divine Love with his creation: "O serene soul! Return to your Lord, joyful and pleasing in his sight. Join My servants and enter My Paradise" (89:27-30).

As we continue to move toward an ever-deepening commitment to God's purpose in our lives, self-knowledge is our greatest ally. The more we become aware of our distractions, our anxieties, and our preoccupations, and the more we know and accept our shortcomings, the more useful we can become. Continuing to be receptive to Divine Love, our commitment slowly deepens, and we find that we are slowly becoming less fascinated with our distractions, less absorbed by our anxieties and preoccupations, and we are slowly finding ways to turn our shortcomings into strengths. And we will find that our deepening commitment is transforming our perception of ourselves and our world. We will find that we are seeing ourselves and our world through the eyes of the Eternal Absolute.

To fulfill our commitment to God's purpose in our lives, we must first begin to discern that purpose and, then, we must begin a courageous, honest, and lifelong process of introspection. We must come face to face with those fears, doubts, and conflicts that stand in the way of our being transformed by Divine Love, embracing our indwelling divinity, and moving toward our unfolding destiny. And we must become aware of those unique gifts we each have been given to do our work as Christ conscious leaders.

Commitment to Our Work

We are all very busy in our lives, doing chores, running errands, caring for loved ones and neighbors, and making every effort to excel at our jobs, but in all this flurry of activity, few of us are engaged in doing our life's work. And because we are not doing our life's work, no matter how we are being rewarded with approval and monetary gains, few of us are fulfilled by all our activity. On the contrary, many of us are dissatisfied with our lives, and to take the edge off that dissatisfaction, most of us simply do more of the same: multiply our activities, multiply our material possessions, and, in time, multiply our dissatisfactions. But this strategy is not working.

Recent studies are showing that the increase in "worker dissatisfaction, demoralization, and alienation" is setting in motion a debilitating spiral of "somatization of personal and social stress," and the chronic physical ailments that result are now responsible for a major portion of disability costs and employee absenteeism. Contributing to this debilitating spiral, "the biomedical health care system is often shown to be dangerous for… somatization patients, because it produces addictions to prescription narcotic analgesic drugs." In addition, many prescribed drugs are leading to dangerous side effects, and various medical and surgical treatments and costly and risky test procedures are causing irreversible complications, as well as "anger and frustration for patients, families, and physicians."[15] Further studies by the World

The mass of men lead lives of quiet desperation. What is called resignation is confirmed desperation.

Walden
Henri David Thoreau[14]

Health Organization indicate that depression is steadily on the increase, up ten percent since 1995 and projected to be up another ten percent by 2020. This rate of increase is expected to "result in depressive disorders becoming the leading cause of disability and overall burden worldwide."[16]

In his poem, "The World Is Too Much with Us," William Wordsworth observes a comparable malaise in industrialized, early nineteenth century England:

> The world is too much with us; late and soon,
> Getting and spending, we lay waste our
>   powers;—
> Little we see in Nature that is ours;
> We have given our hearts away, a sordid
>   boon!
> This Sea that bares her bosom to the moon;
> The winds that will be howling at all hours,
> And are up-gathered now like sleeping
>   flowers;
> For this, for everything, we are out of tune;
> It moves us not. Great God! I'd rather be
> A Pagan suckled in a creed outworn;
> So might I, standing on this pleasant lea,
> Have glimpses that would make me less
>   forlorn;
> Have sight of Proteus rising from the sea;
> Or hear old Triton blow his wreathèd horn.[17]

Whether industrialization and the ensuing consumerism is at fault or whether the unsettling, post-industrial transition into a digital, global economy is to blame for the widespread escalation of depression and somatization, the antidote is well within our reach. For we each can take the time to get to know our true selves, to go below the surface of those images from our childhood and our culture that we use to define who we are. We can also begin to evaluate our current motivations and assess our future goals. And if we find those goals unsatisfying, we can choose to make a conscious effort to discern what God's purpose is in our lives and make a commitment to work toward fulfilling that purpose.

The process of getting to know ourselves is not complicated. It requires only that we spend quiet time with ourselves, listening attentively for our inner truth, for the wisdom of our indwelling divinity, and for God's guidance. Other than finding that quiet time each day, we do not have to change anything in our lives to become introspective and to discover our life's work. We do not have to quit our jobs, sit on a mountaintop in Nepal, consult a guru, or purify ourselves with fasting. We do not have to sign up for a regimen of transcendental meditation and yoga or switch to a macrobiotic diet. While all these external activities may prove beneficial, they are not substitutes for authentic introspection and contemplation; they are not substitutes for having the courage to get to know ourselves. In fact, we often engage in these activities in an unconscious effort to avoid becoming genuinely intimate with ourselves, with our indwelling divinity, and with God. And while we may avoid intimacy with ourselves and avoid asking ourselves questions that could point us in new directions

> *To be completely honest with oneself is the very best effort a human being can make.*
>
> Sigmund Freud[18]

because we fear the answers will lead to a dramatic upheaval in our lives, the price we pay for this avoidance is much more costly than the price we may pay for any changes we may decide to make.

Psychologist Abraham Maslow suggests that we are always torn between "the need to know" about ourselves and "the fear of knowing" about ourselves because we always associate knowing ourselves with having to do something we may not want to do: "the fear of knowing [is] deeply a fear of doing, a fear of the consequences that flow from knowing; a fear of its dangerous responsibilities." He explains further: "Often it is better not to know, because if you *did* know, then you would have to act and stick your neck out." Essentially, Maslow suggests that we are continually engaged in "a struggle between fear and courage," and in this struggle, "the adult human being...is very apt to repress [his fears and anxieties], to deny even to himself that they exist. Frequently, he does not 'know' that he is afraid." Maslow adds: "Freud's greatest discovery is that *the* great cause of much psychological illness is the fear of knowledge of oneself – of one's emotions, one's impulses, memories, capacities, potentialities, of one's destiny."[19]

As we continue to absorb Divine Love and become confident in our unity with the Eternal Absolute, this fear of knowing ourselves will gradually diminish. We will gradually become accustomed to listening to the voice of our indwelling divinity and intuitively discerning

> *Each person....is a unique and special individual, with a calling and a work to do that no one else can accomplish.*
>
> Joseph F. Girzone[20]

God's presence in our lives, and we will gradually begin to discover God's purpose for us and the path of our life's work. We will also discover that we can often do that work no matter what our job may be. Whether we sort mail in the local post office or broker deals in the executive suite of a multinational corporation, whether we are a stay-at-home mom or a high school science teacher, a young minister in Vermont or a surfing instructor in Hawaii, we can know ourselves, be true to our life's work, and fulfill God's purpose anywhere. And the work we are called on to do can be as technical as discovering the process for converting nuclear fusion into a reliable energy source or as ordinary as caring for our families. For our life's work is not a job description or a career; it is a ministry, a calling to serve a unique purpose in the world.

To gain a deeper understanding of the difference between a job and work, we can explore four significant derivations of the Indo-European root *uerg*. As it morphs over four thousand years, this root word, which originally means *work* and *do,* gives rise to the words *organic, energy, synergy,* and *liturgy*.[21] And so, based on its most literal definition, when we are doing our life's work, we are using our organic energy, in synergy with others, and we are also worshiping God. On the other hand, a study of the origins of the word *job*, leads us to a shallow root, connected to the Middle English word *jobben: to peck* – and that is how many jobs are designed. We are often asked to peck away at a job description, and if we perform well, we can anticipate being moved up in the pecking order.[22]

With insight into the difference between our job and our life's work, and with the details of our life's work coming into focus through daily introspection and contemplation, we can move toward making a commitment to do that work. And as we begin to respond to our calling, we will begin to discover that we have all the unique gifts and talents we need to fulfill our commitment. We will discover skills and abilities that we never recognized before, and we may even be mystified by the fact that our capabilities align so perfectly with the new challenges we are facing. And as the challenges of our work continue to unfold and expand, we will discover that every experience we have is preparation for becoming increasingly useful and effective in carrying out our mission.

If we do not discover God's purpose in our life and if we do not make a commitment to do our work, we may go through life without ever realizing the scope of our strengths and talents. Locked into a job and a career path that may have little to do with the expression of our inherent gifts and even less to do with the realization of our reason for being here, we may never experience the ecstasy of getting to know ourselves and exercising our full potential. Behaving like thirsty travelers in an arid desert, we may continue to subsist on the ration of water we carry in our canteens, while, in reality, we have within us an overflowing artesian well.

Now there are varieties of gifts, but the same Spirit; and there are varieties of service, but the same Lord; and there are varieties of working, but it is the same God who inspires them all in every one.

1Corinthians 12:4-6

To find the courage to know ourselves and to make a enduring commitment to our work, we will have to continue to spend quiet, contemplative time with ourselves, and we will have to continue to develop an increasingly intimate relationship with the Eternal Absolute. In our evolution as Christ conscious leaders, we will also have to discover and expand those inherent gifts and life experiences that prepare us to meet the evolving demands of our calling. And we will have to find the passion within ourselves to make a lifelong commitment to our continual transformation.

Commitment to Lifelong Transformation

Early in the twentieth century, with signs of the approaching Russian Revolution in the air, Leo Tolstoy prophetically wrote:

> There can be only one permanent revolution — a moral one; the regeneration of the inner man. How is this revolution to take place? Nobody knows how it will take place in humanity, but every man feels it clearly in himself. And yet in our world everybody thinks of changing humanity, and nobody thinks of changing himself. [23]

Now, a century after the death of Tolstoy and nearly a quarter century after the fall of the Berlin Wall and the end of communism in Russia, we cannot escape the profound truth of these words, and we hear them reaffirmed by Mikhail Gorbachev, the last premier of the Soviet Union:

> The dilemma formulated by wise men of old – to be or to have? – has taken on a new and threatening meaning today....Consumerism and the desire for things...have pushed into the background any desire for spiritual enrichment or cultural progress, the desire for improving or perfecting human thinking and consciousness. This "freedom to have" is regarded as the highest achievement of history, as its grand finale. Yet this is nothing more than the renunciation of all higher aspirations for a better, a genuinely humane future.

Gorbachev warns: "If society enters the future with these current false and distorted values, then it will have no future. It would mean the degeneration of *Homo sapiens*, God's highest creation." Joining many other voices in alerting us to our current realities, he adds: "Because the human race has acquired the ability to destroy itself through nuclear war....for the first time in history we face the challenge of defending human existence itself, not just saving the lives of individuals or nations." And he calls for action: "A return to age-old, spiritual, moral, life-affirming values...is one of the decisive tasks of our era. It is a universal human task. A global one."[24]

Since, as Gorbachev observes, "as ever politics is lagging behind" in answering this call to action,[25] and since we continue to ignore these warnings and continue in the time-honored practice of trying to change the world from outside in, we continue to witness a proliferation of revolutions and political and economic wars raging across the globe. And reflecting on this state of human affairs, we have to consider that we may be so afraid of getting to know ourselves and changing ourselves that we will, ultimately, choose to obliterate each other rather than confront our deep-seated fears and our resistance to altering our perceptions, our motivations, and our behavior.

If we thoughtfully review all of human history and our present precarious position at the edge of potential annihilation, we are forced to conclude, as Tolstoy did more than a century ago, that there is only one path to ensure survival, the inner path to our continual transformation. For no matter how threatening that path may be, and no matter how determined we are to avoid that path, we are now up against a wall that we have put in place, and our choice is to change or die. Tearing down the Berlin Wall is a visible, momentous, external step in that direction, but we now must move forward and tear down the walls that we build inside ourselves.

This critical time in our history is compelling each of us to make a commitment to becoming Christ conscious and to take a leadership role no matter what our position is in our family, our workplace, and our community. And the only way to prepare ourselves to meet the challenges of this responsibility is to make a commitment to a lifetime of personal transformation. For, like an athlete preparing for an Olympic event, our preparation for discerning and fulfilling God's unfolding purpose in our lives requires daily exercise. It requires a lifetime of daily contemplation, of courageous, uncompromising introspection, and of openness to change. It requires a daily expansion of our perception of our oneness with each other and with the Eternal Absolute, and it requires a daily assimilation of Divine Love into our lives. It requires a daily effort to detach from our self-will and from any ingrained, destructive tribal and family influences that may impede our progress. And it requires a daily alignment of our life's work with God's emerging and expanding purpose. Unlike the self-help movements of the late twentieth century, this commitment to daily preparation is not a disciplined dedication to improve oneself for one's own benefit. Rather it is a devout commitment to engage in a profound personal transformation for the benefit of human evolution and survival.

I am the way, and the truth, and the life.

John 14:6

As we have done for thousands of years, today we continue to try to prevail without changing our existing oppositional mindset, without perceiving or acknowledging our unity with each other and with the Eternal Absolute, and without detaching from our familiar attitudes and from our own self-willed goals. And over thousands of years, the price we seem to be willing to pay for this status quo in our perceptions and behaviors continues to be brutal wars, genocide, and personal alienation from our indwelling divinity, from each other, and from God. Since no external political, social, or religious systems we devise and embrace seem to be able to diminish the consequences of living like this, we become inured to these consequences and consider them a necessary part of our human experience, and we continue on as we always have. And unless someone close to us is suffering with brain damage sustained in a recent war, or our immediate family is cut off from an adequate supply of food and clean water, or our neighborhood is being threatened by enemy fire, we ignore these consequences and go about our daily business as if everything is just fine. But everything is not just fine, and if we continue on with our current mindset, we may find that we are running out of time to change. We may find that it is too late to move away from the edge of our own self-ordained destruction.

To move away from that edge of destruction that we are carelessly approaching, we must each make a commitment to change the way we perceive and interact with ourselves, each other, and God. We must each begin a lifelong process of personal commitment to our conscious evolution and to manifesting our indwelling divinity in the world. We must prepare ourselves to become Christ conscious leaders, to reflect, in all our daily actions, the Divine Love of the Eternal Absolute.

8

ACTION
The Fifth Step

In Uruvela, on the Ganges plain of India, near the holy city of Benares, in the year 528 B.C.,[1] the future of what is to become the world's fourth largest religion, with over four million followers,[2] is hanging in the balance. For in that year, Siddhattha Gotama, after struggling for six years, achieving enlightenment, and becoming the first Buddha,[3] decides not to teach the truths he knows to "those that live in lust and hate" because it "would be wearying and troublesome." Considering that "this Dhamma that I have attained to is profound and hard to see, hard to discover....not attainable by mere ratiocination, subtle, for the wise to experience," Gotama Buddha concludes: "But this generation relies on attachment, relishes attachment, delights in attachment.

It is hard for this generation to see this truth." And "his mind favoured inaction and not teaching the Dhamma."[4]

This decision is so upsetting to one Brahma Sahampati that he thinks to himself: "The world will be lost, the world will be utterly lost; for the mind of the Perfect One, accomplished and fully enlightened, favours inaction and not teaching the Dhamma." Deeply perturbed by this crisis, the Brahma decides to approach the Blessed One and pleads: "Lord...let the Sublime One teach the Dhamma....There are beings with little dust in their eyes who are wasting through not hearing the Dhamma. Some of them will gain final knowledge of the Dhamma....some, O Blessed One, will understand."[5]

Hearing the Brahma's fervent request, and "out of compassion for beings," Gotama Buddha reconsiders his decision. He begins to see "beings...with keen faculties and dull faculties, with good qualities and bad qualities, easy to teach and hard to teach, and some who dwelt seeing fear in the other world and blame as well." And he replies to the Brahma: "Let those who hear show faith. If I was minded to tell not the sublime Dhamma I know, it was that I saw vexation in telling," and to himself, Gotama Buddha thought: "To whom shall I first teach the Dhamma?"[7]

Living in a world of almost seven billion souls, some of us feel exactly the same way as the Gotama Buddha. We focus on achieving our personal enlightenment and have no intention of sharing what we have learned

> *Virtues... we acquire ...by having first activated them.... we become just by doing just actions, temperate by doing temperate actions, brave by doing brave actions.*
>
> Nicomachean Ethics
> Aristotle[6]

because it "would be wearying and troublesome." As the Buddha looked at those living "in lust and hate....with much dust in their eyes,"[8] we look at a *third wave* world, as described by futurists Alvin and Heidi Toffler, where all "existing values are being challenged or ignored," where "ideas, images, symbols swirl in a maelstrom, and the individual plucks individual elements with which to form his or her own mosaic or collage,"[9] where "a third to a half of all countries have some hideous weapons of mass murder tucked away in their arsenals...and there simply is no effective *system* to stop the spread of...weapons of mass destruction"[10] – and we think, why bother? Why put any effort into trying to reach out to help others? Why put any effort into making sense of a world that is so erratic, so volatile? In fact, because it requires engaging in a process of getting to know ourselves and transforming the way we think and live, why even bother with a commitment to personal enlightenment? Why not simply go from day to day, focusing on satisfying our immediate needs, and not even thinking about how we can advance our consciousness or influence what is happening in the world around us?

>   This pervasive inclination not to act or to make any commitments, even to one's own personal development, is reaching epidemic proportions, especially among the youth. Several factors are contributing to this, including a growing perception that the individual has little ability to influence the course of events in political, economic, and social matters. In the United States, alone, studies

> *We ourselves feel that what we are doing is just a drop in the ocean. But if that drop was not in the ocean, I think the ocean will be less because of that missing drop.*
>
> Mother Teresa[11]

> *Our society has so many critical problems that it desperately needs as many acting, participating, internal-minded members as possible. If feelings of external control, alienation, and powerlessness continue to grow, we may be heading for a society of dropouts - each person sitting back and watching the world go by.*
>
> Julian Rotter[14]

show that since the 1960s, there is a fifty percent increase in the number of college students who believe that they have no influence over the external forces that shape their lives, and feeling that "you're more likely to get into an accident on the way to the polling place than to have your vote affect the election," only about a quarter of all citizens under the age of twenty-five shows up to vote. This same population rarely reads a newspaper, listens to news broadcasts, or can identify any of today's national challenges, and most believe that the government is "corrupt and evil" and that they can do little to change that.[12]

This sense of impotence is also being felt in a broader range of the population. Since 1970, there has been an eighty percent increase in the number of children between nine and fourteen years of age who feel that they are unable to exert any influence on their environment, as well as a growing number of adults who believe that their opinions have absolutely no impact on the outcome of issues that affect them.[13]

Research psychologist Jean Twenge suggests that "media saturation" is also contributing to this "wave of apathy," and she suggests that media exposure to "disasters, plane crashes, murders of pregnant women, child abductions, stock market crashes" leaves people with the feeling that they have no control over "a huge, complex, confusing, and terrible world." Add to this an overload of information that bombards us from the Internet, emails, and television, "much of it false and not to be believed," and we become even more cynical and apathetic.[15] Twenge concludes that, as a consequence of this distrust of existing institutions and this feeling of overwhelming powerlessness, "young people don't have a sense of personal responsibility, and blame others for their problems."[16]

Research psychologist Peter Gray provides further perspective, suggesting that the shift from "intrinsic to extrinsic goals," promoted by a popular culture that advertises happiness as dependent upon "good looks, popularity, and material goods," also contributes to this breakdown in personal responsibility and to the alarming increase in depression and anxiety disorders in America's youth. Indicating that this psychopathology is now five to eight times more prevalent than it was fifty years ago, he explains: "To the extent that my emotional sense of satisfaction comes from progress toward intrinsic goals I can control my emotional wellbeing." He adds: "To the extent that my satisfaction comes from others' judgments and rewards, I have much less control over my emotional state."[17]

Always expecting all our problems to be solved externally, with a new government policy, a new economic structure, a new religious movement, or a new political revolution, we continue to blame outside forces for what goes wrong inside our lives, and it follows logically that, as the outer world becomes increasingly complex, we feel increasingly powerless to get our needs met or to effect change. And rather than shifting our behavior and looking inward and setting internal goals that we can meet, we persist in looking for satisfaction outside of ourselves, and we become increasingly disenchanted and depressed as the degree of satisfaction we are able to glean from this behavior continues to diminish.

Even the heroes we admire today lack the ability to rescue us from our predicaments. Our faith in yesterday's brave, selfless, wise, and inspiring heroes who venture into the unknown, overcome herculean challenges, and bring redeeming wisdom back to save the society is being replaced by belief in "a synthetic product," created by "whoever controls the microphones and printing presses [which] can make or unmake belief overnight."[18] These "synthetic products" that we believe in and respect include not only celebrated sports figures and movie stars but also fictional characters: Batman, Spiderman, and Captain Kirk of the USS *Enterprise*. Revealing our current mindset, a recent survey of hundreds of people finds that more than forty percent name a person in these categories as their hero, while fewer than six percent name a humanitarian: Mahatma Gandhi, Martin Luther King, or Mother Teresa.[19]

Betrayed by both the malfunctioning of our institutions and the ineptness of our heroes, we still insist on denying responsibility for our behavior and looking outside ourselves to be rescued from our dilemmas. Like two-year-olds in "the magic years" of childhood, we continue to believe that the world is a magical place, and that no matter how often we imperil ourselves, someone will come along and rescue us as we careen toward the edge of a cliff.[20] And when we find that we are not being rescued by any of our institutions, our leaders, or our heroes, we again confirm to ourselves that something is very wrong with the world, but nothing is wrong with us.

Seeking others to rescue us, we seize upon every opportunity to convert the most pedestrian relationships into potentially magical affairs. We do this with everyone and everything we encounter, and so we expect the education system magically to convert our sons and daughters into scholars, and we expect the church we attend magically to convert us into saints. When this does not happen, we blame the teacher and the minister, and we enroll our children in a new school, while we join a new church. And we bring these magical expectations into our marriages. Once the honeymoon is over, if we find that we are not living happily ever after, we blame our partners rather than examining our own inability to find fulfillment in ourselves. Again putting the burden of our satisfaction on someone outside of ourselves, we determine that we chose the wrong partner and we head to the divorce courts, only to bring our magical expectations into the next marriage. As a consequence of this "marriage-go-round" pattern of behavior, by the age of fifteen, forty percent of all children in the United States witness the end of their parents' relationships in a marriage or a cohabitation arrangement, and nearly fifty percent of all children in the United States experience the arrival of a new significant other in their homes within three years of the end of a parent's last relationship, either in a marriage or other cohabitation arrangement.[21]

Locked into this two-year-old rescue fantasy, we also bring our unrealistic expectations to our doctors, expecting instant, magic cures for what ails us, and the doctors, locked into their own rescue fantasies, try to comply. Caught up in this "power trip," the physicians see themselves as heroes who can "snatch the patient from the jaws of death."[22] The impact of this rescue fantasy on sound medical procedure is significant. Howard Brody, Director of the Institute for Medical Humanities, explores this phenomenon: "Most patients visiting a primary-care physician either have nothing medically wrong with them, or have something that will go away if left to itself, or have something chronic that can be managed but never cured." But because "good medicine" is equated "with always trying to rescue, no matter how low the chances of success or how severe the burdens imposed," and because "to give up the rescue fantasy would be felt subconsciously as the giving up of a vital part of the physician's self-image – the sense of the power to control bad outcomes," this power fantasy, inadvertently instilled in the physicians during their early training, can lead to misguided medical treatment,[23] as well as unethical decisions by the medical team.[24] Brody explains the patient's role in collaborating with the physician to keep the rescue fantasy intact: "The patient herself may not have wanted to hear about [any] degree of medical impotence, and the rescue fantasy may initially have been as much a function of her needs as the physicians'."[25] As the patient experiences the rescue fantasy, according to Brody, the "powerful physician... is the one person who can save him from the harm that threatens."[26] And Brody also points out the dangers of this rescue fantasy in psychology: "An inappropriate assumption of power by the therapist, who may believe that only he can 'fix' the client's problem...delays the better therapeutic outcome in which the client comes to accept responsibility for making changes in his own life."[27]

While magical thinking is best left to our nursery years, we obviously can carry it into our dotage, creating endless rescue fantasies as either the conquering hero or the rescued victim, but, at no time in our lives, are these fantasies effective tools for clearly assessing our realities or for moving toward a meaningful path of growth and action. Only when we make a commitment to rescuing ourselves from these fantasies can we hope to become emotionally and spiritually mature, prepared to engage in activities that will benefit ourselves and others.

Mythologist Joseph Campbell suggests that the genuine hero's journey, which we all must take, represents a "rite of passage": a separation from "the world of common day into a region of supernatural wonder"; an initiation during which "fabulous forces are there encountered and a decisive victory won"; and a return, when "the hero comes back from this mysterious adventure with the power to bestow boons on his fellow man."[28] And Campbell asserts that the first step in this journey is "detachment or withdrawal...a radical transfer of emphasis from the external to the internal world...a retreat from the desperations of the waste land to the peace of the everlasting realm within." Campbell defines this internal realm as "the infantile unconscious," where we find "all the ogres and secret helpers of our nursery... all the magic of childhood. And more important, all the life-potentialities that we never managed to bring to adult realization, those other portions of ourself, are there." Assuring us that "such golden seeds do not die," Campbell offers us hope: "If only a portion of that lost totality could be dredged up into the light of day, we should experience a marvelous expansion of our powers, a vivid renewal of life."[29]

The word *hero* derives from an Indo-European root word, *kleu*, meaning *to hear, to hearken*.[30] If we are ever to realize our "life-potentialities," leave behind our apathy and our magical fantasies of being rescued by external forces, and be prepared to become active participants in our own destiny and the destiny of humanity, it is critical that we become true heroes; it is critical that we learn to hear. And the first sound we will need to hear is the voice of our indwelling divinity, the voice of the Eternal Absolute guiding us toward our work and toward God's purpose in our lives. We will also need to hearken to the needs of others, hearing in those needs the subtle voice of God inviting us to be useful, to use our unique gifts to improve our world and

> *Hearken to me...*
> *my deliverance will*
> *be for ever, and*
> *my salvation to all*
> *generations.*
>
> Isaiah 51:7-8

our relationships with one another. For as God always hears us and hearkens to our needs, he also empowers us to meet those needs, to hearken to our calling, and to do our work.

To become genuine heroes prepared to take those actions that are needed to do our life's work, we will have to give up the age-old illusion that there are external solutions to our problems, that there are external heroes who will rescue us, and that we are the helpless victims of external forces that are beyond our ability to influence. We will have to begin to look inward for guidance and direction to discern our calling and to find the willingness to respond to that calling, however ordinary or extraordinary that calling may seem. And we will have to come to realize that whatever ordinary or extraordinary action we are called upon to do, that action performed is part of God's plan and moves all of humanity closer to realizing God's kingdom on earth.

The Call to Action

Every call to action is designed to realize God's purpose, to bring all of humanity into unity with Christ, the Eternal Absolute, and in so doing, to build the kingdom of God on earth as we each manifest our indwelling divinity in the world. To prepare us to do our part, God graces each of us with Divine Love and spiritual gifts. So for each one of us, the first and most important call to action is the call to receive God's grace. Whether zealously spiritual or skeptical and indifferent, we cannot participate in God's plan if we refuse God's invitation to receive this grace, if we are so externally focused that we are not even aware of the gifts that are being offered, or if, upon becoming aware of these gifts, we place no value on them. And until we become aware of God's invitation to receive grace and accept that invitation, we are incapable of answering any other call for advancing God's purpose.

As we observe the world we live in and find little to suggest that we are living in God's kingdom come to earth, we can accurately conclude that most of us are not receptive to God's gifts and that many of us may not even include the existence of these gifts in our perception of reality. Oblivious to grace, we may go through the routines of each day, even go to church on Sunday, and never notice that God is patiently waiting for us to accept the gifts that are available to us. Or we may erroneously believe that God is only interested in providing grace to those who become saints or to holy men and women who live hidden away in ashrams in the Himalayas and in cloistered convents and monasteries. Or as we pursue our careers and amass our goods and services, we may find we have no use for God's grace. Worse, we may think that our material success is evidence enough of God's grace in our lives and we have no interest in receiving any other expression of grace, nor do we have any interest in advancing God's kingdom

> *He who abides in me, and I in him, he it is that bears much fruit, for apart from me you can do nothing.*
>
> John 15:5

on earth. Proud of our external accomplishments, we ignore the nagging sense that something is missing, and we accumulate more and more goods and services to try to quiet the unrelenting dissatisfactions we feel. And as we continue to ignore God's grace, our souls – and the world – continue to suffer.

If we can overcome our resistance and become open to answering the first and fundamental call to action, to receive God's grace, we can then begin to answer the second call to action, to be Christ conscious. United with the Eternal Absolute through the grace of Divine Love, we are now conscious of our indwelling divinity and of the indwelling divinity in everyone we encounter, and we are able to love and honor the indwelling divinity in everyone we encounter. As practiced in both Hindu and Buddhist cultures, we are able to greet everyone we meet with the ancient Sanskrit greeting, *namaste*, pressing our palms together, with our fingers touching and pointing upward in front of our chest, and bowing slightly in reverence, affirming that our indwelling divinity acknowledges and honors their indwelling divinity.[31] And in being conscious of our shared divinity, we also are able to affirm our unity with each other within the Eternal Absolute.

Being a model of Christ consciousness, recognizing and loving the indwelling divinity in every human being, we are also able to help others become Christ conscious. And as we help one person at a time become Christ conscious, we also contribute to the conscious evolution of mankind; we contribute to realizing the kingdom of God on earth. In Ephesians (4:15-25), the apostle Paul explains: "Speaking the truth in love," we are able to help others "put on the new nature, created after the likeness of God," and we are able to contribute to building the universal body of Christ: "joined and knit together by every joint with which it is supplied, when each part is working properly." We are able to "let every one speak the truth with his neighbor, for we are members one of another."

If we diligently answer these first two calls to action, receiving God's grace and being Christ conscious, we will be able to manifest our indwelling divinity in all our actions. No matter what we are doing from day to day, our activities will become instruments for advancing all human consciousness. If we are parents, we will come to cherish and love the indwelling divinity in our children, and we will find it impossible to abuse them, no matter how challenging and demanding their behavior may be, for we will be aware that we would be abusing God. And we will find new ways to love our children as God loves us. If we are educators, we will begin to respond to and honor the indwelling divinity in our students and we will realize that our work is a ministry and that our students, no matter how unruly and fractious they may become, are disciples of God. And we will find new ways to teach our students as God teaches us. If we are members of the clergy, we will treasure and respect the indwelling divinity in our parishioners and we will find our calling to shepherd the flock reignited by our heightened compassion for the struggles of the souls in our care, no matter how mortal their sins may be. And we will find new ways to forgive our parishioners as God forgives us. And as Christ conscious leaders, if we lay the foundation of this new awareness for our youth, we will be inspiring a new generation of Christ conscious leaders. We will be inspiring a new generation of medical professionals who will acknowledge and value the indwelling divinity of their patients, a new generation of lawyers who will appreciate and respect the indwelling divinity of their clients, a new generation of bankers and corporate executives who will recognize and have regard for the indwelling divinity of their employees and their customers, and a new generation of government officials who will remember that they are elected to serve and to hold sacred the indwelling divinity of the people.

    Answering the call to action, to be receptive to God's grace and to be Christ conscious, we will also be able to inspire our peers. As role models, we will find opportunities to reveal God's gifts of wisdom and faith, gifts that may attract others to look inward and seek their own calling. If we are graced with the unique gifts of healing or knowledge, we will find that we are called to meet the needs of those who require these distinct gifts, those who may require physical, emotional, or spiritual support, or those who may require our particular expertise. And while some of us may identify our gifts and look for opportunities to offer those gifts to others, it

> *One person becomes a model for other persons,*
> *one family for other families,*
> *one town for other towns,*
> *one country for other countries,*
> *one empire for all empires.*
>
> Tao Te Ching 54

is not always necessary to seek out those who need us. We may find ourselves becoming spontaneously aware of those we can help through our daily encounters, or others may seek us out directly, and we will be able to recognize their needs and respond to them. For some of us, our gifts will lead to a specific vocation of service. On the other hand, many of us will find that we are simply available whenever a need arises to do our work, to answer an unexpected call to action. And every time that we make ourselves available to serve others, to share our gifts and our strengths, whether as part of our chosen ministry or as part of our chance encounters, we will reaffirm for ourselves and for those we assist that we are all united in the Divine Love of the Eternal Absolute.

To answer the call to action, we will first have to become aware of God's grace, of the Divine Love and spiritual gifts that empower us to become Christ conscious leaders, and we will have to open our minds and our hearts to receive that grace. We will have to reflect on how we perceive the purpose of our lives, how we plan to spend our days, and what kind of world we want to leave behind. We will have to consider how receiving God's grace can transform our aspirations and our interactions with each other. And we will have to assess our willingness to respond to whatever call to action we discern as we unite with the Eternal Absolute in advancing human consciousness and building the kingdom of God on earth.

Willingness and Response

Empowered by God's grace and inspired by Christ consciousness, we are now abundantly prepared to do our work and to answer any call to action we discern. We are prepared to join in a partnership with the Eternal Absolute, to manifest our indwelling divinity in all our actions, and to focus on our potential for attaining unity and peace. Realizing the lesson in the Svetasvatara Upanishad (4.14) that "in the midst of disorder...the creator of the universe...[is] the Benign One," we are prepared to "attain unending peace." We are also prepared to fulfill the promise in the Tao Te Ching (38), where we are told: "A truly great man conforms to the spirit, and not to external appearance. He bears fruit – not just blossoms." Acknowledging our dependence on God's grace, we become like Moses, "very meek, more than all men...on the face of the earth," and in our humbleness, we are, like Moses, "entrusted" with serving God (Numbers 12:3-7). We are prepared to answer Jesus' call in the Sermon on the Mount: "You are the light of the world....Let your light so shine before men, that they may see your good works and give glory to your Father who is in heaven" (Matthew 5:14-16). And we are prepared to be charitable, realizing, as the Koran (2:177) teaches, that "righteousness does not consist in whether you face towards the East or the West."

For all that we may be called to do to advance our conscious evolution and realize unity and peace in

> *And God is able to provide you with every blessing in abundance, so that you may always have enough of everything and may provide in abundance for every good work.*
>
> 2 Corinthians 9:8

> *After three days they found him in the temple...and his mother said to him... "Behold, your father and I have been looking for you anxiously." And he said to them, "How is it you sought me? Did you not know that I must be in my Father's house?"*
>
> Luke 2:46-49

the world, we are empowered and abundantly prepared, but are we willing? Are we willing to detach from family and tribe and, like Jesus, be about our Father's business? Are we willing to engage in introspection and contemplation, to come to know ourselves, and to make a commitment to a lasting and intimate relationship with the Eternal Absolute? Are we willing to put aside our private fantasies so that we are intellectually, emotionally, and spiritually available to do our work? Are we willing to relinquish our addictions to self-will and self-gratification and shift our motivations from making sure that we always find a way to feel good to making sure that we always find a way to be useful? Are we willing to welcome the unfamiliar and endure the upheaval of our fixed routines and career plans? Are we willing to embrace crisis and suffer through those deconstructing turning points in our lives that lead to reconstruction and new directions? Are we willing to be led into uncharted territory where we will continually be strengthened and transformed to fulfill God's unfolding and expanding purpose in our lives? And are we willing to do all this every day of our lives, not only on Sundays and holy days?

Our personal destiny and the destiny of humanity depends on our willingness to respond not only to a personal call to action but also to the public call to action that surrounds us; for we live in a time that cries out for our response. We live in a time when the rate of incarceration in the United States is two hundred and forty percent higher than it was thirty years ago, and the total budget for corrections is seventy-five billion dollars, spent mostly on incarceration.[32] At the same time, attempts at rehabilitation are disregarded because of a determination by the courts that "the efforts of the criminal justice system to achieve rehabilitation of offenders had failed."[33] We live in a time when we spend more than eleven billion dollars a year on the cost of unintended pregnancies, with the majority of the cost being spent on abortions,[34] while spending less than two hundred million annually on sex education.[35] And we live in a time when the global expenditures for defense are over one and half trillion dollars,[36] while the United Nations' budget for feeding the world's poor is just over five billion dollars.[37] We live in a time when our energies and our resources are being eroded to protect ourselves against each other rather than being replenished and invested in our well-being and progress, a time when our concern for life, itself, appears to be eroding.

There is a way which seems right to a man, but its end is the way to death.

Proverbs 14:12

If we are not willing to respond, if we remain indifferent because we feel we have more important things to do than to be concerned with God's purpose in our lives, we may notice that not only does the world seem stuck in a downward spiral, but we also are stuck in a downward spiral, experiencing neither growth nor fulfillment. Focusing on those who choose to ignore the call to action, Joseph Campbell observes: "Often... we encounter the dull case of the call unanswered; for it is always possible to turn the ear to other interests.

> *Have you not seen those who repay the grace of God with unbelief?*
>
> The Koran 14:28

Refusal of the summons converts the adventure into its negative." And Campbell vividly describes the consequences of this choice: "Walled in boredom, hard work, or 'culture,' the subject loses the power of significant affirmative action and becomes a victim to be saved. His flowering world becomes a wasteland of dry stones and his life feels meaningless." And because he is hiding from his unresolved childhood conflicts, afraid to confront his personal ghosts and goblins, Campbell predicts: "Whatever house he builds, it will be a house of death: a labyrinth of cyclopean walls to hide from his Minotaur. All he can do is create new problems for himself and await the gradual approach of his disintegration."[38]

Like the invited guests in Jesus' parable about the wedding feast, we find all sorts of excuses for not accepting the invitation to receive God's grace, for not being willing to answer the call, for not attending to our life's work. How well this description of the invited guests fits us: "But they made light of it and went off, one to his farm, another to his business, while the rest seized his servants, treated them shamefully, and killed them" (Matthew 22:1-14). Invited to share our lives with God, we, too, make light of it and go off to pursue our own interests, thinking nothing of harming each other, of treating each other "shamefully," at times, even killing each other. And like the guest who came inappropriately dressed for the wedding feast and had to be thrown out, we, too, will carelessly show up for life without considering what is required of us to partake in the celebration of our relationship with God. If "many are called, but few are chosen," it is not because God does not want to choose all of us; it is because we are not willing to be chosen: we are not willing to accept God's invitation to receive grace; we are not willing to be Christ conscious leaders; we are not willing to enter into a partnership with the Eternal Absolute.

Possibly the most effective excuse we tell ourselves is that receiving the grace of Divine Love is an abstract ideal, that being a Christ conscious leader is an abstract ideal, that a partnership with the Eternal Absolute is an abstract ideal. And since this is what we conveniently tell ourselves, we can dismiss these abstract ideals as something that philosophers contemplate and saints achieve, and as something that has absolutely nothing to do with us. So we complacently sit back and watch ourselves snatching bits of momentary pleasure as we casually meander through our lives, and we watch the world itself begin to crumble under the weight of all that we are not willing to do.

As we observe ourselves and become aware of our unwillingness to do our part in building the kingdom of God on earth, we may be reassured that God's grace is unconditionally and eternally available. But we may also find that we are discouraged by our deep-rooted fear of change and our willful resistance to turning ourselves around, receiving God's grace, and acknowledging our inherent partnership with the Eternal Absolute.

To become willing to respond to God's call, we will have to realize that we are always abundantly prepared by the gift of Divine Love to do our work, to fulfill our purpose, and that the only obstacle we face is our own reluctance. We will have to realize that the kingdom of God on earth is not an irrelevant ideal disconnected from our reality. And we will have to realize that partnering with the Eternal Absolute to build the kingdom of God on earth not only promises the fulfillment of our soul's deepest yearnings but also provides the only alternative we have for survival at this crossroad in our evolution.

The Kingdom of God on Earth

To realize evolutionary change in the world, we can rely on only one forum: the sacred space where Divine Love dwells in each of us. It is from this forum, and none other, that we can build the kingdom of God on earth. From this forum, and none other, we can come to know "complete freedom" (Brhadaranyaka Upanishad 3.1.5); we can come to know "eternity…seeing the big picture" with a "breadth of vision [that] brings nobility… [which] is close to divinity" (Tao Te Ching 16). From this forum, and none other, we can experience "the living God" (Psalms 42:2); and we can become "merciful… and pure in heart," and we can become "peacemakers" (Matthew 5:1-9). And from this forum, and none other, we can become "true servants of the Merciful…those

---

Only when people will be able to roll up the sky like a piece of leather will suffering come to an end, without first knowing God.

Svetasvatara Upanishad 6.20

who walk humbly on the earth and say: 'Peace!' to the ignorant who accost them" (The Koran 25:63).

Our history confirms that we have tried every other possible forum available to us to attain peace, but the closest we have ever come to attaining peace so far is "a form of contract ending a quarrel or a war and normatively regulating relationships between human beings,"[39] a contract that, while ending one war, often sets up the dynamics for starting the next war. We see evidence of this from the beginning of recorded time, from the Peace of Phoenice in 205 B.C., which ends the First Macedonian War and triggers the Second Macedonian War only five years later,[40] to the Peace Treaty of Versailles in 1919, which marks the end of the First World War but sets up new conflicts that lead to the start of the Second World War.[41]

Even our most optimistic and most organized attempts at peace seem to falter. At the end of World War I, United States President Woodrow Wilson, determined to make this the "war that will end war,"[42] proposes a Draft Covenant of the League of Nations at the Paris peace conference, "intended to harmonize relations and enforce peace among the nations of the world." The twenty-six articles of this document cover a broad range of reforms, including disarmament and international enforcement of "the political independence and territorial integrity of League members against external aggression, and it required members to take action, even to the extent of using military force, against violators of this guarantee."[43] Although the League of Nations is adopted by the nations represented at the peace conference and moves forward to try to fulfill its mission, the Versailles Treaty, along with the provision for the League of Nations, is never ratified by the United States Congress, which is strongly opposed to relinquishing its isolationist policies.[44] And without the membership of the United States, and without any military strength, the League proves ineffective as a deterrent to the next great war.[45]

Winner of the 1987 Alternative Nobel Prize for his groundbreaking work in peace and conflict studies, Norwegian sociologist Johan Galtung suggests that the reason we are unable to achieve peace is that all our efforts are negative, based on one nation, or an organization of United Nations, that uses coercive power to maintain stability. Without universal disarmament, Galtung believes that this approach, which includes arms control, international conventions, such as the Geneva conventions, and balance of power strategies, is destined to fail.[46] Galtung also proposes that, in addition to direct violence that we all recognize in war, genocide, and suicide, there is widespread structural violence in society that undermines peace and, ultimately, leads to direct violence, including racism, state imperialism, cultural imperialism, exploitation, and repression. Galtung emphasizes that *"violence of any kind breeds violence of any kind,"*[47] and he further suggests that "the idea of one theory, *the* theory, is an invitation to cultural violence –

neglecting all other truths, trying to fit reality into one truth only, lumping all the others as 'non-Western', 'non-Christian', 'non-Marxist.'"[48] Nor does the absence of direct violence indicate the existence of "positive peace" in a culture. Without the "absence of structural and cultural violence," all a society can hope to achieve is "negative peace."[49]

To achieve more than "negative peace," Galtung maintains that *"direct positive peace* would consist of verbal and physical kindness, good to the body, mind and spirit of Self and Other," and he insists: "Love is the epitome of this." Galtung explains: "symbiosis and equity in human relations" must be present in the culture. And he elaborates: "Structured positive peace would substitute freedom for repression and equity for exploitation, and then reinforce this with *dialogue* instead of penetration, *solidarity* instead of fragmentation, and *participation* instead of marginalization." He adds, "this also holds for *inner peace*," and he concludes: *"Positive peace is the best protection against violence."*[50]

Wolfgang Dietrich, political science professor and chair of the UNESCO Peace Studies initiative at the University of Innsbruck in Austria, agrees and proposes that peace emanates from more than the "norms which legitimize themselves via God, reason, law, power, or morals...a construction of normative, moral precepts or proscriptions."[51] For peace to be sustainable, according to Dietrich, it must include "an energetic experiencing of being," which one perceives "via the dynamics of life and

> *Peace I leave with you; my peace I give to you; not as the world gives do I give to you.*
>
> John 14:27

the connectivity of all beings, and interprets...as mystic, harmonious, and aesthetic resonance." And insisting that each culture has its own interpretations of peace and that there are many "peaces" and many "peace heroes" in every culture, he calls for a "reintegration of spirituality into rational...interpretations...which indicates that peace is in a permanent flow, that it has to be reshaped every moment in every context and can never be kept in the cage of a rigid rational structure."[52]

We can find many examples of how the "permanent flow" of "positive peace" can bridge cultural differences and diminish cultural violence. Both committed to non-violence as preached by Jesus in the Sermon on the Mount, the excommunicated Russian Orthodox writer Leo Tolstoy and the devout Hindu lawyer Mahatma Gandhi build a bridge of inspiration that fortifies the work of the "peace hero" of India.[53] And sitting in a South African jail, Nelson Mandela, born of African royalty and educated in colonial British schools,[54] gains strength from the stories he hears about the courage of an American "peace hero," Rosa Parks, whose early education was in a rural schoolhouse in America's segregated south.[55] But we find the best example of the "permanent flow" of "positive peace" over two thousand years ago, when Jesus of Nazareth, a carpenter's son, attracts one of the most diverse groups of twelve people ever assembled – four fishermen, a tax collector, an assortment of other artisans and professionals, and later, a tentmaker and a physician – to a ministry of peace.

For where two or three are gathered in my name, there am I in the midst of them.

Matthew 18:20

Sustainable peace has only one source, the indwelling divinity in each of us. As we each continue to build our relationship with the Eternal Absolute, and as we each find peace in that relationship, we each contribute to world peace. And every time we interact with each other and acknowledge the divinity in each other, we begin to erode those deep-rooted oppositional barriers that fuel our violence toward each other. From this solid foundation of individual peace, we can accomplish what is always alluding us, namely, a way to end the entrenched and escalating violence within ourselves, within our culture, and within our world. We see graveyards filled with evidence from the past, and we see graveyards that we are still filling with evidence today, that nothing else works to curb our violence toward ourselves and each other.

To generate an enduring peace, we will each have to continue to make progress as Christ conscious leaders, becoming increasingly aware of our unity with others and expanding our ability to receive Divine Love and be a vehicle for Divine Love. We will each have to detach from any impediments in our tribes, our families, and our own self-will that deter us from a commitment to fulfill God's purpose in our lives, to do our work, and to continue our lifelong transformation as Christ conscious leaders. And we will have to come to realize that, in partnership with the Eternal Absolute, we each have the power - and the calling - to build the kingdom of God on earth.

> *The kingdom of God is not coming with signs to be observed; nor will they say, "Lo, here it is!" or "There!" for behold, the kingdom of God is in the midst of you.*
>
> Luke 17:20-21

SECTION THREE

YOUR CHRIST CONSCIOUS LEADERSHIP PROFILE

This day, O Soul, I give you a wondrous mirror;
Long in the dark, in tarnish and cloud it lay – But the cloud has
pass'd, and the tarnish gone;
...Behold, O Soul! it is now a clean and bright mirror,
Faithfully showing you all the things of the world.

This Day, O Soul
Walt Whitman

9

INTROSPECTION AND CREATIVE ACTION PLANS

As we move forward in our evolution as Christ conscious leaders, we may find it useful to identify our strengths and our challenges, to assess our progress, and to consider actions that will help us reach our goals. The exercises on the following pages will provide an opportunity for introspection, contemplation, and action planning, and they will lead to new insights about ourselves and new perceptions about our life's purpose. They will also help us to identify those beliefs and motivations that are so much a part of our mental map that we never even think about them, although they influence all our thoughts and actions.

INSIGHTS

CHRIST CONSCIOUS LEADERSHIP

There are major differences between traditional leadership and Christ conscious leadership. How did you define effective leadership before reading this book?

_____
_____
_____
_____
_____
_____

How do you define effective leadership now?

_____
_____
_____
_____
_____
_____

Do you know a Christ conscious leader? If yes, describe this person's most outstanding characteristics. If not, describe five (5) characteristics that you consider essential for being a Christ conscious leader.

Compare the characteristics of the Christ conscious leader with the characteristics of other leaders you know.

Characteristic	Christ Conscious Leader	Other Leaders

Which of these Christ conscious leadership characteristics do you have?

_____
_____
_____
_____
_____
_____

Which of these Christ conscious leadership characteristics would you like to develop? List these characteristics in order of importance to you, on a scale of 1-5, with 1 being the highest importance.

1. _____
_____

2. _____
_____

3. _____
_____

4. _____
_____

5. _____
_____

How would developing these characteristics of Christ conscious leadership improve your effectiveness in your personal and professional interactions?

Characteristic	Improved Effectiveness – Personal

Characteristic	Improved Effectiveness – Professional

What obstacles, if any, in your personality and/or perceptions could keep you from developing these characteristics?

_____
_____
_____
_____
_____
_____
_____

What obstacles, if any, in your personal and/or professional life could keep you from developing these characteristics?

_____
_____
_____
_____
_____
_____
_____

UNITY – *The First Step*

Quantum physics has proven that all elements in the universe are interconnected and interdependent.
List five (5) examples of being interconnected in your personal and/or professional life. For each example, indicate why you view being interconnected as positive and/or negative.

Examples of Being Interconnected	Positive

Examples of Being Interconnected	Negative

INSIGHTS

List five (5) examples of being interdependent in your personal and/or professional life. For each example, indicate why you view being interdependent as positive and/or negative.

Examples of Being Interdependent	Positive

Examples of Being Interdependent	Negative

Below are four progressive stages of readiness for being a Christ conscious leader in an interconnected, interdependent world. To help you assess your readiness, score each of the statements below from 1-5 [1- completely disagree; 2 – disagree somewhat; 3 – neither agree nor disagree; 4 – agree somewhat; 5 – completely agree].

Survival - The First Stage

Statement	Score
I have no control over what is happening in the world.	___
I live in the center of a hostile world.	___
My main concerns are meeting my physical needs: food, shelter, pleasure.	___
My main concern is my safety and security.	___
My main concern is my survival.	___
Average Score	

Developmental - The Second Stage

Statement	Score
I find it difficult to cope with the world.	___
My main concern is gaining the approval of my family.	___

I want to succeed so that I will be accepted
by my peers. _____

My main concern is building my skills and
my self-confidence. _____

I want to feel like I belong. _____

Average Score

Participative – The Third Stage

Statement	Score
I must participate in the world and make a contribution.	_____
My main concern is my vocation and my service to others.	_____
My main concern is my life, my self-actualization, and my creativity.	_____
My main concern is my independence and integrity.	_____
I am concerned about personal accountability and mutual responsibility.	_____

Average Score

Transcendent – The Final Stage

Statement	Score
I am a part of the world and am responsible for its well-being.	_____

My main concern is advancing global harmony. _____

My main concern is expanding my awareness
and wisdom. _____

My main concern is advancing interdependence
in the world. _____

I value solitude, introspection, and
contemplation. _____

Average Score

To get your average score in each category, add up your score in each category and divide by 5. The highest average score indicates your current stage of readiness.

Based on your current stage of readiness, list your strengths and challenges for being a Christ conscious leader in an interconnected, interdependent world.

Your Stage of Readiness	Strengths	Challenges

Consider five (5) ways that you can apply your strengths in your personal/professional life.

_____
_____
_____
_____
_____
_____
_____
_____
_____
_____
_____
_____
_____
_____
_____
_____
_____

Consider five (5) ways that you can improve your readiness for being a Christ conscious leader in an interconnected, interdependent world.

INSIGHTS

LOVE – *The Second Step*

Divine Love is always available, compassionate, and unconditional. Human love, on the other hand, is usually conditional, sometimes judgmental, and not always available. What condition/s do you place on others in order for you to love them? Identify the person/s and the condition/s below.

Person/s	Condition/s

What examples do you have of judging others? Identify the person/s and judgment/s below.

Person/s	Judgment/s

What examples do you have of not being available to love others? Identify the person/s and the occasion/s below.

Person/s	Occasion/s

What condition/s do you believe others place on you in order for you to secure their love? Identify the person/s and the condition/s below.

Person/s	Condition/s

What examples do you have of others judging you? Identify the person/s and judgement/s below.

Person/s	Judgment/s

What examples do you have of others not being available to love you? Identify the person/s and the occasion/s below.

Person/s	Occasion/s

If you have experienced receiving available, compassionate, and unconditional love from another person, list that person/s and describe the occasion/s. If you have never received Divine Love from another person, how would you explain that? Write your explanation below.

Person/s	Occasion/s

If you have experienced receiving available, compassionate, and unconditional love from God, list the occasion/s. If you have never received Divine Love from God, how would you explain that? Write your explanation below.

___
___
___
___
___
___

List the occasion/s when you have provided available, compassionate, and unconditional love to others and indicate who they were. If you never have provided available, compassionate, and unconditional love to anyone, how would you explain that? Write your explanation below.

Person/s	Occasion/s

Check off the statements below that best describe your feelings.

___ I have difficulty enjoying myself unless I'm surrounded by lots of other people.

___ I always find fault with myself.

___ I always find fault with others.

___ I don't have any real close friends, but I have many friendly acquaintances.

___ If people really got to know me, I don't think they would like me very much.

___ People often say things that hurt my feelings and make me angry.

___ I always try to do my best so that people will like me.

___ I am most comfortable when I can help someone who needs me.

___ I don't like surprise and change. I like to know exactly what's happening next.

___ I like people to do things the way I like them to be done.

___ When someone I'm close to leaves for work, I feel anxious.

___ I'm always worried that something terrible will happen to a loved one.

___ When someone has a problem, I always feel that somehow I'm to blame.

___ It's very hard for me to refuse a request, even if I don't want to do something.

___ I always feel that people don't really care about me.

If you checked off any of these statements, explain how these feelings may have an effect on your ability to receive Divine Love and become a vehicle for Divine Love.

_____

_____

_____

_____

Think of a person who you find very difficult to get along with, someone you really don't like but someone who you have to interact with on a regular basis. Make a list of all the characteristics of this person that annoy you. Also make a list of <u>at least two</u> characteristics of this person that you can admire. For the next two months, think only of the admirable characteristics of this person every time you interact. Keep a record of how your relationship with this person changes and if and how this person's behavior changes.

Characteristics you find annoying: _____
_____
_____

Characteristics you find admirable: _____
_____
_____

Change in relationship: _____
_____
_____

Change in person: _____
_____
_____

DETACHMENT – *The Third Step*

INSIGHTS

The motivations, expectations, and behaviors that are shaped in early childhood by our culture and our family, and reinforced by our own self-will throughout our lives, are so much a part of us that we often cannot even identify them. Yet they influence all our thoughts and actions. In the exercises below, you will have an opportunity to identify those ingrained motivations, expectations, behaviors, thoughts, and feelings, those chains that bind you.

In the space below, identify what motivates you in your relationship with yourself, your work, those in your personal life, and others.

Motivations

Self _____

_____

_____

_____

_____

Work _____

_____

_____

_____

_____

Personal _____
_____
_____
_____
_____

Others _____
_____
_____
_____
_____

In the space below, identify your expectations of yourself, your work, your personal relationships, and others.

Expectations

Self _____
_____
_____
_____
_____

Work _____
_____
_____

_____

_____

Personal _____

_____

_____

_____

_____

Others _____

_____

_____

_____

_____

In the space below, identify your patterns of behavior, the way you behave toward yourself, those at work, people in your personal life, and others.

Behavior

Self _____

_____

_____

_____

_____

Work _____

_____

_____

_____

_____

Personal _____

_____

_____

_____

_____

Others _____

_____

_____

_____

_____

_____

In the space below, identify your ingrained thoughts and feelings and how they influence the way you think and feel about yourself, those at work, people in your personal life, and others.

Ingrained thoughts and feelings

Self _____

_____

INTROSPECTION AND CREATIVE ACTION PLANS

_____
_____
_____

Work _____
_____
_____
_____
_____

Personal _____
_____
_____
_____

Others _____
_____
_____
_____
_____

INSIGHTS

Commitment – *The Fourth Step*

We can use several approaches to defining our life's work and purpose. Through contemplation, we may discern a specific purpose that God has for us, and through introspection and self-assessment, we can identify our specific talents and core competencies. When there is an alignment of our discernment of God's purpose with our specific talents and core competencies, we have a solid indication of what our work might be. In addition, we may find that we have already had experiences in our lives that have prepared us further to be effective in the work we will be doing. Above all, if we find a profound sense of fulfillment in the work, we can be certain that this is, in fact, our life's work and that we are fulfilling God's purpose.

To begin the process of defining your life's work, make a list of your core competencies. Core competencies are not job descriptions. They are skills that you have in your "tool box," the deliverables that you can take with you into any industry. Here are some examples: proven excellence in project management; exceptional ability to build and facilitate collaborative teamwork; outstanding oral and written communication skills.

Core Competencies: _____
_____
_____
_____
_____

Next, list your special gifts and talents: _____
_____
_____
_____
_____

Next, list pertinent life experiences: _____
_____
_____
_____
_____

Next, list your discernments in contemplation: _____
_____
_____
_____
_____

Considering your core competencies, your special gifts and talents, your life experiences, and your discernments in contemplation, the next step is to try to define what your life's work or purpose may be. Here are some examples: servant leadership; developing human potential; education and training. This is not an attempt to define a career or job. It is an attempt to define your life's work, which you can do in any number of different careers and jobs.

Once we identify our life's work and purpose, making a commitment to doing that work and fulfilling God's purpose calls for accepting continual change in our lives. Our tolerance for change will determine our ability to sustain that commitment.

Our motivations, expectations, behaviors, and ingrained thoughts and feelings often determine our self-willed goals. If we want to detach from our self-will and become available to fulfill God's purpose in our lives and do our work, we may have to change many of our motivations, expectations, behaviors, and ingrained thoughts and feelings.

In the space below, identify your life's work and purpose and identify the changes you will have to make.

Life's Work and Purpose: _____

_____

_____

_____

Necessary Changes

Motivations _____

_____

_____

_____

_____

Expectations _____

_____

_____

_____

_____

Behaviors _____

_____

_____

_____

_____

Ingrained thoughts and feelings _____
_____
_____
_____

Tolerance for change differs from one person to another. To assess your tolerance for change, review each of the changes you will have to make to fulfill your life's work and purpose, as indicated in the exercise above. Next to each change indicate your resistance to making that change in a range from 1 to 5 [1 – little resistance; 5 – high resistance].

Commitment to doing our life's work and the continual transformation that we experience as part of that commitment requires that we learn how to be open systems, to live in the question without always knowing how our purpose will emerge and evolve.

To gain insight into your readiness to live in the question, check the statements below in Group A and Group B that best reflect your thoughts and feelings.

Group A

___ I am a cosmic dot and nothing I say or does really matters.

___ It's every person for himself.

___ I have no idea how to find my place in this chaotic world.

___ Everything in life is a roll of the dice. It doesn't matter how much talent you have or how much effort you exert.

___ I just want to get everything I can out of life and have a real good time.

___ I like to know what's going to happen on the road ahead. I don't like surprises.

___ I've been trained to do my job, and that's what I want to do.

___ If I work hard at my job, I will have guaranteed security and happiness.

___ I like a job that offers a clear description of my responsibilities.

___ If a problem doesn't affect me or my family, it's not my problem.

Group B

___ The world is made up of cosmic dots and each dot is important to the whole of creation.

___ I am here to contribute my part to the evolution of humanity.

___ My greatest joy in life is changing and growing.

___ Life is an adventure without a road map.

___ We are all here to help one another grow and realize our greatest potential.

___ I am totally responsible for my thoughts, words, and actions.

___ Everything is in a constant process of change, and so am I.

___ I have goals, but I hold them loosely and am always prepared to relinquish them as more significant goals emerge.

___ With lifelong learning, I can continually expand my capabilities and fulfill my unfolding purpose.

___ I have no clear picture of my career path and am comfortable with an open-ended future.

If the majority of the statements that reflect the way you think and feel are in Group A, your mental map is not well prepared for living in the question. If the majority of the statements that reflect the way you think and feel are in Group B, you are an open system and well prepared to live in the question.

ACTION: *The Fifth Step*

If we are willing to answer the call to action, we will find ourselves relying upon all our gifts and talents. High on the list of abilities that we will need to use is our ingenuity: our ability to know, to be, and to create. And we will need to use our intellectual, emotional, and intuitive tools of perception for discerning and fulfilling our unfolding purpose. See diagram below.

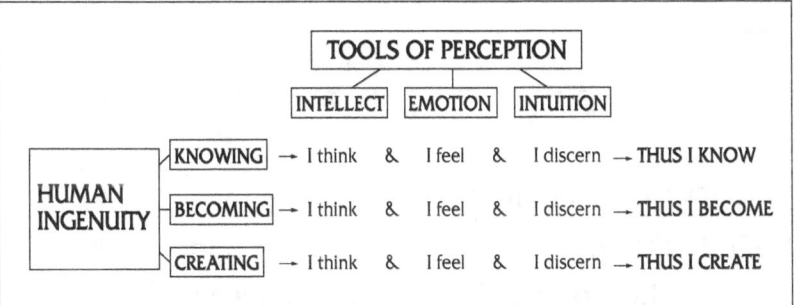

The following exercise is designed to acquaint you with these three distinctively different tools of perception. Since each perception provides a completely different view of the same problem or goal, it is important to be able to utilize and integrate all three perceptions in developing Creative Action Plans and moving forward to answer the call to action.

INSIGHTS

STEP ONE - Intellectual Perceptions

Working alone in a quiet room, list all the colors you see, the sounds you hear, the thoughts you are thinking, and the feelings you are feeling.

_____

_____

_____

_____

_____

_____

STEP TWO - Emotional Perceptions

Next, list all the colors you *hear*, the sounds you *see*, the thoughts you are *feeling*, and the feelings you are *thinking about*.

_____

_____

_____

_____

_____

_____

[Note: If you are very uncomfortable doing this step in the exercise, you are probably not accustomed to responding emotionally without using your intellectual tools of perception, and you may feel more secure when you perceive and interact with the world with your intellect.]

STEP THREE - Intuitive Perceptions
Put down your paper and pen. Close your eyes and sit quietly for as long as you can comfortably do this. Do not attempt to do anything or think about anything. Just sit quietly. When you become uncomfortable doing this, open your eyes. Record what you experienced with your eyes closed, including any discernments or insights. Also record the nature of discomfort that caused you to open your eyes.

_____

_____

_____

_____

_____

_____

[Note: Intuitive perceptions cannot be planned or ordered on demand. We can only record them when we discern them.]

Repeat these exercises as often as possible to strengthen your ability to identify each of your three perceptual tools and to utilize them effectively in decision making and creative action planning.

THE CREATIVE ACTION PLAN

Using your tools of perception, identify a specific problem you want to solve or a specific goal you would like to reach on your way to becoming a Christ conscious leader. Using the Creative Action Plan below, determine what your first step will be.

Step One – Assessing and Determining the Problem or Goal

– State the problem or goal: _____

_____

_____

– Using your intellectual perceptions, restate the problem or goal: _____

_____

_____

– Using your emotional perceptions, restate the problem or goal: _____

_____

_____

– Using your intuitive perceptions, restate the problem or goal: _____

_____

_____

– Integrating all three perceptions and the restatements of the problem or goal, redefine the problem or goal:

_____

_____

_____

Step Two – Proposing an Action

Propose the action you will have to take to solve the problem or reach the goal: _____

_____

_____

– Using your intellectual perceptions, restate the proposed action: _____

_____

_____

– Using your emotional perceptions, restate the proposed action: _____

_____

_____

– Using your intuitive perceptions, restate the proposed action: _____

_____

_____

– Integrating all three perceptions and the restatements of the proposed action, redefine the action: _____

_____

_____

_____

Step Three – Insight, Transformation, and Action

What new insights do you have about your problem or goal and about your proposed action?

_____

_____

_____

_____

_____

What specific point of transformation in your perception of your problem or goal led to your decision about the first step you will take to solve your problem or reach your goal?

_____
_____
_____
_____
_____
_____

What will your first step be?

_____
_____
_____
_____
_____
_____

NOTES

SECTION ONE
THE GOOD NEWS – EVOLVING AND SURVIVING

Chapter 1: Christ: The Eternal Absolute

[1] Patrick Olivelle, trans., *The Upanishads* (New York: Oxford University Press, 2008), 15-19.

[2] Lao Tzu, *Tao Te Ching* (Lexington, KY: Ancient Renewal, 2009), 52.

[3] *The Holy Bible: The Revised Standard Version* (New York: Thomas Nelson & Sons, 1953.), 58.

[4] N. J. Dawood, trans., *The Koran* (New York: Penguin Books, 2006), 11.

[5] Louis Renou, ed., *Hinduism* (New York: George Braziller, 1961), 95.

[6] Hieromonk Damascene, *Christ the Eternal Tao* (Platina, CA: Valaam Books, 2004), 219.

[7] Richard Hooper, ed., *Jesus, Buddha, Krishna, Lao Tzu: The Parallel Sayings* (Sedona, AZ: Sanctuary Publications, Inc., 2007), 144.

[8] Damascene, 220.

[9] N. J. Girardot, *Myth and Meaning in Early Taoism* (Berkeley, CA: University of California Press, 1983), 98.

[10] *Catechism of the Catholic Church,* English translation (Citto del Vaticano: Liberia Editrice Vaticana, 1994), #374-375.

[11] Ibid., #397-400.

[12] Renou, 20.

[13] Ibid., 96.

[14] Girardot, 74.

[15] Joseph T. Shipley, *The Origins of English Words* (Baltimore: The Johns Hopkins University Press, 1984), 56.

[16] John Milton, *Paradise Lost and Paradise Regained* (New York: New American Library, 1968), 356.

[17] Rene Girard, *I See Satan Fall Like Lightning* (Maryknoll, NY: Orbis Books, 2001), 8-9.

[18] Rene Girard, *Things Hidden Since the Foundation of the World* (Stanford, CA: Stanford University Press, 1978), 285.

[19] Henri J. M. Nouwen, *Reaching Out* (New York: Doubleday, 1975), 24-25.

[20] http://www.themoneytimes.com/featured/20100620/cdc-statistics-reveal-misuse-prescription-pain-drugs-111-4-years-id-10118140.html

[21] Substance Abuse and Mental Health Services Administration, *Results from the 2009 National Survey on Drug Use and Health: Volume I. Summary of National Findings* (Rockville, MD: Office of Applied Studies, NSDUH Series H-38A, HHS Publication No. SMA 10-4586 Findings, 2010), 3.

[22] Ibid., 1-2.

[23] Thomas Merton, *The Seven Storey Mountain* (New York: Harcourt Brace & Co., 1948), 148.

[24] Substance Abuse and Mental Health Services Administration, 1-2.

[25] Ibid.

[26] Ibid.

[27] St. Teresa of Avila, *Interior Castle,* trans. E. Allison Peers (New York: Doubleday, 1989), 47.

[28] Ibid.

[29] http://www.eastlakefoundation.org/sites/courses/view.asp?id=346&page=27971

[30] http://www.eastlakefoundation.org/sites/courses/view.asp?id=346&page=8796

[31] http:// purposebuiltcommunities.org/

[32] Hesiod, *Theogony,* trans. Norman O. Brown (Indianapolis: Bobbs-Merrill, 1953), 56.

[33] Joseph Girzone, "Daily Postings," April 7, 2011. http://joshuamountain.org/postings/?cat=1

[34] Bob Deffinbaugh, "Israel and Aaron at the Hand of Moses (Exodus 32:15-35)," http://bible.org/seriespage/israel-and-aaron-hand-moses-exodus-3215-35

[35] Fritjof Capra, *The Web of Life* (New York: Doubleday, 1996), 190.

[36] Wes White, "Who were the mysterious MAGI that visited Jesus?" http://www.biblestudy.org/basicart/who-were-mysterious-magi-that-visited-baby-jesus.html

[37] Helen K. Bond, *Caiaphas: Friend of Rome and Judge of Jesus?* (Louisville, KY: Westminster John Knox Press, 2004), 26-28.

[38] Joseph Girzone, *Jesus* (New York: Doubleday, 2009), 18.

[39] Ibid., 31-34.

[40] Thomas Wolfe, *You Can't Go Home Again* (New York: HarperCollins, 1998), 103, 119.

[41] Gerd Theissen and Annette Merz, *The Historical Jesus: A Comprehensive Guide,* John Bowden, trans. (Minneapolis, MN: Augsburg Fortress, 1998), 304-305.

[42] Geoffrey W. Bromiley, ed., *International Standard Bible Encyclopedia* (Grand Rapids, MI: William B. Eerdmans Publishing Co., 1979), 487.

[43] Bond, 54.

44 Quoted in Donald Goergen, *Fire of Love: Encountering the Holy Spirit* (Mahwah, NJ: Paulist Press, 2006), 93.

45 Bart D. Ehrman, *God's Problem* (New York: HarperCollins, 2008), 143-44.

46 Girardot, 98.

47 John Briggs and F. David Peat, *Seven Life Lessons of Chaos* (New York: HarperCollins, 1999), 28-29.

48 John Alden Williams, ed., *Islam* (New York: George Braziller, 1961), 59 - 63.

49 Ibid.

50 John L. Esposito, *Islam: The Straight Path* (New York: Oxford University Press, 1988), 5.

51 Muhammad Zafrulla Khan, *Muhammad: Seal of the Prophets* (London, UK: Routledge & Kegan, 1980), 2-3.

52 Williams, 60.

53 Michael H. Hart, *The 100: A Ranking of the Most Influential Persons in History* (New York: Kensington Publishing, 1992), 4.

54 Dawood, 2.

55 Williams, 62.

56 Ibid.

57 Ibid., 63-65.

58 Hart, 4.

59 Williams, 63.

60 Esposito, 7.

61 Dawood, 7.

62 Williams, 73.

63 Ibid., 74.

64 Ibid., 75.

65 Ibid., 80.

66 Hart, 5.

67 "The Future of the Global Muslim Population: Projections for 2010-2030" (Washington, D.C: The Pew Forum on Religion & Public Life, January 27, 2011), 1.

68 Toby Mac and Michael Tait, *Under God* (Bloomington, MN: Bethany House Publishers, 2004), p. 62.

69 "Pioneer of Civil Rights" Interview (Washington, DC: Academy of Achievement, June 2, 1995) http://www.achievement.org/autodoc/page/par0int-1

70 Ibid.

71 Maya Angelou, *The Complete Collected Poems of Maya Angelou* (New York: Random House, 1994), 269.

72 Rosa Parks, *Quiet Strength* (Grand Rapids, MI: Zondervan Publishing House, 1994), 49.

73 Ibid., 91.

74 Ibid., 21.

75 Mac and Tait, 63.

76 F. Erik Brooks, "The Civil Rights Movement," September 19, 2007, 1. http://www.encyclopediaofalabama.org/face/Article.jsp?id=h-1355

77 Michel W. Potts, "Arun Gandhi Shares the Mahatma's Message" *India - West,* February 1, 2002, A34.

78 Parks, 17.

79 Brooks, 2.

80 Ibid.

81 Mac and Tait, 63.

82 Ibid., 64.

83 James Burke, *The Pinball Effect* (New York: Little, Brown and Company, 1996), 7.

84 "Pioneer of Civil Rights" Interview.

85 Ibid.

86 Ibid.

87 Martin Luther King, Jr., *Stride Toward Freedom: The Montgomery Story* (Boston: Beacon Press, 1958), 31.

88 Rosa Parks et al., "40 Years Later," *Ebony,* August 2003, 164.

89 Parks, *Quiet Strength,* 92.

90 Ruth Ashby, *Rosa Parks: Freedom Rider* (New York: Sterling Publishing, 2008), 1.

91 John Kifner, "Preparations Are Hectic for Mandela's U.S. Tour," *New York Times,* June 18, 1990.

92 Ashby, 1.

[93] F. David Peat and John Briggs, "Interview with David Bohm," *Omni Magazine,* January 1987.

[94] Richard Wrangham, *Catching Fire: How Cooking Made Us Human* (New York: Basic Books, 2009), 103.

[95] Niklas Luhmann, *Social Systems* (Stanford, CA: Stanford University Press, 1995), 80.

[96] Bill Joy, "Why the Future Doesn't Need Us," *Wired,* April 2000, 56.

[97] Ibid, 57.

[98] Ibid, 58-60.

[99] Fritjof Capra and David Steindl-Rast, *Belonging to the Universe* (San Francisco, CA: HarperSanFranscisco, 1991), 30.

[100] Edwin Hubbell Chapin, *Living Words* (Boston: A. Thompkins, 1860), 77.

Chapter 2: Consciousness and the Soul

[1] Gerald M. Edelman and Giulio Tononi, *The Universe of Consciousness* (New York: Basic Books, 2000), 7.

[2] Gerald M. Edelman, *Wider Than the Sky* (New Haven, CT: Yale University Press, 2004), 161.

[3] Thomas H. Huxley, *Collected Essays: Volume 1* (Chestnut Hill, MA: Adamant Media Corporation, 2001), 227.

[4] Julian Jaynes, *The Origin of Consciousness in the Breakdown of the Bicameral Mind* (New York: Houghton Mifflin Company, 1990), 17.

[5] Francis Crick, *The Astonishing Hypothesis: The Scientific Search for the Soul* (New York: Simon and Schuster, 1994), 3.

[6] Ibid., 268.

[7] Carl G. Jung, *The Archetypes and the Collective Unconscious* (Princeton, NJ: Princeton University Press, 1981), 3-5.

[8] Ibid., 38.

[9] Crick, 6.

[10] Edelman and Tononi, 220-222.

[11] John C. Eccles, *Evolution of the Brain: Creation of the Self* (New York: Routledge, 1996), 247-253.

[12] Theos Bernard, *Hindu Philosophy* (New York: The Philosophical Library, 1947), 70.

[13] Carl G. Jung, *The Structure and Dynamics of the Psyche* (Princeton, NJ: Princeton University Press, 1970), 276-279.

[14] Alan Henry, "Robots Successfully Invent Their Own Language," *Extreme Tech*, May 17, 2011.

[15] Edelman and Tononi, 193-194.

[16] Ludwig Wittgenstein, *Philosophical Investigations* (West Sussex, UK: Wiley-Blackwell, 2009), 462.

[17] Roger Penrose, *Shadows of the Mind: A Search for the Missing Science of Consciousness* (New York: Oxford University Press, 1994), 11.

[18] Aldous Huxley, *Brave New World* (New York: HarperCollins, 1998).

[19] Derek Denton, *The Primordial Emotions: The Dawning of Consciousness* (New York: Oxford University Press, 2006), 4.

[20] Charles Darwin, *The Expression of the Emotions in Man and Animals* (Chicago: Chicago University Press, 1965), 360-366.

[21] Francis D. Burton, *Fire: The Spark That Ignited Human Evolution* (Albuquerque, NM: University of New Mexico Press, 2009), 16.

[22] Richard Wrangham, *Catching Fire: How Cooking Made Us Human* (New York: Basic Books, 2009), 1-15.

[23] Aeschylus, *Prometheus Bound,* trans. James Scully and C. J. Harrington (New York: Oxford University Press, 1990), 29.

[24] Derek Bickerton, *Adam's Tongue: How Humans Made Language; How Language Made Humans* (New York: Hill and Wang, 2009), 18.

[25] Robert Ornstein, *The Evolution of Consciousness* (New York: Prentice Hall Press, 1991), 45-47.

[26] Terrence William Deacon, *The Symbolic Species: The Co-Evolution of Language and the Brain* (New York: W. Norton and Company, 1998), 24.

[27] Bickerton, 213-215.

[28] Guy Deutscher, *The Unfolding of Language* (New York: Henry Holt and Company, 2009), 212.

[29] Jonathan G. Wynn et al., "Geological and Palaeontological Context of a Pliocene Juvenile Hominin at Dikika, Ethiopia," *Nature,* September 21, 2006.

[30] Noam Chomsky, *The Chomsky Reader* (New York: Pantheon, 1987), 193.

[31] Steven Pinker, *The Language Instinct: How the Mind Creates Language,* 3rd ed. (New York: Harper Perennial Modern Classics, 2007), 6.

[32] Jean Piaget et al., *The Child's Conception of the World* (Lanham, MD: Rowman & Littlefield, 2007), 127.

[33] Benedicte de Boysson-Bardies, *How Language Comes to Children: From Birth to Two Years* (Cambridge, MA: MIT Press, 2001), 71.

[34] Ibid., 45.

[35] Ibid., 142.

[36] Jean Piaget, *The Psychology of Intelligence* (London, UK: Routledge Classics, 2001), 8.

[37] Bruce G. Charlton, *Psychiatry and the Human Condition* (Oxford, UK: Radcliffe Medical Press, 2000), 232.

[38] Peter W. Jusczyk, *The Discovery of Spoken Language* (Cambridge, MA: MIT Press, 2000), 169.

[39] Joseph T. Shipley, *The Origins of English Words: A Discursive Dictionary of Indo-European Roots* (Baltimore, MD: The Johns Hopkins University Press, 1984), 348.

[40] Harry Newton, *Glossary of Computer Terms* (Point Pleasant, PA: The Computer Language Company, 1997).

[41] Piaget, *The Psychology of Intelligence,* 136.

[42] Deacon, 452.

[43] Bickerton, 5.

[44] Louis Untermeyer, ed., *Modern American Poetry* (New York: Harcourt, Brace & World, 1962), 401.

[45] Lev S. Vygotsky, *Thought and Language* (Cambridge, MA: The MIT Press, 1986), 256.

[46] Jared Diamond, *The Rise and Fall of the Third Chimpanzee* (London, UK: Vintage Books, 1991), 225.

[47] Shipley, 129-133.

[48] Ibid.

[49] Ibid.

50 Ibid., xxix.

51 Bernard Grant-Campbell, *Human Evolution – An Introduction to Man's Adaptations* (Piscataway, NJ: Aldine Transaction, 1998), 305.

52 Eugene Linden, *The Octopus and The Orangutan: More Tales of Animal Intrigue, Intelligence, and Ingenuity* (New York: Penguin Group, 2002), 16-17.

53 Steven Mithen, *The Prehistory of the Mind* (London, UK: Thames & Hudson, 1999), 11.

54 John H. Lienhard, *The Engines of Our Ingenuity: An Engineer Looks at Technology and Culture* (New York: Oxford University Press, 2003), 96.

55 Steven Pinker, *Evolution of the Mind* (WGBH Educational Foundation and Clear Blue Sky Productions, 2001), PBS transcript.

56 Lienhard, 60.

57 Ibid., 133.

58 Ibid., 142.

59 Zhongwei Zhao, ANU, and Wei Chen, "China's rising sex ratio at birth," *East Asia Forum,* June 19, 2011.

60 "China's unwanted girls," BBC News, August, 2001. http://news.bbc.co.uk/2/hi/asia-pacific/1506469.stm

61 Tan Ee Lyn, "Up to 12 million girls aborted in India over last 30 years," *Reuters,* May 24, 2011.

62 Thomas Homer-Dixon, *The Ingenuity Gap: Can We Solve the Problems of the Future* (New York: Alfred A. Knopf, 2000), 23.

63 Daniel Brian O'Leary, *Escaping the Progress Trap* (Westmount, QC, Canada: Geozone Communications, 2006), 38.

64 David Bohm, *Thought as a System* (New York: Routledge, 1994), 103.

[65] O'Leary, 43.

[66] Ibid., 45-46.

[67] Ibid., 49.

[68] Homer-Dixon, 399.

[69] O'Leary, 46.

[70] Denton, 8.

[71] Antonio Damasio, *Descartes' Error: Emotion, Reason, and the Human Brain* (New York: Penguin Putnam, 1994), xv.

[72] *Water - The Great Mystery*, producer, Saida Medvedeva, DVD, Intention Media Inc., 2008.

[73] Angie Best-Boss with David Edelberg, M.D., *The Everything Digestive Health Book* (Avon, MA: F & W Media, 2009), 120.

[74] http://ga.water.usgs.gov/edu/earthhowmuch.html

[75] Bohm, 150.

[76] Shipley, 409.

[77] St. Teresa of Avila, *Interior Castle,* trans. E. Allison Peers (New York: Doubleday, 1989), 80-84.

[78] Frances E. Vaughan, *Awakening Intuition* (New York: Doubleday, 1979), 152-153.

[79] Sam M. Intrator and Megan Scribner, eds., *Teaching with Fire: Poetry That Sustains the Courage to Teach* (San Francisco, CA: Jossey-Bass, 2003), 88.

[80] St. Teresa of Avila, 145.

[81] Orest Bedrij, *Exodus III: Great Joy and Glory to the Most High as You* (Bloomington, IN: Xlibris, 2011), 21.

[82] Quoted in James Bailey, *After Thought: The Computer Challenge to Human Intelligence* (New York: BasicBooks, 1996), 6.

[83] Quoted in Kirsten Gibson, "Social media creates interest in uprising," *The Exponent ONLINE,* June 29, 2011.

[84] Bailey, 6.

[85] Ibid., 18.

[86] S. I. Hayakawa, *Language in Thought and Action* (New York: Harcourt, Inc., 1990), 11.

[87] Ibid., 76.

[88] Denis Brian, *The Voice Of Genius: Conversations with Nobel Scientists and Other Luminaries* (New York: Basic Books, 2000), 127.

[89] Thomas Homer-Dixon, *The Upside of Down* (Washington, DC: Island Press, 2006), 144.

[90] James Howard Kunstler, *The Long Emergency* (New York: The Atlantic Monthly Press, 2005), 24.

[91] Homer-Dixon, *The Upside of Down,* 81.

[92] Kunstler, 6.

[93] William Sullivan, *The Secret of the Incas* (New York: Three Rivers Press, 1996), 6.

[94] Homer-Dixon, *The Upside of Down,* 186.

[95] Ervin Laszlo, ed., *The Consciousness Revolution* (London, UK: Elf Rock Productions, 2003), 5.

[96] Homer-Dixon, *The Upside of Down,* 198.

[97] Ibid., 63.

[98] Quoted in Charles Hugh Smith, *An Unconventional Guide to Investing in Troubled Times* (Berkeley, CA: Oftwominds.com, 2011), Chapter Two.

[99] Homer-Dixon, *The Upside of Down*, 115.

[100] Jared Diamond, *Guns, Germs, and Steel: The Fates of Human Societies* (New York: W. W. Norton & Company, 1997), 291-292.

[101] Quoted in Laszlo, 2.

[102] Ibid., 3.

[103] Grant-Campbell, 448.

[104] Robert Ornstein and Paul Ehrlich, *New World New Mind* (New York: Simon & Schuster, 1989), 12.

[105] Sir David Brewster, *The Kaleidoscope: Its History, Theory, and Construction* (Charleston, SC: BiblioBazaar, 2009), 132-133.

[106] Orest Bedrij, *'1': The Foundation and Mathematization of Physics* (Bloomington, IN: Xlibris, 2008), 29.

[107] Ibid., 84.

[108] Brewster, 5.

[109] Ibid.

[110] Fritjof Capra and David Steindl-Rast, *Belonging to the Universe* (New York: HarperCollins Publishers, 1991), 35.

[111] Richard P. Feynman, *The Meaning of It All* (Reading, MA: Addison-Wesley, 1998), 14-15.

[112] Michio Kaku, *Hyperspace* (New York: Oxford University Press, 1994), 333.

[113] Richard Hooper, ed., *Jesus, Buddha, Krishna, Lao Tzu: The Parallel Sayings* (Sedona, AZ: Sanctuary Publications, Inc., 2007), 52.

[114] Rene Girard, *Things Hidden since the Foundation of the World* (Stanford, CA: Stanford University Press, 1978), 286.

[115] Ibid., 444.

[116] Alan McGlashan, *The Savage and Beautiful Country* (Einsiedeln, Switzerland: Daimon Verlag, 1988), 55.

[117] Deacon, 22.

[118] David Bohm, *Wholeness and the Implicate Order* (London, UK: Routledge, 1995), 147-149.

[119] Paul van Tongeren et al., eds., *Eros and Eris* (Dordrecht, The Netherlands: Kluwer Academic Publishers, 2010), 2-8.

[120] Jaynes, 318.

[121] Ibid., 313.

[122] Richard Rohr and Joseph Martos, *The Great Themes of Scripture* (Cincinnati, OH: St. Anthony Messenger Press, 1988), 1.

[123] Carl Jung, *Memories, Dreams, Reflections,* trans. Richard and Clara Winston (New York: Vintage Books, 1989), 336.

[124] Ibid., 327.

[125] Steven Runciman, *The First Crusade* (Cambridge, UK: Cambridge University Press, 2005), 1-33.

[126] Christopher Hatch MacEvitt, *The Crusades and the Christian World of the East* (Philadelphia, PA: University of Philadelphia Press, 2008), 27.

¹²⁷ Rabindranath Tagore, trans., *The Songs of Kabir* (New York: The Macmillan Company, 1915), 82.

¹²⁸ Jung, *Memories, Dreams, Reflections,* 360.

¹²⁹ Jaynes, 319.

¹³⁰ St. Teresa of Avila, 31.

¹³¹ Caryll Houselander, *A Rocking Horse Catholic* (Westminster, MD: Christian Classics, 1988), 57-58.

¹³² Jung, 328.

¹³³ Ken Wilber et al., *Transformations of Consciousness* (Boston, MA: New Science Library, 1986), 158.

Chapter 3: Leadership at a Crossroad

¹ Desmond M. Tutu, "Believing in the Dignity of All," World Economic Forum, *Fora TV Conference Channel,* February 1, 2009. http://fora.tv/2009/02/01/Desmond_Tutu_Believing_in_the_Dignity_of_All

² Jared Diamond, *Guns, Germs, and Steel: The Fates of Human Societies* (New York: W. W. Norton & Company, 1997), 267-270.

³ Ibid.

⁴ John Stuart Mill, *On Liberty* (London, UK: Penguin Books Ltd., 1974), 62-62.

⁵ Robert Longley, "How to Lose but Win an Election." http://usgovinfo.about.com/od/thepoliticalsystem/a/electcollege_2.htm

⁶ Adolf Hitler, *Mein Kampf,* trans. Abraham Foxman (Boring, OR: CPA Book Publisher, 1942), 75.

[7] Diamond, 276.

[8] Ibid.

[9] Claire Soares, "Revolution! Another coup in the world's most unstable country," *The Independent,* March 26, 2008.

[10] Barbara Benjamin et al., *Leadership in the Interactive Age* (South Salem, NY: Intuitive Discovery Productions, 2005), 1-3.

[11] Joseph T. Shipley, *The Origins of English Words* (Baltimore: The Johns Hopkins University Press, 1984), 49.

[12] William Sullivan, *The Secret of the Incas* (New York: Three Rivers Press, 1996), 6.

[13] Karl-Erik Sveiby and Tex Skuthorpe, *Treading Lightly: The Hidden Wisdom of the World's Oldest People* (Crows Nest NSW, Australia: Allen & Unwin, 2006), 28.

[14] Ibid., xviii.

[15] Ibid., 27.

[16] Johnny Ryan, *A History of the Internet and the Digital Future* (London, UK: Reaktion Books, 2010), i.

[17] Ibid., ii.

[18] Paul Leicester Ford, ed., *The Writings of Thomas Jefferson, Vol. X* (New York: G.P. Putnam's Sons, 1899), 161.

[19] Ryan Rifai, "Tunisia's uprising: Chronicle of nationwide demonstrations over the country's unemployment crisis," *Al Jazeera,* January 23, 2001.

[20] Colin Delany, "How Social Media Accelerated Tunisia's Revolution: An Inside View," *Huffington Post,* February, 2011.

[21] http://blog.backtype.com/2011/01/analysis-of-the-tunisia-twitter-trend/

[22] Delany.

[23] Evgeny Morozov, *The Net Delusion: The Dark Side of Internet Freedom* (New York: PublicAffairs, 2001), xvi.

[24] Craig Kanalley, "Egypt's Internet Shut Down, According To Reports," *Huffington Post,* January 27, 2011.

[25] CBS News, "Internet freedom: world's strictest regimes," *ZDNetUK,* February 1, 2011.

[26] Morozov, 205.

[27] Quoted in Thomas Freiling, *Walking with Lincoln: Spiritual Strength from America's Favorite President* (Grand Rapids, MI: Revell, 2009), 176.

[28] Edward N. Lorenz, *The Essence of Chaos* (Seattle, WA: University of Washington Press, 1993), 7.

[29] Ibid.

[30] Ibid., 181.

[31] Margaret J. Wheatley, "Is the Pace of Life Hindering Our Ability to Manage?" *Management Today,* March, 2004.

[32] Angelique Christafis, "Tunisian dissident blogger takes job as minister," *The Guardian,* January, 18, 2011.

[33] Robert Mackey, "Tunisian Blogger Joins Government," *The New York Times,* January 18, 2011

[34] Ibid.

[35] Zied Mhirsi, "Slim Amamou," May 4, 2011, http://www.tunisia-live.net

36 Kathleen Madigan, "It's Man vs. Machine and Man Is Losing," *Wall Street Journal,* September 28, 2011.

37 Richard Rothstein, "College graduates: supply and demand," *Economic Policy Institute,* July 21, 2009.

38 John McCarthy, "3.3 Million U.S. Service Jobs to Go Offshore," *Forrester Research,* November 11, 2002.

39 Richard Vedder, "Why Did 17 Million Students Go to College?" *The Chronicle of Higher Education,* October 20, 2010.

40 United States Department of Education, National Center for Education Statistics (2010), *Digest of Education Statistics,* 2010 (NCES 2011-015), chap. 3.

41 "Are They Ready to Work? Employers' Perspective on the Basic Knowledge and Applied Skills of New Entrants to the 21st Century U.S. Workforce" *The Conference Board, Corporate Voices for Working Families, Partnership for 21st Century Skills, and Society for Human Resource Management,* 2006, 7-14.

42 Derek Scissors, "The United States vs. China — Which Economy Is Bigger, Which Is Better," *Backgrounder,* The Heritage Foundation, April 14, 2011, 5.

43 "An entire system of global trade is at risk," *The Telegraph,* October 8, 2011.

44 Scissors.

45 Hannah Richardson, "Nuclear family 'in decline,' figures show," *BBC News,* July 2, 2010.

46 Stephanie Coontz, *The Way We Never Were: American Families and the Nostalgia Trap* (New York: Basic Books, 1992), xx.

47 National Science Foundation, *Human Resources for Science and Technology: The Asian Region,* NSF 93-303 (Washington, DC, 1993). 35-38.

48 Coontz, 239.

⁴⁹ Jacob Kohn, *Evolution as Revelation* (New York: Philosophical Library, 1963), 50.

⁵⁰ David A. Price, *Love and Hate in Jamestown* (New York: Vintage Books, 2003), 4.

⁵¹ Davis W. Houck, *FDR and Fear Itself: The First Inaugural Address* (College Station, TX: Texas A & M University Press, 2002), 3.

⁵² Erich Fromm, *Escape from Freedom* (New York: Avon Books, 1965), 46-47.

⁵³ Alston Chase, *Harvard and the Unabomber: The Education of an American Terrorist* (New York: Norton & Company, 2003), 21.

⁵⁴ "Norway shooting: Anders Behring Breivik plagiarized 'Unabomber'," *The Telegraph*, October 19, 2011.

⁵⁵ Chase, 356.

⁵⁶ Ibid., 18.

⁵⁷ *The Jerusalem Bible* (Garden City, NY: Doubleday & Company, 1971), 886.

⁵⁸ Joel Arthur Barker, *Paradigms: The Business of Discovering the Future* (New York: HarperCollins, 1992), 15-17.

⁵⁹ Steve Shifferes, "The Decline of Detroit," *BBC News*, February 19, 2007.

⁶⁰ Thomas J. Watson, Jr., *Father, Son & Co.* (New York: Bantam Books, 1990), 207.

⁶¹ Ibid., 218.

⁶² Richard S. Tedlow, *The Watson Dynasty: The Fiery Reign and Troubled Legacy of IBM's Founding Father and Son* (New York: HarperCollins, 2003), 265-272.

⁶³ Fromm, 263.

⁶⁴ Ibid., 266.

65 Aldous Huxley, *Ends and Means* (New York: Harper & Brothers, Publishers, 1937), 99.

66 Shipley, 327.

67 Jiddu Krishnamurti, *You Are the World* (New York: HarperCollins, 1989), 39-44.

68 Shipley, 327.

69 Rene Girard, *Battling to the End: Conversations with Benoit Chantre* (East Lansing, MI: Michigan State University Press, 2010), 217.

70 Thomas Marc Parrott, ed., *Shakespeare, Twenty-three Plays and the Sonnets* (New York: Charles Scribner's Sons, 1953), 687.

71 Joseph Chilton Pearce, *The Death of Religion and the Rebirth of Spirit* (Rochester, VT: Park Street Press, 2007), 111.

72 Ibid., 112.

73 Ibid., 117.

74 Clancy D. McKenzie, M.D., *Babies Need Mothers: How Mothers Can Prevent Mental Illness in their Children* (Bloomington, IN: Xlibris, 2009), 116.

75 Jody Becker, "Behind the Autism Statistics," *The Atlantic,* November 12, 2011.

76 http://www.cdc.gov/violenceprevention/pdf/Suicide_DataSheet-a.pdf

77 http://www.fbi.gov/news/stories/2009/february/ngta_020609

78 http://www.nationalchildrensalliance.org/NCANationalStatistics

79 http://www.streetchildren.org.uk/_uploads/resources/Street_Children_Stats_FINAL.pdf

80 http://www.internationalstreetkids.com/statistics.php

81 http://www.cdc.gov/niosh/blog/nsb041408_teacher.html

82 http://nces.ed.gov/fastfacts/display.asp?id=49

83 Quoted in Paul G. Harwood and Victor Asal, *Educating the First Digital Generation* (New York: Praeger, 2007), 51.

84 Ibid., 51-52.

85 http://www2.ed.gov/about/overview/budget/history/edhistory.pdf

86 "High School Dropouts: How They Affect Taxpayers and the Economy," *Huffington Post,* November 13, 2011. http://www.huffingtonpost.com/2011/07/25/high-school-dropouts-how_n_908600.html

87 Debra Lau Whelan, "Most Students Unprepared for College," *School Library Journal,* June 1, 2007.

88 "U.S. Education Spending and Performance vs. The World," *Master of Arts in Teaching, University of Southern California,* February 8th, 2011. http://mat.usc.edu/u-s-education-versus-the-world-infographic/

89 Paul Freston, *Evangelicals and Politics in Asia, Africa, and Latin America* (Cambridge, UK: Cambridge University Press, 2001), 140-142.

90 Vali Nasr, *The Shia Revival: How Conflicts within Islam Will Shape the Future* (New York: W. W. Norton & Company), 24-34.

91 Douglas Allen, ed., *Religion and Political Conflict in South Asia: India, Pakistan, and Sri Lanka* (Westport, CT: Greenwood Press, 1992), 7-8.

92 John M. Robertson, *A Short History of Christianity* (Ithaca, NY: Cornell University Press , 2009), 278.

93 Robert Knecht, *The French Religious Wars* (Oxford, UK: Osprey Publishing, 2002), 91.

[94] Rabindranath Tagore, *Sadhana - The Realization of Life* (New York: The Macmillan Company, 1913), 111.

[95] Michael Maccoby, "Narcissistic Leaders: The Incredible Pros, the Inevitable Cons," *The Harvard Business Review,* January-February, 2000.

[96] Pearce, 23.

[97] Ibid., 15-16.

[98] Quoted in *Quest: The Church of the Larger Fellowship, Unitarian Universalist,* October 2011, 3.

[99] Shipley, 186.

SECTION TWO
THE WAY TO CHRIST CONSCIOUS *LEADERSHIP*

Chapter 4: Unity – *The First Step*

[1] Rupert Gethin, *The Foundations of Buddhism* (Oxford: Oxford University Press, 1998), 9.

[2] G. M. Strong, *The Udana: The Solemn Utterances of the Buddha* (Forgotten Books, 2007), 97-99. http://www.forgottenbooks.org/

[3] Quoted in Nick Herbert, *Quantum Reality: Beyond the New Physics* (New York: Anchor Books, 1985), 178.

[4] Swami Nikhilananda, trans., *Gospel of Sri Ramakrishna* (New York: Ramakrishna-Vivekananda Center, 2000), 191.

[5] John Godfrey Saxe, *The Poems of John Godfrey Saxe* (Boston: Ticknor and Fields, 1868), 259-261.

[6] Rene Girard, *I See Satan Fall Like Lightning* (Maryknoll, NY: Orbis Books, 2001), 10-11.

[7] Joseph Chilton Pearce, *The Biology of Transcendence: A Blueprint of the Human Spirit* (Rochester, VT: Park Street Press, 2002), 134.

[8] Peter L. Rudnytsky, *Freud and Oedipus* (New York: Columbia University Press, 1992), 35.

[9] Herbert Spencer, *The Principles of Biology, Vol. 1* (London, UK: Williams and Norgate, 1864), 112.

[10] Michael Le Page, "Evolution myths: 'Survival of the fittest' justifies 'everyone for themselves'," *NewScientist,* April 16, 2008.

[11] Edward Connery Lathem, ed., *The Poems of Robert Frost* (New York: Henry Holt and Company, 1969), 34.

[12] David Bohm, *On Dialogue* (New York: Routledge, 1996), 59.

[13] Louis Untermeyer, ed., *Modern American Poetry* (New York: Harcourt, Brace & World, 1962), 62.

[14] Bohm, 67-68.

[15] Michio Kaku, *Parallel Worlds: A journey through creation, higher dimensions, and the future of the cosmos* (New York: Anchor Books, 2006), 16-18.

[16] Peter Byrne, *The Many Worlds of Hugh Everett III* (New York: Oxford University Press, 2010), 97.

[17] Alvin Toffler, *Future Shock* (New York: Bantam Books, 1971), 414.

[18] Byrne, 98-99.

[19] Quoted in Herbert, 18.

[20] David Bohm, *Wholeness and the Implicate Order* (New York: Routledge, 1980), 158.

[21] Ibid., 191.

[22] Byrne, 98.

[23] Herbert, 174.

[24] Erwin Schrodinger, *What is Life? with Mind and Matter and Autobiographical Sketches* (Cambridge, UK: Cambridge University Press, 2003), 127.

[25] Niels Bohr, *Atomic Theory and the Description of Nature* (Cambridge, UK: Cambridge University Press, 1934), 119.

[26] Ibid., 5.

[27] Schrodinger, 18.

[28] Richard P. Feynman, *The Strange Theory of Light and Matter* (Princeton, NJ: Princeton University Press, 1985), 10.

[29] Thomas Heath, *The Copernicus of Antiquity – Aristarchus of Samos* (New York: The Macmillan Company, 1920), 39.

[30] Arthur Koestler, *The Sleepwalker: A History of Man's Changing Vision of the Universe* (New York: Penguin Books, 1990), 84.

[31] Stuart Kauffman, *At Home in the Universe* (New York: Oxford University Press, 1995), 5.

[32] Ibid.

[33] Koestler, 154-156.

[34] Ingrid D. Roland, *Giordano Bruno: Philosopher/Heretic* (Chicago, IL: University of Chicago Press, 2009), 90.

[35] Ibid., 4-6.

[36] J. Dobrzycki, ed., *The Reception of Copernicus' Heliocentric Theory* (Dordrecht, Holland: D. Reidel, 2010), 280.

[37] Ibid., 279.

[38] Maurice A. Finocchiaro, ed., *The Galileo Affair: A Documentary History* (Berkeley, CA: University of California Press, 1989), 14.

[39] Koestler, 468.

[40] Finocchiaro, 35.

[41] Ibid., 38.

[42] Ibid. 39.

[43] David Weintraub, *Is Pluto a Planet* (Princeton, NJ: Princeton University Press, 2007), 67.

[44] Ibid., 43.

[45] Max Planck, *Scientific Autobiography and Other Papers* (New York: Philosophical Library, 1949), 33-34.

[46] Herbert, 18.

[47] Fritjof Capra, *The Tao of Physics* (New York: Bantam Books, 1975), 129.

[48] Jean Lipman-Blumen, *The Connective Edge: Leading in an Interdependent World* (San Francisco, CA: Jossey-Bass Publishers, 1996), 6.

[49] Quoted in Conrad P. Pritscher, *Re-opening Einstein's Thought* (Rotterdam, The Netherlands: Sense Publishers, 2008), 14.

[50] Rene Girard, *The Scapegoat* (Baltimore, MD: The Johns Hopkins University Press, 1986), 21.

[51] Paul Ehrlich and Robert Ornstein, *Humanity on a Tightrope: Thoughts on Empathy, Family, and Big Changes for a Viable Future* (Lanham, MD: Rowman & Littlefield, 2010), 13-15.

[52] Benjamin Jowett, trans., *Plato: Six Great Dialogues* (Mineola, NY: Dover Publications, 2007), 18.

[53] John Archibald Wheeler with Kenneth Ford, *Geons, Black Holes, and Quantum Foam: A Life in Physics* (New York: W. W. Norton & Company, 1998), 338.

[54] Thomas Merton, *New Seeds of Contemplation* (New York: New Directions Publishing, 1972), 47-48.

[55] Rainer Maria Rilke, *Letters to a Young Poet,* trans. Stephen Mitchell, (New York: Random House, 1986), 34-35.

[56] Kieran Kavanaugh, O.C.D. and Otilio Rodriguez, O.C.D., trans., *The Collected Works of Saint John of the Cross* (Washington, D.C.: ICS Publications, 1991), 160-161.

[57] Morihei Ueshiba, *The Art of Peace* (Boston, MA: Shambhala Publications, 2002), 26-40.

[58] Ann Nyland, trans., *The Gospel of Thomas* (Smith and Stirling, 2004), 24.

[59] Quoted in William C. Chittick, *The Sufi Doctrine of Rumi* (Bloomington, IN: World Wisdom, 2005), 74.

[60] John Wheeler, "Genesis and Observership," in Robert E. Butts and Jaakko Hintikka, eds., *Foundation Problems in the Special Sciences, Vol. 1* (Dordrecht, Holland: D. Reidel, 1977), 27.

[61] Quoted in Chittick, 37.

Chapter 5: Love – *The Second Step*

[1] Krishna Kripalani, ed., *All Men Are Brothers: Life and Thoughts of Mahatma Gandhi as Told in His Own Words* (Paris, FR: UNESCO, 1958), 4.

[2] Sanjoy Majumder, "Mahatma Gandhi's fading dream," *BBC News,* March 31, 2004. http://news.bbc.co.uk/2/hi/south_asia/3581555.stm

[3] Pierre Teilhard de Chardin, *Toward the Future* (London, UK: William Collins Sons & Co. and Harcourt, 1973), 86-87.

[4] Kripalani, 5-11.

[5] Mahatma Gandhi, *An Autobiography: The Story of My Experiments with Truth* (Boston, MA: Beacon Press, 1957), 68-69.

[6] Kripalani, 5.

[7] Gandhi, 34.

[8] Ibid., 33.

[9] Kripalani, xiv.

[10] "The life and death of Mahatma Gandhi," *BBC News,* January 29, 1998. http://news.bbc.co.uk/2/hi/50664.stm

[11] Ibid.

[12] Simone Panter-Brick, "Gandhi's Dream of Hindu-Muslim Unity and Its Two Offshoots in the Middle East," *Durham Anthropology Journal,* 16, 2 (2009), 55.

[13] "The life and death of Mahatma Gandhi"

[14] Mahatma Gandhi, *Non-Violent Resistance* (New York: Dover Publications, 2001), 3.

[15] Ibid., 13-16.

[16] Ibid., 36.

[17] Martin Luther King, Jr., *Toward Freedom* (Boston, MA: Beacon Press, 1958), 84.

[18] Louis Fisher, ed., *The Essential Gandhi: An Anthology of His Writings* (New York: Vintage Books, 1962), 80.

[19] http://www.bbc.co.uk/history/historic_figures/mountbatten_lord_louis.shtml

[20] Gandhi, *Non-Violent Resistance,* 76.

[21] Thomas Merton, ed., *Gandhi on Non-Violence* (New York: New Directions Publishing, 1965), 68.

[22] Gandhi, *Non-Violent Resistance,* 298.

[23] John Dear, ed., *Mahatma Gandhi: Essential Writings* (New York: Orbis Books, 2002), 77.

[24] Gandhi, *Non-Violent Resistance,* 298.

[25] Nirmal Kumar Bose, *Selections from Gandhi* (Ahemadabad, India: Jitendra T. Desai, 1960), 3.

[26] Dear, 77.

[27] Ishaan Tharoor, "Remembering Why Gandhi Starved Himself," *Time,* August 17, 2007.

[28] http://www.bbc.co.uk/history/historic_figures/mountbatten_lord_louis.shtml

[29] "The life and death of Mahatma Gandhi"

[30] Ibid.

[31] Karan Thapar, "How Nathuram Godse died," *Hindustan Times,* January 1, 2001.

[32] Majumder, "Mahatma Gandhi's fading dream."

[33] Merton, 25.

[34] Gandhi, *An Autobiography,* 329.

[35] Ibid., 504.

[36] Juan Mascaro, *The Upanishads* (New York: Penguin Books, 1965), 31-35.

[37] Stephen Mitchell, trans., *Bhagavad Gita* (New York: Three Rivers Press, 2000), 26.

[38] Ibid., 119.

[39] Ibid., 73.

[40] Kieran Kavanaugh, O.C.D. and Otilio Rodriguez, O.C.D., trans., *The Collected Works of Saint John of the Cross* (Washington, D.C.: ICS Publications, 1991), 676.

[41] Richard Rohr, O.F.M., *Jesus' Plan for a New World: The Sermon on the Mount* (Cincinnati, OH: St. Anthony Messenger Press, 1996) 117.

[42] Clancy McKenzie, "Love Energy: The Life Force," *Theosophy Forward,* November 22, 2011.

[43] Ceslaus Spicq, O.P., *Agape in the New Testament - Volume II* (St. Louis, MO: B. Herder Book Company, 1965), 315.

[44] Leo Tolstoy, *The Law of Love and the Law of Violence* (Mineola, NY: Dover Publications, 2010), 32-33.

[45] Paramahansa Yogananda, *The Yoga of Jesus* (Los Angeles, CA: Self-Realization Foundation, 2007), 66.

[46] Quoted in William C. Chittick, *The Sufi Doctrine of Rumi* (Bloomington, IN: World Wisdom, 2005), 20.

Chapter 6: Detachment – *The Third Step*

[1] Ann Gibbons, "Comparative Genetics: Which of Our Genes Make Us Human," *Science,* September 4, 1998.

[2] "Putting DNA to Work," *National Academy of Sciences,* 2012. http://www.koshland-science-museum.org/exhibitdna/intro01.jsp

[3] Jasmine McCammon and Hazel Sive, "How fish can help find causes of autism," *Simons Foundation Autism Research Initiative,* August 29, 2011. http://sfari.org/news-and-opinion/viewpoint/2011/how-fish-can-help-find-causes-of-autism

[4] Quoted in Jennifer Viegas, "Embryos Show All Animals Share Ancient Genes," *Discovery News,* December 8, 2010.

[5] Michael Purdy, "First analysis of chicken genome offers many new insights," *Washington University in St. Louis Newsroom,* December 8, 2004. http://news.wustl.edu/news/Pages/4421.aspx

[6] Viegas.

[7] "Fruit fly gene success," *BBC News,* February 18, 2000. http://news.bbc.co.uk/2/hi/science/nature/647139.stm

[8] Peter Gluckman and Mark Hanson, *The Fetal Matrix: Evolution, Development, and Disease* (Cambridge, UK: Cambridge University Press, 2005), 30-31.

[9] Ibid.

[10] Silvina Epsztejn-Litman et al., "*De novo* DNA methylation promoted by G9a prevents reprogramming of embryonically silenced genes," *Nature Structural & Molecular Biology* 15 (2008), 1176-1183.

[11] M. K. Richardson, "Heterochrony and the phylotypic period," *Developmental Biology* (December 1995), 412-421.

[12] Stephen Jay Gould, *Ontogeny and Phylogeny* (Cambridge, MA: The Belknap Press of Harvard University Press, 1977), 9.

[13] Ibid., 405-406.

[14] Ibid., 399.

[15] Ibid., 403.

[16] Margaret Power, *The Egalitarians, Human and Chimpanzee: An anthropological view of social organization* (Cambridge, UK: Cambridge University Press, 1991), 62.

[17] Delbert D. Thiessen, *Bittersweet Destiny: The Stormy Evolution of Human Behavior* (New Brunswick, NJ: Transaction Publishers, 1996), 106-107.

[18] http://php.med.unsw.edu.au/embryology/index.php?title=Mouse_Timeline_Detailed

[19] Takefumi Kikusui et al., "Maternal deprivation by early weaning increases corticosterone and decreases hippocampal BDNF and neurogenesis in mice," *Psychoneuroendocrinology* 34, 5 (2009), 762-772.

[20] Thiessen, 106.

[21] Lee A. Fuiman and Robert G. Werner, *Fishery Science: The Unique Contribution of Early Life Stages* (Oxford, UK: Blackwell Publishing Company, 2002), 3-20.

[22] Robert E. Kohler, *Lords of the Fly: Drosophila Genetics and the Experimental Life* (Chicago, IL: Univesity of Chicago Press, 1994), 21-28.

[23] http://quest.nasa.gov/projects/flies/lifeCycle.html

[24] Jill B. Becker, S. Marc Breedlove, and David Crews, eds., *Behavioral Endocrinology* (Cambridge, MA: The MIT Press, 1992), 224-225.

[25] http://www.massaudubon.org/Nature_Connection/wildlife/index.php?subject=Birds:%20Nests%20and%20Young&id=42

[26] Raman Sukumar, *The Living Elephants* (New York: Oxford University Press, 2003), 255.

[27] Ibid., 125.

[28] Otto Rank, *The Trauma of Birth* (New York, Harper & Row, 1973), 123.

[29] Quoted in Ruth Leys, *Trauma: A Genealogy* (Chicago, IL: University of Chicago Press, 2000), 146.

[30] Andrew R. Eisen and Charles E. Schaefer, *Separation Anxiety in Children and Adolescents* (New York: The Guilford Press, 2005), 4.

[31] Ibid., 42.

[32] Vijaya Manicavasagar et al., "Parent-child concordance for separation anxiety: a clinical study," *Journal of Affective Disorders* 65, 1 (June 2001), 81-84.

[33] Vijaya Manicavasagar et al., "Is there an adult form of separation anxiety disorder? A brief clinical report," *The Australian and New Zealand Journal of Psychiatry* 2 (April 31, 1997), 299-303.

[34] Harriet J. Smith, *Parenting for Primates* (Cambridge, MA: Harvard University Press, 2005), 166.

[35] John A. Hostetler, *Amish Society* (Baltimore, MD: The Johns Hopkins University Press, 1993), 303.

[36] Ayala Fader, *Mitzvah Girls: Bringing Up the Next Generation* (Princeton, NJ: Princeton University Press, 2009), 25.

[37] Paul Ehrlich and Robert Ornstein, *Humanity on a Tightrope* (Lanham, MD: Rowman & Littlefield, 2010), 12.

[38] Harvey Arden, *Dreamkeepers: A Spirit-Journey into Aboriginal Australia* (New York: HarperCollins, 1994), 9.

[39] Ibid., 7.

[40] Ibid., 10.

[41] Mark E. Thibodeaux, S.J., *God's Voice Within: The Ignatian Way to Discover God's Will* (Chicago, IL: Loyola Press, 2010), 153.

[42] Michael Heim, *The Metaphysics of Virtual Reality* (New York: Oxford University Press, 1993), 10.

[43] Ibid., 131.

[44] Ibid., 61.

[45] Ibid., xii.

[46] Ibid., 134-135.

[47] Ron Rhodes, *The Challenge of Cults and New Religions* (Grand Rapids, MI: Zondervan, 2001) 41-43.

[48] Bill Hoffman and Cathy Burke, *Heaven's Gate: Cult Suicide in San Diego* (New York: HarperPaperbacks, 1997), 316.

[49] Walter Martin, *Kingdom of Cults* (Bloomington, MN: Bethany House Publishers, 2003), 23.

[50] J. Gordon Melton, *Encyclopedic Handbook of Cults in America* (New York: Garland Publishing, 1992), 12.

[51] Ibid., 9.

[52] Rhodes, 15.

[53] James A. Kenny and Lori Groves, *Bonding and the Case for Permanence: Preventing Mental Illness, Crime, and Homelessness Among Children in Foster Care and Adoption* (Rensselaer, IN: ACT Publications, 2010), 20-23.

[54] Ibid., 47-48.

[55] Russell W. Beck, "Possessions and the Extended Self," *The Journal of Consumer Research* 15, 2 (September 1988), 160.

[56] Ibid., 156.

[57] Kahlil Gibran, *The Prophet* (New York: Alfred A. Knopf, 1973), 18.

[58] Ram Chandra Prasad, *The Upanayana: The Hindu Ceremonies of the Sacred Thread* (Delhi, India: Motilal Banarsidass Publishers, 2004), 142.

[59] Ibid., 158-160.

[60] Arnold Van Gennep, *The Rites of Passage* (East Essex, UK: Psychology Press, 2004), 59.

[61] H. Byron Earhart, ed., *Religious Traditions of the World* (New York: HarperCollins, 1993), 921.

[62] Joseph Campbell, *The Power of Myth* (New York: Anchor Books, 1991), 152.

[63] Herman Hesse, *Siddhartha* (New York: New Directions Publishing, 1971), 10-12.

[64] Fenggang Yang, *Religion in China* (New York: Oxford University Press, 2012), 148-152.

[65] Vanessa L. Fong, *Only Hope: Coming of Age under China's One-Child Policy* (Stanford, CA: Stanford University Press, 2004), 90.

[66] Ibid, 202.

[67] Ibid., 87.

[68] George Robinson, *Essential Judaism* (New York: Pocket Books, 2000), 157.

[69] *Quam Singulari,* Decree of the Sacred Congregation of the Discipline of the Sacraments on First Communion, August 8, 1910. http://www.papalencyclicals.net/Pius10/p10quam.htm

[70] *Catechism of the Catholic Church,* English trans. (Citto del Vaticano: Liberia Editrice Vaticana, 1994), #1309.

[71] Sarah Levete, *Coming of Age* (New York: The Rosen Publishing Group, 2010), 20-23.

[72] Nathan Stone, *Names of God* (Chicago, IL: Moody Publishers, 2010), 58.

73 St. Teresa of Avila, *Interior Castle,* trans. E. Allison Peers, (New York: Doubleday, 1989), 112-113.

74 Ibid., 224.

75 Ibid., 107.

76 Translated in Edward Dowden, ed., *The Poetical Works of William Wordsworth,* vol. 3, (Rye Brook, NY: Elibron Classics, 2005), 17-18.

Chapter 7: Commitment – *The Fourth Step*

1 Kieran Kavanaugh, O.C.D. and Otilio Rodriguez, O.C.D., trans., *The Collected Works of Saint John of the Cross* (Washington, D.C.: ICS Publications, 1991), 150.

2 Ibid., 114-115.

3 Rudolf Steiner, *Knowledge of the Higher Worlds and its Attainment: An Esoteric Spiritualism* (New York: Classic Books International, 2010), 12.

4 Joseph T. Shipley, *The Origins of English Words: A Discursive Dictionary of Indo-European Roots* (Baltimore, MD: The Johns Hopkins University Press, 1984), 425.

5 Stuart Kauffman, *At Home in the Universe* (New York: Oxford University Press, 1995), 26-27.

6 Ibid., 21.

7 Rollo May, *The Courage to Create* (New York: W. W. Norton, 1994), 12-13.

8 Robert Ernest Hume, *The Thirteen Principle Upanishads* (Charleston, SC: BiblioLife, 2009), 6.

9 N. J. Girardot, *Myth and Meaning in Early Taoism* (Berkeley, CA: University of California Press, 1983), 47.

[10] Thomas Marc Parrott, ed., *Shakespeare: Twenty-three Plays and the Sonnets* (New York: Charles Scribner's Sons, 1953), 704.

[11] Donald Senior, ed., *The Catholic Study Bible: New American Bible, The New Testament* (New York: Oxford University Press, 1990), 11.

[12] Ibid.

[13] Ibid.

[14] Henry David Thoreau, *Walden* (Mineola, NY: Dover Publications, 1995), 4.

[15] Arthur Kleinman and Byron J. Good, eds., *Studies in the Anthropology and Cross Cultural Psychiatry of Affect and Disorder* (Berkeley, CA: The University of California Press, 1985), 435-436.

[16] Myrna M. Weissman, ed., *Treatment of Depression: Bridging the 21st Century* (Washington, DC: American Psychiatric Press, 2001), 41.

[17] Ernest Bernbaum, ed., *Anthology of Romanticism* (New York: The Ronald Press, 1948), 236.

[18] Quoted in Abraham H. Maslow, *Toward a Psychology of Being* (New York: John Wiley & Sons, 1999), 71,

[19] Ibid., 71-78.

[20] Joseph Girzone, "Daily Postings," January 30, 2012. http://joshuamountain.org/postings/?cat=1

[21] Shipley, 439.

[22] Judith Andreyev, *Wondering about Words* (Paris, FR: Breal, 2005), 67.

[23] Quoted in Percy Redfern, *Tolstoy: A Study* (London, UK: A. C. Fifield, 1907), 100.

[24] Mikhael Gorbachev, *Mikhael Gorbachev: On My Country and the World,* trans. George Shriver (New York: Columbia University Press, 2000), 269.

[25] Ibid., 270.

Chapter 8: Action – *The Fifth Step*

[1] Bhikkhu Nanamoli, *The Life of the Buddha: According to the Pali Canon* (Onalaska, WA: Pariyatti Publishing, 2001), 1.

[2] Sarah Janssen, ed., *The World Almanac and Book of Facts* (New York: Infobase Learning, 2012), 697.

[3] Nanamoli, 2.

[4] Ibid., 38.

[5] Ibid.

[6] Aristotle, *Nicomachean Ethics*, trans. Terence Irwin (Indianapolis, IN: Hackett Publishing, 1999), 18-19.

[7] Nanamoli, 38-39

[8] Ibid.

[9] Alvin and Heidi Toffler, *War and Anti-War: Making Sense of Today's Global Chaos* (New York: Warner Books, 1993), 25.

[10] Ibid., 236.

[11] Quoted in John-Thor Dahlburg, "Mother Teresa, 87, Dies; Devoted Her Life to Poor," *Los Angeles Times*, September 6, 1997.

[12] Jean M. Twenge, *Why Today's Young Americans Are More Confident, Assertive, Entitled – and More Miserable Than Ever Before* (New York: Free Press, 2006), 138-145.

[13] Ibid., 140.

[14] Quoted in Twenge, 158.

[15] Ibid., 146.

[16] Ibid., 138.

[17] Peter Gray "Freedom to Learn," *Psychology Today*, January 26, 2010.

[18] Sidney Hook, *The Hero in History: The Study of Limitation and Possibility* (New Brunswick, NJ: Transaction Publishers, 1992), 5.

[19] Scott T. Allison and George R. Goethals, *Heroes: What They Do and Why We Need Them* (New York: Oxford University Press, 2011), 25-26.

[20] Selma H. Fraiberg, *The Magic Years* (New York: Simon & Schuster, 1996), 90.

[21] Andrew J. Cherlin, *The Marriage-Go-Round* (New York: Alfred A. Knopf, 2009), 207.

[22] Howard Brody, *The Healer's Power* (New Haven, CT: Yale University Press, 1992), 139.

[23] Ibid., 139-140.

[24] Ibid., 152.

[25] Ibid., 152-156.

[26] Ibid., 141.

[27] Ibid., 137.

[28] Joseph Campbell, *The Hero with a Thousand Faces* (Princeton, NJ: Princeton University Press, 1949), 23.

[29] Ibid., 12.

30 Joseph T. Shipley, *The Origins of English Words: A Discursive Dictionary of Indo-European Roots* (Baltimore, MD: The Johns Hopkins University Press, 1984), 187.

31 Michael Jaquish, *Namaste: Greeting the Light Within* (Gig Harbor, WA: Country Cop Books, 2007), 5.

32 John Schmitt, Kris Warner, and Sarika Gupta, "The High Budgetary Cost of Incarceration," Washington, D.C., *Center for Economic and Policy Research*, June 2010, 1-10.

33 Jerome G. Miller, "The Debate on Rehabilitating Criminals: Is It True that Nothing Works?" *Washington Post*, March 1989.

34 Emily Monea and Adam Thomas, "Unintended Pregnancy and Taxpayer Spending," *Perspectives on Sexual and Reproductive Health* 43, 2 (June 2011), 2.

35 Joerg Dreweke and Rebecca Wind, "Strong Evidence Favors Comprehensive Approach to Sex Ed," *Media Center*, May 23, 2007. mediaworks@guttmacher.org

36 http://armscontrolcenter.org/policy/securityspending/articles/US_vs_Global/

37 Louis Charbonneau, "U.N. Passes Leaner 2012-2013 Budget amid Economic Turmoil," *Reuters*, December 24, 2011.

38 Campbell, 49.

39 Wolfgang Dietrich, *Interpretations of Peace in History and Culture* (London, UK: Palgrave Macmillan, 2012), 4.

40 Arthur M. Eckstein, *Rome Enters the Greek East: From Anarchy to Hierarchy in the Helenistic Mediterranean, 230-170 B.C.* (Malden, MA: Blackwell Publishing, 2008), 117-123.

41 Gordon Martel, ed., *The Origins of the Second World War Reconsidered* (New York: Routledge, 1999), 13-19.

[42] W. Warren Wagar, *H. G. Wells: Traversing Time* (Middletown, CT: Wesleyan University Press, 2004), 152.

[43] John Milton Cooper, *Breaking the Heart of the World: Woodrow Wilson and the Fight for the League of Nations* (Cambridge, UK: Cambridge University Press, 2001) 10-11.

[44] Ibid., 330.

[45] Thomas J. Knock, *To End All Wars: Woodrow Wilson and the Quest for a New World Order* (Princeton, NJ: Princeton University Press, 1992), 272-273.

[46] Johan Galtung, "An Editorial," *Journal of Peace Research* 1, 1 (March 1964), 1-4.

[47] Johan Galtung, *Peace by Peaceful Means* (Thousand Oaks, CA: Sage Publications, 1996), 32-33.

[48] Ibid., 21.

[49] Ibid., 14.

[50] Ibid., 32.

[51] Wolfgang Dietrich, *Interpretations of Peace in History and Culture* (Basingstoke, Hampshire, England, UK: Palgrave Macmillan, 2012), 4-8.

[52] Wolfgang Dietrich et al., eds., *The Palgrave International Handbook of Peace Studies: A Cultural Perspective* (Basingstoke, Hampshire, England, UK: Palgrave Macmillan, 2011), xxix.

[53] Mahatma Gandhi, *An Autobiography: The Story of My Experiments with Truth* (Boston, MA: Beacon Press, 1957), 137-138

[54] Richard Stengel, *Mandela's Way* (New York: Crown Publishers, 2009), 4.

[55] Rosa Parks, *Quiet Strength* (Grand Rapids, MI: Zondervan Publishing House, 1994), 11.

INDEX

Abandonment
   of children, 133-134
   fear of, 98-99, 188, 202-205
   of self, 96, 98-99, 229
Abernathy, Ralph, 47
Aborigines, 141, 207
   Nhunggabarra, 106-107, 115
Abortion(s), 74, 214
Abrahamic religion(s), 12, 39, 166, 195, 218
Action(s), xix-xxii, 4-5, 7-8, 17-19, 33, 36, 48, 50-53, 90, 112-113, 123, 128-129, 140, 164, 180, 193, 219, 223, 236, 240, 249, 252-279, 315
   call to action, xix, xxi, 263-265, 267-271
   kingdom of God on earth, xxi, 274-279
   willingness and response, 269-274
Aeschylus, *Prometheus Bound*, 63
Agape, 96
AIDS, 17, 53, 133-134
Al Jazeera, 110
Alienation, 76, 94, 190, 242, 252, 256
Allah, 3-4, 7, 37, 41
Amamou, Slim, 115
   Friedrich-Ebert Foundation Award, 115
Angelou, Maya, "On the Pulse of Morning," 46
Anxiety, 15, 217, 257
   separation anxiety, 121, 131-132, 203-204
Archetypes, 57-58
Arden, Harvey, 207
Aristarchus of Samos, 154-155
   Pythagorean school of mathematics, 154
Aristotle, 154
   geocentric philosophy, 154
   Nicomachean Ethics, 254
Armageddon, xvii
Asiatic Registration Act, 172

Bailey, James, 84
Bania caste, 170

Banyacya, Sr., Thomas, "Prophecy from the Hopi Nation," 140
Barker, Joel, 123-124
Beck, Russell W., 214
Bedrij, Orest, *Exodus III*, 82
   dimensionless point of pure awareness and quantum potentialities, 88
Ben Ali, Zine al-Abidine, 109-110
Bergman, Yehudit 197
Berlin Wall, 248, 250
Bernard, Theos, *Hindu Philosophy*, 59
Bhagavad Gita, 178
Bhatt, Shamal, 171
Bickerton, Derek, 64, 68
Bohm, David, 52, 150, 152
   Thought as a System, 76
Bohr, Niels, 153
Brahma Sahampati, 254
Brahman, 3-5, 8, 72, 165, 183, 222, 234
Briggs, John and Peat, F. David, *Seven Life Lessons of Chaos*, 36
British colonial rule in India, 170, 172-173, 175-176
Brody, Howard, 260-261
Brown, Judy, "Fire," 81
Bruno, Giordano, 155-156
Buddha, Gotama 253-255
   Brahma Sahampati, 254
   Dhamma, 253-254
Buddhist (tales, traditions, and culture), 145, 216, 265
   monks and nuns in China, 217
Burke, James, *The Pinball Effect*, 48

Caiaphas, 33
Campbell, Joseph, 261-262, 271-272
   The Power of Myth, 216
Capra, Fritjof, 55
   The Web of Life, 24

Catechism of the Catholic Church, 7
Change(s), xiv, xvii-xviii, xx, 16-17, 19, 25, 38, 44, 47, 60, 62, 73, 75, 93-94, 115-116, 119-120, 129, 137, 140, 151, 198-199, 205, 209-211, 226, 231, 244-245, 256-257, 261, 274
    resistance to change, 9, 21, 32, 35-36, 41, 82 84, 86-87, 105, 120-130, 161, 169, 250-252, 273
    See also Chaos; Consciousness; Evolutio and development; Transformation
Chaos, 51, 110, 131, 230
    generating chaos, 19-44
    Lorenz, Edward, chaos theory, 113
Chapin, Edwin Hubbell, *Living Words*, 55
Charlton, Bruce G., *Psychiatry and the Human Condition*, 66
Chernobyl nuclear disaster, 74
Childhood (children), 97, 118, 120-122, 149, 162, 185-186, 199-202, 205, 215, 216, 218-220, 266, 272
    in crisis, xvii, 18, 22, 27, 85-86, 133-136, 202-204, 213-215, 256, 259
    language development, 66-68
    "magic years," 258, 262
    See also Family; Infant development
China, 74, 85, 103, 108, 111, 118, 130, 216-217
Christ, the Eternal Absolute, xv, xix, 3-55, 90-92, 95-99, 137-138, 141, 143, 147, 158-159, 161, 164-168, 177, 182-183, 186-89, 190, 193-194, 196, 210, 212, 216, 219-220, 223, 226-228, 230-231, 233-234, 240, 245, 251-252, 262-263, 265-266, 268-270, 273-274, 279
    generating chaos, 19-44
    shaping the future, 44-51
    stirring the soul, 13-19
    unifying time, 51-55
Christ conscious leaders (leadership), xiv, xix-xx, xxii, 140-141, 151, 169, 177, 196, 206, 220, 225, 227, 232, 241, 248, 252, 267-268, 273, 279, 283-288

Christ consciousness, xiii-xiv, xxi-xii, 229, 250, 265-267, 269
Christian Byzantine Empire, 37
Christianity (Christians), 3-7, 36-37, 39-40, 49, 95, 138, 171-172, 207, 219, 277
    See also Disciples; Jesus; New Covenant; New Testament
Clergy (as leaders), xii, 137-140, 266
Collective unconscious, 57-58
Commandment(s), 24, 31-32, 179, 218
    New Testament, xxi, 4, 11, 33-34, 181, 194-195
    Ten Commandments, 23-25, 32-33
Commitment(s), xxi, 17, 44, 49, 55, 139, 141, 172, 177, 210, 217, 219, 226-252, 255, 261, 270, 279, 308
    to God's purpose, 233-241
    to lifelong transformation, 248-252
    to our work, 242-248
Communism, 126, 249
Compassion, 4, 16-17, 41, 139, 178-179, 180-183, 185-189, 192, 195-196, 206, 254, 267, 296, 299-300
Consciousness, 14, 16, 20, 129, 135, 141, 154, 160-161, 184, 220, 227, 249, 255, 268-269
    Christ consciousness, xiii-xiv, xxi-xii, 229, 250, 265-267, 269
    consciousness and the soul, 56-99
    consciousness and survival, 62-69
    evolution of, xviii-xx, 93-99
    Evolution of Ingenuity and Consciousness, The (Diagram B), 75
    evolving consciously, xix-xx, 55, 82-91, 128, 252, 265, 270
    ingenuity and emerging consciousness, 69-82
    See also Language; Soul(s)
Constitutional republic, 101-102
Contemplation, 70, 80, 98, 228, 244, 247, 251 270, 281
Copernicus, Nicolaus, 155-158
    De Revolutionibus, 155-156, 158
    On the Infinite Universe and Worlds, 155

See also Geocentric theory of the universe; Heliocentric theory of the universe
Courage, 46, 137, 189, 216, 228, 251, 278
  to become a creative force, 231-232
  to change, 141, 169, 196,
  to face fears, 98-99, 134, 188, 245
  to get to know ourselves, 244-245, 248, 251
Cousins, Tom, 18-19
Creative Action Plan, 315-321
Crick, Francis, 57-58
Crucifixion of Jesus, 11, 35, 95, 98-99, 181, 239
Crusades, 95, 138
Cults (modern), 211
Cyberspace, 113, 209-210
  cyberspace citizen(s), 112, 140

Damascene, Hieromonk, *Christ the Eternal Tao*, 5-6
Damasio, Antonio, *Descartes' Error: Emotion Reason, and the Human Brain*, 79
Darwin, Charles, 62, 65
Deacon, Terrence, 64
Denton, Derek, *The Primordial Emotions: The Dawning of Consciousness*, 62
Descartes, Rene 77, 79
Detachment and differentiation, xxi, 58, 197-225, 234, 262, 303
  from the family, 212-220
  in human cells (embryogenesis), 197-198 202, 205
  from self-will, 221-225
  from the tribe, 206-212
  See also Rite(s) of Passage; Separation
Deutscher, Guy, 64
Dhamma, 253-254
Diamond, Jared, *Guns, Germs, and Steel: The Fates of Human Societies*, 103-104
Dietrich, Wolfgang, 277
Disciples (New Testament), 29, 35-36, 167, 181, 193-196, 238-240
  Andrew, 28
  James, 238
  John, xiv, 4, 11, 28-29, 34-35, 166-167, 178, 180-181, 183, 192, 194, 220, 238-239, 251, 264, 277
  Judas Iscariot, 238
  Luke, 26-30, 35, 99, 166, 180-181, 184, 192, 194, 211, 223, 238-239, 270, 279
  Mark, 35, 96, 167, 181, 191-193, 238
  Matthew, xv, 4, 10, 26-27, 33-35, 41-42, 93, 98, 134, 166-167, 175, 181, 192-193, 213, 237-240, 269, 272, 275, 278
  Paul, xii-xiv, xix, 36, 53, 93, 99, 141, 167-168, 194, 203, 220, 240, 247, 266, 269
  Peter, 28, 193, 238-239
  Philip, xiii, 28
  Thomas, 239
  Timothy, 238
  See also New Testament
Distraction(s), 16-17, 98, 234, 240-241
Divine, the, 93, 152, 165, 168-169
Divine Love, xxi, 177-196, 206, 212, 216, 227-228, 231, 233, 235-236, 241, 245, 251-252, 263, 265, 268, 273-274, 279, 296, 299, 301
  receptive to, 183-189
  vehicle for, 189-196
  See also Love
Drosophila, 201
Drugs, 15, 18, 139, 198, 242
Duality, 4-8, 93, 146
  end of, 151-160
  See also Oppositional behavior; Quantum physics
Durr, Clifford, 47

East Lake Foundation, 18
Eccles, Sir John, 58-59
Edelman, Gerald, 58
Education, 77, 85, 103, 173, 204, 259, 266, 271, 278
  college graduates in America, 116-117
  comparative costs of, 136-137
  religious, 215, 219
Educators (as leaders), 135-137, 266

Egypt (ancient), 20-25, 27, 44, 100, 179
Egyptian revolution (2011), 110-111, 127
Ehrlich, Paul, 88
  Humanity on a Tightrope, 205
Einstein, Albert, 147, 161
Electoral College, 102
Eliot, T. S., "Ash-Wednesday," 69
Embryogenesis, 197-198, 202, 205
Emotion(s), emotional development, 62, 76-81, 82, 97, 132, 161, 182, 185, 205, 206, 213, 229, 231, 245, 257, 261, 267, 270
  emotional perceptions, xx, xxii, 71, 75-76, 79, 151, 315-320
Everett, Hugh, 145, 151-152
Evolution and development (human), 25, 36, 55, 59, 61-62, 68, 73, 75, 76, 78, 112-113, 119, 141, 150, 162, 178, 205, 232, 251-252, 274, 281
  adaptation(s), xviii, 62, 82, 87-88, 90
  detachment, 197-206
  Evolution of Ingenuity and Consciousness, The (Diagram B), 75
  hominids, 62-65, 71, 199
  Homo erectus, 52, 63, 90
  Homo habilis, 52, 63
  Homo neanderthalensis, 71, 90
  Homo sapiens, 62-64, 70, 86, 91, 249
  Homo sapiens sapiens, 70
  language, evolution of, 60-71, 82, 84
  pair-bonding, 199
  See also Consciousness; Ingenuity

Facebook, 109
Family, 132, 162, 185, 204-205, 212-213, 216, 220-221, 226, 250-252, 267, 270
  infant and childhood dependency on, 148-150, 162, 199-205, 216
  See also Detachment and differentiation
Fear(s), 47, 50, 79, 96-99, 131-134, 140-141, 162, 187-190, 237, 239, 241, 254, 269, 270
  of change, 21-23, 31-32, 35-36, 39, 120-123, 126-130, 273

of God, 12, 31, 93-94, 184
  primal fear (of abandonment), 98-99, 188, 202, 205
  of self-knowledge, 244-245, 250
Feynman, Richard P., 89
  The Strange Theory of Light and Matter, 153
Free will, 5-6, 8, 57, 221, 224
Freedom, 4, 7, 25, 49-51, 72, 90, 115, 140, 173, 220, 225, 249, 274, 277
  and the ability to lead, 120-130
  Indo-European root word, *prai*, 128-129
  See also Fromm; Leaders
French Catholics and Huguenots, 138
French Revolution, 104
Freud, Sigmund, 202, 244-245
Friedrich-Ebert Foundation Award, 115
Fromm, Erich, 121, 126
  Escape from Freedom, 121
Frost, Robert, 148-149
Fukushima nuclear disaster, 52, 74

Galilei, Galileo, 77, 152, 156-158
  A Dialogue Concerning the Two Chief World Systems, 157
  The Two New Sciences, 157
  See also Heliocentric theory of the universe
Galtung, Johan, 276-277
Gandhi, Mahatma, 47, 55, 147, 170-177, 258, 278
  antagonism between Hindus and Muslims, 174-175
  Asiatic Registration Act, 172
  assassination, 175
  Bania caste, 170
  Bhatt, Shamal, 171
  British colonial rule in India, 170, 172-173, 175-176
  Indian National Congress, 172
  Porbandar, India, 170, 176
  Satyagraha (non-violence), 173-176
  See also Love
Garden of Eden, 10, 12-13
  lost paradise, 6-8

Genocide, 105, 130, 251, 276
Geocentric theory of the universe, 154-155
    Aristotle, 154
    Orphic Mystery Cult, 154
    Ptolemy, 154
Gibran, Kahlil, *The Prophet*, 215
Girard, Rene, 14, 90, 130
Girardot, N. J., *Myth and Meaning in Early Taoism*, 35
Girzone, Joseph F., 19-20, 246
    Joshua and the City, 19
Gluckman, Sir Peter, 198
God's grace, 5, 11, 13, 165, 176, 264-269, 272-274
Gorbachev, Mikhail, 55, 249
    Berlin Wall, 248
Gospel of Mary (Gnostic Gospels), 89
Gospel of Thomas (Gnostic Gospels), 168
Gould, Stephen Jay, 199
Gray, Peter, 257

Hayakawa, S. I., *Language in Thought and Action*, 84
Heim, Michael, *The Metaphysics of Virtual Reality*, 209-210
Heitler, Walter, 152
Heliocentric theory of the universe, 155-157, 160
    Aristarchus of Samos, 154-155
    Bruno, Giordano, 155-156
    Copernicus, Nicolaus, 155-158
    Galilei, Galileo, 77, 152, 156-158
    See also Inquisition
Heroes, 55, 258-260, 262-263, 278
Hesiod, *Theogony*, 19
Hesse, Herman, *Siddhartha*, 216
Hierarchy, xx, 35, 96, 105-109, 114, 193
Hinduism (Hindus), 3-5, 8, 59, 93, 138, 145-46, 165, 170-172, 174-176, 178, 216, 222-233, 278
    Bhagavad Gita, 178
    Brahman, 3-5, 8, 72, 165, 183, 222, 234
    namaste, 265
    Veda(s), the, 93, 216

    See also Gandhi; Upanishads
Hitler, Adolf, *Mein Kampf*, 103
Holy Spirit (Holy Ghost), 3, 36, 183, 208, 219
Homer, *The Iliad*, 91-92
Homer-Dixon, Thomas, 78, 86
Hominids, 62-65, 71, 199
Homo erectus, 52, 63, 90
Homo habilis, 52, 63
Homo neanderthalensis, 71, 90
Homo sapiens, 62-64, 70, 86, 91, 249
Homo sapiens sapiens, 70
Houselander, Caryll, *A Rocking-Horse Catholic*, 97
Hubris, 95-96, 98
Humanity, xiv, 11, 17, 81, 112, 130, 138, 248, 262-263
    challenges to survival, xviii, 54-55, 112, 128-130, 145-151, 269-270
    oneness of all, 17, 137, 205
    unity with the Divine, 3, 5, 8-9, 11, 94, 165-169, 189-190, 196, 233-235, 263
    See also Survival
Humility, 9-10, 98-99, 229, 232
Huxley, Aldous
    Brave New World, 61
    Ends and Means, 126
Huxley, Thomas, *Collected Essays*, 56

Ibrahim, Harun, 86
Idols, 32, 37, 43
    Golden Calf, 22-23
    at Ka'ba, in Mecca, 37
Illusion of control, 8, 96, 98-99, 120, 162
India, 74, 86, 130, 134, 138, 170-172, 174-176, 253, 278
Indian National Congress, 172
Indo-European (root words), xxii, 9, 67, 69, 80, 105, 128-129, 140, 230, 246, 262
Industrial Age, 105
Indwelling divinity, 3, 36, 99, 177, 232, 262-263, 265-267, 269
    alienation from, 96, 196, 211-212, 225, 241, 244-245, 252

source of sustainable peace, 279
Infant development, 131-133
　language development, 62, 65-69
　primal attachment(s), 202
　primal fear (of abandonment), 98-99, 188,
　See also Family
Information, 64, 79, 106, 151, 161, 178
　technology, 61, 82-84, 105, 108, 110, 114, 116, 119, 208-210, 256
　unlimited access to, xx, 107-109
Ingenuity, 69-76, 82, 90, 137
　Dynamics of Human Ingenuity and Perception, The (Diagram A), 71
　Evolution of Ingenuity and Consciousness, The (Diagram B), 75
　See also Perception
Inquisition, the, 155-157, 160
　his Holiness Paul V, 156
　his Holiness Urban VIII, 156
　See also Bruno; Copernicus; Galileo; Heliocentric theory of the universe
Intellect, 76, 78-81
　intellectual perceptions, xx, xxii, 71, 75, 79, 82
Interactive Age, 105
Interconnectedness, xx, 52, 107, 112, 117-119, 123, 127, 137, 140, 159, 162, 259, 289
　See also Unity; Universe
Interdependence, 17, 55, 117-118, 127, 137, 140, 160, 162, 289
　See also Unity; Universe
Internet, 68, 75, 107-108, 110-114, 116, 130, 208, 211, 256
　cyberspace, 112-113, 140, 209-210
　Facebook, 109
　Twitter, 109-110, 115
　See also Egyptian revolution; Information; Tunisian revolution
Introspection, 98, 228, 241, 244, 247, 251, 270, 281
Intuition, 71, 77-78, 80-82, 231
　intuitive perceptions, xx, xxii, 71, 75-76, 79-82, 96, 99, 120, 151, 190, 209, 245, 315, 317, 319-320

Islam (Muslims), 3,6, 12, 39-44, 95, 111, 138, 168, 172, 174-176, 181, 207, 217, 219
　Allah, 3-4, 7, 37, 41
　Koran, the, 4, 7, 12-13, 40-42, 181-183, 195, 228, 240-241, 269, 272, 275
　See also Muhammad ibn Abdullah
Israel (Israelites), 4, 10, 20-25, 27-28, 30-33, 35, 39-40, 93-94, 179
　Exodus, 4, 20-23, 32, 82
　See also Judaism

Jamestown colony, 120
Jaynes, Julian, 56, 93, 95-96
Jefferson, Thomas, 108
Jesuits, 76
Jesus, xiii-xv, 3, 11-12, 25-36, 52-53, 141, 187, 191-196, 208, 237-239, 269-270, 272
　Caiaphas, 33
　Crucifixion, 11, 35, 95, 98-99, 181, 239
　Last Supper, 34, 167, 181, 194-195
　love, xlv, xxi, 4, 33-34, 173, 180-181, 183, 191-192, 194-195, 213, 237
　Mary (Mother of Jesus), 26, 40
　Nazareth (Nazarenes), 26-29, 31, 33, 35, 93, 278
　Nicodemus, 29
　Pharisee(s), 25, 29, 31, 33-34, 36, 93, 167, 180, 192-193
　Pilate, Pontius, 33
　Resurrection, 11, 25, 36, 99, 194
　Sanhedrin, 26, 31-32
　Sermon on the Mount, 171, 269, 278
　unity, 166-167
　See also Christianity; Commandments; Disciples; Divine Love; Judaic-Christians; New Covenant; New Testament
Joy, Bill, 53-54
Judaic-Christians, 7, 11
　Messiah, 10-11, 26, 28-31, 40
　See also Commandments
Judaism (Jews), 3-4, 6 26, 37, 43, 166, 172
　Israel (Israelites), 4, 10, 20-25, 27-28, 30-33, 35, 39-40, 93-94, 179

Mosaic laws, 32, 34, 93
Yahweh, 3-4, 93, 166
See also Moses; Old Testament
Jung, Carl, 57, 59, 94-95

Ka'ba, 37, 39, 42-43
Kaczynski, Theodore (The Unibomber), 122
Kaku, Michio, 89
Kaleidoscope, 88
Kardiner, Abraham, 202
Kauffman, Stuart, 154, 230
Kennedy, John F., 135
Kepler, Johannes, *Epitome of Copernican Astronomy*, 158
Khadija, 37, 39
King, Jr., Martin Luther, 47-51, 258
Toward Freedom, 173
See also Parks, Rosa
Kingdom of God, xix, xxi, 11, 20, 29, 211, 220, 239-240, 263, 266, 268, 273, 274-279
Kleptocracy (kleptocrats), 104
Kohn, Jacob, *Evolution as Revelation*, 119
Koran, the, 4, 7, 12-13, 40-42, 181-183, 195, 228, 240-241, 269, 272, 275
Krishnamurti, Jiddu, *You Are the World*, 128

Lahab, Abu, 41
Language, evolution of, 60-71, 82, 84
Lingodroids, 60-61
Last Supper, 34, 167, 181, 194-195
Le Bovier de Fortenelle, Bernard, 158
Le Page, Michael, 147-148
Leaders (leadership), xi-xv, 18-19, 42, 44, 49, 160, 250, 259
Christ conscious leaders (leadership), xiv, xix-xx, xxii, 140-141, 151, 169, 177, 196, 206, 220, 225, 227, 232, 241, 248, 252, 267-268, 273, 279, 283-288
freedom and the ability to lead, 120-130
hierarchical leaders (leadership), 105, 107, 109, 114
kleptocrats (kleptocracy), 104
leadership at a crossroad, 100-141
leading into the unknown, 112-120
Nhunggabarra Aborigines, 106-107, 115
parents, educators, clergy (as leaders), 134-140, 266
totalitarian leaders, 103
world awaits its leaders, the, 130-140
League of Nations, 275
Lienhard, John H., 72-73
Lifton, Robert J., 214
Lincoln, Abraham, 112
Lingodroids, 60-61
Lipman-Blumen, Jean, 160
Lorenz, Edward, 113
Love, xxi, 170-196, 229, 235, 266, 296
for each other, xiv, xxi, 4, 17, 33, 137-139, 170-177, 265
emotion of, 79
"energies of love" (Teilhard de Chardin), 170
for God, xii, 4, 33, 36, 213
God's love for man, 4, 10, 16, 24, 34-36, 94, 225, 228, 236-23
"law of love" (Mahatma Gandhi), 173
parental love, 14, 97, 134, 215
power of love, 172, 225
See also Divine Love
Luhmann, Niklas, *Social Systems*, 52

Mall of America, 14
Mandela, Nelson, 50-51, 178, 278
See also Parks, Rosa
Margulis, Lynn, 82
Marriage, 74, 204, 214, 259-260
Mary (Mother of Jesus), 26, 40
Maslow, Abraham, 245
Matei, Sorin, 83
May, Rollo, 231
McGlashan, Alan, *The Savage and Beautiful Country*, 90
McKenzie, Clancy, 132, 186
Mecca, 36-37, 39, 41-44, 219
Medina, 42-43

Merton, Thomas, 163-164
  The Seven Storey Mountain, 15
Messiah, 10-11, 26, 28-31, 40
Michelangelo, 224
Middle East conflicts, xi, 83, 109-111, 114, 127, 130, 207
Milton, John, *Paradise Regained*, 11
Monotheism, 37
Montgomery Improvement Association, 47
  Montgomery bus boycott, 45-48
Morozov, Evgeny, *The Net Delusion: The Dark Side of Internet Freedom*, 110
Moses, 4, 20, 22-25, 166, 237, 269
  Mosaic laws, 32, 34, 93
  Mount Sinai, 22, 24, 166
Mother Teresa, 55, 255, 258
Motivation(s), 76, 169, 232, 235, 244, 281, 283, 303, 310
  and commitment, 228-229, 232, 270
  detachment from self-will, 221-225
  fear-based, 128-129, 250
  and survival, 161, 164
  See also Commitment; Oppositional behavior
Mount Hira, 38, 40
Mount Sinai, 22, 24, 166
Mubarak, Hosni, 110-111
Muhammad ibn Abdullah, 37-44, 219
  Christian Byzantine Empire, 37
  Ka'ba, 37, 39, 42-43
  Khadija, 37, 39
  Lahav, Abu, 41
  Mecca, 36-37, 39, 41-44, 219
  Medina, 42-43
  Mount Hira, 38, 40
  Quraysh tribe, 37-43
  Talib, Abu, 37, 41-42
  See also Idols; Islam
Multiverse, 151, 152, 159

NAACP (National Association for the Advancement of Colored People), 46-47, 49
Namaste, 265

Natural resources, xv, xvii-xviii, 13, 85-87, 91, 127, 271
  See also Water
Nazareth (Nazarenes), 26-29, 31, 33, 35, 93, 278
New Covenant, 94, 96, 98
New Testament, 36, 94, 166. 171, 180, 184, 187, 191, 237
  Acts, 36, 240
  Colossians, xix, 141, 167, 220
  Corinthians, 53, 99, 167, 203, 247, 269
  Ephesians, 93, 168, 194, 266
  Romans, xii
  See also Christianity; Disciples; Jesus; Judaic-Christians; New Covenant
Newton, Harry, *Glossary of Computer Terms*, 67
Newton, Isaac, 77, 152
  Mathematical Principles of Natural Philosophy, 158
  Newtonian physics, 89
Nhunggabarra Aborigines, 106-107, 115
Nicodemus, 29
Nixon, Edgar, 47
Nouwen, Henri J. M., *Reaching Out*, 14
Nuclear energy, 52, 73-74, 85, 246
  Chernobyl, 74
  Fukushima, 52, 74
  threat of nuclear weapons, xvii, 130

O'Leary, Daniel, *Escaping the Progress Trap*, 76-77
Oedipal rivalries, 14, 147
Old Testament, 10, 166, 179, 184, 191, 195, 236
  Deuteronomy, 25, 237
  Ecclesiastes, 236
  Exodus, 4, 20-23, 32, 82
  Ezekiel, 32, 191
  Genesis, 5-7, 27, 166, 214, 221, 233
  Hosea, 236
  Isaiah, 11, 166, 262
  Jeremiah, 31, 38, 179, 236
  Joshua, 43
  Nehemiah, 179
  Numbers, 24-25, 269

Proverbs, 184, 271
Psalms, 10, 80, 184, 236-237, 274
Song of Songs, 188
Wisdom, 123
Zechariah, 191
Zephaniah, 183
See also Israel; Judaism; Moses
Oppositional behavior, 163-164, 251, 279
    between religions, 138-140
    dangers of, xvii, 14,130-131
    Girard, Rene, "mimetic desire," 14
    and leadership, 100
    Oedipal rivalries, 14, 147
    paradigm shift, 55, 89, 159-160, 169
    in relationship with God, 96, 146
    for survival, 141, 147-148
    See also Duality; Quantum physics
Ornstein, Robert, 205
    New World New Mind, 88

Pair bonding, 199, 201
Paradise, lost, 8-9, 11-12, 40, 165, 241
Parents (parenting), 27, 66, 97, 110, 120, 133, 201-203, 213-215, 259
    as leaders, 134-135, 266
Paris Peace Conference, 275
Parks, Rosa, 45-51, 278
    Durr, Clifford, 47
    King, Jr., Martin Luther, 47-51, 258
    Klu Klux Klan, 46
    Jim Crow laws, 47
    Mandela, Nelson, 50-51, 178, 278
    Montgomery bus boycott, 45-48
    Montgomery Improvement Association, 47
    NAACP (National Association for the Advancement of Colored People), 46-47, 49
    Nixon, Edgar, 47
PC (Personal Computer), 125
Peace, xv, xxii, 11-12, 17, 22, 41, 128-129, 135, 137, 154, 166, 168, 175, 262, 269-270
    failure to attain peace, 274-277
    global peace, xv, xxii,

Nhunggabarra, 106-107
peace heroes, 278
"positive peace," 277-279
Pearce, Joseph Chilton, 131-132
Peat, F. David, 36
Penrose, Roger, *Shadows of the Mind*, 61
Perception(s), xviii, xx-xxii, 5, 17, 24, 52, 57, 68, 88-91, 93, 95, 98, 118, 129, 145, 148-151, 153, 160-162, 164, 169, 185, 204-206, 210, 220, 222, 224, 228, 241, 250-251, 255, 264, 281
    Dynamics of Human Ingenuity and Perception, The (Diagram A), 71
    emotional perceptions, xx, xxii, 71-72, 75-76, 79, 151, 315-320
    intellectual perceptions, xx, xxii, 71, 75, 79-82
    intuitive perceptions, xx, xxii, 71, 75-76, 79-82, 96, 99, 120, 151, 190, 209, 245, 315, 317, 319-320
Pharisee(s), 25, 29, 31, 33-34, 36, 93, 167, 180, 192-193
Pilate, Pontius, 33
Pinker, Steven, *Evolution of the Mind*, 73
Planck, Max, *Scientific Biography and Other Papers*, 158
Population, escalating world, xvii-xviii, 44, 85-87
    gender imbalance in China and India, 74
    global workforce, 118
    See also Natural resources
Porbandar, India, 170, 176
Positional leader(s), 105, 114
Ptolemy, 154, 157
P-trap pipe, 186
Purpose Built Communities, 19
Purpose, xxi, 16, 53, 55, 162, 190, 205-206, 208
    commitment to God's purpose, 225-274, 279, 308
    and life's work, xxi, 53, 213, 224, 226, 231, 238, 241, 242-248, 251, 262-263, 266, 268-270, 272, 274, 279, 308
    in the world of cyberspace, 210-212
Pythagorean school of mathematics, 154

Quantum physics, xxi, 52, 88-89, 91, 141, 150 153, 159, 168, 289
   Bohm, David, 52, 76, 150, 152
   Bohr, Niels, 153
   Briggs, John and Peat, F. David, *Seven Life Lessons of Chaos*, 36
   Einstein, Albert, 147, 161
   Everett, Hugh, 145, 151-152
   Feynman, Richard P., *The Strange Theory of Light and Matter*, 153
   Heitler, Walter, 152
   Kaku, Michio, 89
   multiverse, 151, 152, 159
   Planck, Max, *Scientific Biography and Other Papers*, 158
   Russell, Peter, 87
   Schrodinger, Erwin, 152-153
   Wheeler, John, 85, 168
Quraysh tribe, 37-43

Ramadan, 38, 219
Rank, Otto, 202
Renaissance, 76, 224
Rescue fantasy, 260-261
Resurrection of Jesus, 11, 25, 36, 99, 194
Revolutions, 105, 250, 257
   American, 104
   French, 104
   Middle East, xi, 83, 109-111, 114, 127, 130, 207
   Russian, 248
Rilke, Rainer Maria, 164
Rite(s) of passage, 216-220, 261
   in Buddhist tradition, 216
   in the Catholic Church (First Communion, Confirmation), 219
   in Hindu society (ceremonies of the sacred thread, the *upanayana*), 216
   in Judaic tradition (*bar mitzvah, bat mitzvah*), 218
   in the Muslim community, 219
Robertson, Alex, 19
Robots, 60-61

Rohr, Richard, 94, 184
Rome, ancient, 26-27, 32-33, 87, 92, 156
Roosevelt, Franklin Delano, 121
Rotter, Julian, 256
Rumi, Mawlana, 168-169, 190
Russell, Peter, 87
Ryan, Johnny, 107-108

Sanhedrin, 26, 31-32
Satan, 12, 28, 95
Satyagraha (non-violence), 173-176
Saxe, John Godfrey, 146
Schrodinger, Erwin, 152-153
Schultz, Ruth, 60
Self-will, 220-226, 251, 270, 279
Separation
   anxiety, 127, 203-204
   artificial separation between the past, present, and future, 54
   from the Eternal Absolute, 5-13, 165
   in infant and child development, 66, 121-122, 132, 165, 202-204, 261
   "inseparable whole" in quantum physics, 152-153, 159, 161, 165
   See also Detachment and differentiation
Shakespeare, William, *Hamlet*, 131, 236
Siddhartha, 216-217
Six blind men and the elephant, tale of the, 145-146
Smith, Harriet J., 203
Smith, Janet Farrell, 214
Social media, 83
   Facebook, 109
   Twitter, 109-110, 115
Socrates, 162
Songs of Kabir, The, 95
Soul(s), xviii, xx, 4, 5, 8, 10, 16-21, 25-26, 33, 36, 173, 178, 181-182, 223, 230, 241, 274, 281
   consciousness and the soul, 56-99
   "dark night of the soul," 227-228
   empowering the soul, 91-99
   stirring the soul, 13-19

Sparks, Glenn, 83
Spicq, O.P., Ceslaus, *Agape in the New Testament*, 187
St. John of the Cross, 165, 183, 227
    "dark night of the soul," 227-228
St. Teresa of Avila, 16, 80, 96, 223-224
    Interior Castle, 16, 96
Steiner, Rudolf, *Knowledge of the Higher Worlds and Its Attainment*, 229
Stone, Nathan, *Names of God*, 222
Suicide, 148, 211, 276
    youth and young adults in China, 217-218
    youth and young adults in the United States, 133
Sullivan, William, *The Secret of the Incas*, 105
Survival (humanity), 46, 112, 132, 200, 274, 291
    challenges to, xviii, 54-55, 59-61, 112, 128-130, 145-151, 269-270
    and change, 32, 120, 162, 202, 205, 212-213, 250-251
    as a competitive activity, 13-14, 16, 100-103, 141, 147-148, 161-162
    and ingenuity, 71, 73-79
    and the role of consciousness, 61-69, 90
    See also Humanity
Sveiby, Karl-Erik, 106

Tagore, Rabindranath, *Sadhana - The Realization of Life*, 138
Talib, Abu, 37, 41-42
Tao, Taoism, 3-6, 9-10, 35, 179, 191, 235
    See also Tzu, Lao
Technology (technologies), 13, 67-68, 87-88, 90, 105, 125, 211
    and conscious evolution, 87-88
    and economic change, 116-119
    ethical challenges of, 53-54, 59-61, 208-209
    and ingenuity, xx, 70-82
    and political change, 82-83, 107-108
    See also Information
Teilhard de Chardin, Pierre, 33
    Toward the Future, 170
Ten Commandments, 23, 25
Tennyson, Alfred Lord, "Ring Out, Wild Bells," 143
Thibodeaux, S.J., Mark E., *God's Voice Within*, 208
Thiessen, Delbert, 200
Thoreau, Henri David, *Walden*, 242
Time, 88, 131, 140, 170, 270-271
    race against time, xviii, 252
    real-time information, 110, 119
    space and time, 48, 68
    unifying time, 51-55
    zeitgeist (the spirit of the time), 49
Toffler, Alvin and Heidi, 255
    Future Shock, 151
Tolstoy, Leo, 189, 248, 250, 278
Tonini, Giulio, 58
Transformation, xiii-xv, xxi-xxii, 24-25, 55, 91, 162, 173, 230
    commitment to lifelong, 232, 248-252, 279
    by Divine Love, 177-178, 187-188, 190, 206
    in human consciousness, 93, 98
Tribalism (tribal groups), 103, 105-106, 120, 141, 146, 202
    allegiances and conflicts, 37-44, 61, 100-101, 141, 159-162, 173-177, 204-206
    detachment from the tribe, 206-212, 220-221, 226, 251, 270, 279
Tunisian revolution, 109-110, 115, 127
    Amamou, Slim, 115
    Ben Ali, Zine al-Abidine, 109-110
    Twitter, 109-110, 115
    See also Social media
Tutu, Desmond M., 100
Twenge, Jean, 256-257
Twitter, 109-110, 115
Tyranny, 25, 101, 108, 126-127, 172
Tzu, Lao, 166, 235
    Tao Te Ching, 4, 9, 11, 13, 19, 44, 93, 166, 174, 179, 183, 191, 230, 235, 267, 269, 274

Ueshiba, Morihei, *The Art of Peace*, 166
United Nations, 271, 276
    General Assembly, 50
    UNICEF (United Nations Children's Fund), 134

United States (America), 15, 45, 49-50, 72, 85, 111, 116-118, 124-125, 133, 206-207, 211, 257, 259, 271, 276
   American Revolution, 104
   constitutional republic, 101-103
   Department of Education, 136
   Electoral College, 102
   Jamestown colony, 120
Unity, 43, 111, 114, 137-138, 141, 145-169, 170, 176, 269-270, 279, 289
   end of duality, 150-160
   of humanity and the Divine, xv, xix, xxi, 3-5, 8-10, 13, 25, 52, 55, 93-96, 147, 165-169, 172-174, 182, 190, 233-236, 245, 251, 263, 265
   individual in an undivided universe, 161-164
   See also Quantum physics
Universe, 33, 59, 70, 78, 97-98, 173, 178, 183-184, 226, 233
   and chaos, 20, 24, 36, 269
   heliocentric theory of, 154-159
   interdependence and interconnection with, 17, 52, 69, 81, 85, 89-90, 141, 146, 150-152, 159, 161-165, 169, 231, 235
Upanishads, 4, 93, 182
   Brhadaranyaka, 165-166, 222, 274
   Brihadaranyaka, 6
   Byhadaranyaka, 234
   Chandogya, 8, 159, 190, 234
   Isa, 18
   Katha, 51, 233
   Kausitaki, 89
   Mundaka, 178, 183, 234
   Svetasvatara, 235, 269, 275
   Taittiriya, 72, 190

Vaughan, Frances, 81
Veda(s), the, 93, 216
Vygotsky, Lev S., 69

Walsch, Neale Donald, *Conversations with God*, 17
Waraqa, 39

Water, 79-81, 95, 171, 186-188, 252
   diminishing resources, xvii, 52, 85-87, 252
   in the New Testament, 28-29, 34, 180, 183
   in the Old Testament, 21, 23, 25, 188
Watson, James, 57
Watson, Sr., Thomas, 125
Wheatley, Margaret J., 114
Wheeler, John, 85, 168
Whitman, Walt, "Song of Myself," 150
   "This Day, O Soul," 280
Wilber, Ken, *Transformation of Consciousness*, 98
Willingness to evolve, 160, 169, 206
   response to our calling, 263, 268-274
Wilson, Woodrow, 275
Wisdom, 4, 53, 56, 81, 96, 99, 141, 209, 215, 237, 240, 244, 258, 267
   literature, iv, vii, 159
Wittgenstein, Ludwig, 61
Wolfe, Thomas, *You Can't Go Home Again*, 30
Wordsworth, William, 243
Workers in a global economy, 116-120
   dissatisfaction of, 242-244
World Health Organization, 243

Yahweh, 3-4, 93, 166
Yeats, William Butler, "The Second Coming," 2
Yoganda, Paramahansa, Yogi, 190

Zedong, Mao, 103
Zhenwu, Zhai, 74

ABOUT THE AUTHOR

A consultant, educator, executive mentor, international retreat leader, and author, Barbara Benjamin is the director of the Center for Christ Conscious Leadership, which offers online certificate courses and individual, group, and organizational consulting. From 1990 until 2010, she was the founding director of Intuitive Discovery, Inc. In that capacity she designed and facilitated programs in leadership, human resources, innovation, and creative and spiritual development for Fortune 500 companies, non-profit organizations, and universities.

Ms. Benjamin has also designed, directed, and instructed graduate distance learning programs in organizational and interactive leadership for the School of Business at Mercy College and for the National Technological University. In 1998, Ms. Benjamin organized and directed The Third Millennium Leadership Assembly in Campobello, New Brunswick, Canada.

Ms. Benjamin's publications include *Leadership in the Interactive Age: A Skills Development Workbook* and the accompanying CDs, *The Leadership Lecture Series*; *The Joshua Priest: A Biography of Faith*; and *A Modern Prayer Guide to St. Teresa of Avila's "Interior Castle."* *Face to Face*, Ms. Benjamin's most recent volume of mystical poetry, was nominated for a Pulitzer Prize in 2009.

www.ingramcontent.com/pod-product-compliance
Lightning Source LLC
Chambersburg PA
CBHW051206290426
44109CB00021B/2366